TWISTED SCRIPTURES

TWISTED SCRIPTURES

MARY ALICE CHRNALOGAR

Whitaker House

TWISTED SCRIPTURES

Mary Alice Chrnalogar
Control Techniques, Inc.
P.O. Box 8021
Chattanooga, TN 37414-8021
(423) 698-9343

ISBN: 0-88368-514-0
Printed in the United States of America
Copyright © 1997 by Mary Alice Chrnalogar

Whitaker House
30 Hunt Valley Circle
New Kensington, PA 15068

Editorial Consultant: Paul M. Howey
Chief Editors: Tim Brauns M.A., Stephen D. Martin M.Div.
Contributing Editors: Kathleen M. Buttrey, Karen M. Parker, Moira Tingle,
Mary Woodard
Publishing Consultant: Publishers Support Services
Copy Editing: Technic Group, Pty.
Proofreading: Bonnie Trenga, Robin Quinn
Cover Design: Lynlie Hermann
Graphs and Figures: Dennis L. Meinart

1 2 3 4 5 6 7 8 9 10 11 12 / 06 05 04 03 02 01 00 99 98 97

Many references to Holy Bible translations and commentaries are used with the gracious permission of the publishers of *The Word (The Bible in 26 Translations)* (Curtis Vaughn, Th.D., General Editor—Mathis Publishers, Inc., Moss Point, MS: 1993). See p. xiii of *The Word* for a complete explanation of the codes used. The following translations from *The Word* are quoted:

ABPS The Holy Bible Containing the Old and New Testaments: An Improved Edition (American Baptist Publication Society)

ASV The American Standard Version

BER The Berkeley Version of the New Testament (Gerrit Verkuyl)

KJV The King James Version

NKJV New King James Version

Knox Monsignor Roland Knox

NAB The New America Bible

NASB New American Standard Bible by Thomas Nelson, Inc.

NEB The New English Bible

RSV The Revised Standard Bible

RV The Holy Bible: Revised Version

Wms The New Testament—A Translation in the Language of the People (Charles B. Williams)

Tay Living Letters (Kenneth N. Taylor)

Wey The New Testament in Modern Speech (Richard Francis Weymouth)

The following version was also used

DOUAY Douay Version translated from the Latin Vulgate by the London Catholic Society (1609)

DEDICATION

To Reed Hughes,
the instrument God used to inspire this book,
so that others may be freed
from the bondage of abusive discipleship.

ACKNOWLEDGEMENTS

In writing this book, I benefited greatly from the guidance and assistance of two dedicated and knowledgeable theologians and Biblical scholars:

> Timothy Brouns, M.S., is a Baptist minister in Roslindale, Massachusetts, with the American Baptist Church, and a graduate of Gordon-Conwell Theological Seminary. Brauns, himself, was once trapped in an abusive discipleship group (University Bible Fellowship) while attending college.

> Stephen D. Martin, M.Div., is a graduate of Nazarene Theological Seminary in Kansas City, Missouri, and was a pastor for two years. He has worked as a staff member in rehabilitating ex-cult members at Wellspring Retreat and Resource Center near Athens, Ohio. Wellspring is a unique and restorative place for victims of controlling groups.

You should note that these men and I have vastly different theological and denominational backgrounds. It is especially important to know that, despite our differences, we agree on this important and controversial issue—that Christ's message is sometimes abused as a device to gain personal power over others.

2

Table of Contents

INTRODUCTION

This is important! This book is designed to restore a loved one's ability to think without being unduly influenced by a particular group. For many, this book will break the psychological control exerted by an abusive discipling relationship or controlling church. That is why there is overlapping of information and repetition of ideas. The victim's strongly biased mind needs this repetition if family, friends, or therapists are to be successful in restoring objectivity.

You may be reading this now because someone close to you suspects you are being hurt, rather than helped, by your discipling relationship. It is normal to feel somewhat defensive or resentful when questioned about the possibility of abuse in our own churches or ministries. Remember, the Apostle Paul tells us, "examine everything carefully" (1 Thess. 5:21 NASB). I am not asking you to accept my opinion about your church or group. Instead, evaluate what is happening to you and around you. After reading this book, you should be able to decide for yourself if there is reason to be concerned.

Friends and family: If you have a loved one caught up in what you suspect is a controlling ministry, collect information about the group, then ask the victim to read this book from cover to cover. Use the checklists at the end of each chapter as a starting point for conversation. Finally, discuss the information with him or her away from the group and with former members if possible.

Freedom exists through discipline and obedience—obedience not to yourself or another human, but to God. Many disciples think they are being taught the right way of obedience; but they are deceived into giving up their desires, wishes, and goals for those of another mortal being—their discipler.

PREFACE

I know that after I leave, savage wolves will come in among you and will not spare the flock. Even from among your own number men will arise and distort the truth in order to draw away disciples after them. So be on your guard! Remember that for three years I never stopped warning each of you night and day with tears. The Apostle Paul (Acts 20:29-31)

Authentic discipleship is something I hold very dear, but I am vehemently against discipleship that is destructive (i.e., non-Biblical discipleship). If your first reaction to this book is to think that I am attacking discipleship, please take the time to digest my entire presentation with the Bible verses I use to explain my points. You may be surprised to find that your discipleship may be straying far from Scripture. This information can cause you to think more clearly or free yourself from a controlling environment in which you may find yourself. Once you are aware of it, you can make the proper changes in order for you to have balanced discipleship once again.

Even though I agree that there are many positive aspects of discipling even in abusive groups, this book will not focus on these positive aspects. Discipling, even abusive discipling, can lead people away from materialism, bad influences, and sinful habits. Disciples can be led to grow spiritually. In this world where God's commandments are ever more violated, it is easy to overlook abuse in discipleship because of the good influences it can bring about. Still, this is no reason to avoid eliminating the non-Biblical ideas and controlling behavior that can creep into any discipleship.

Proper perspective is difficult to achieve, especially when we are involved. It is important, therefore, to take the time you need to develop an accurate perspective of your discipleship group. Please give yourself, as well as others who might be sharing this information with you, time to lay out all the pieces of the puzzle until you see the full picture. I encourage you to take a break from your group in order to reflect. The group may be important to you, but your life and your soul are even more important.

I have used fictitious names to protect the identities of some of those I describe and quote. In some instances, I have combined their experiences to present a composite picture of typical situations.

In this book, the word "disciple" will be used when speaking of someone who is in a learning, obedient, or submissive position as a Christian. The word "discipler" will be used for someone who is in a teaching, authoritative, or leadership position in a discipling relationship. "Abusive discipleship" refers to the practice of the subtle and coercive methods I describe throughout this book.

Many observers decide that a discipling group is destructive on the basis of what they describe as "weirdness." Bizarre and eccentric behaviors are most commonly only symptoms of the underlying problem. You must go to the core of the system that causes the weirdness. Don't judge a destructive group merely by how strange the leader's doctrine is or by some bizarre actions that may take place in the group. Such failure to look beyond the symptoms is the reason many miss discovering the control or abusive elements that cause those symptoms. This book will take you into the inner workings of abusive and controlling groups to show you how they control members. I will make clear the mind games that many of the major destructively controlling groups have in common.

We don't have to wait until a person is totally involved with alcohol to diagnose alcoholism, because we have documented evidence of what to look for in the beginning stages of alcoholic addiction. Similarly, learning to see the framework of controlling actions will enable you to identify an abusive church even at the the beginning stages.

Learn about these mind control games and free yourself with the power of the information you will find in this book.

Chapter 1

THE DISCIPLESHIP GAME

You agree to wait for confirmation from your
discipler before making important decisions.
This works out to be getting permission.

Let's start by playing a game. Below are twelve items, six of which you are to pick:

    1 2 3 4 5 6 7 8 9 10 11 12

What you don't know is that I have decided I don't want you to choose items 4, 7, or 10. On the other hand, I do want you to take items 2 and 5. The rest are of no consequence to me. What are the chances you will pick the ones I want you to choose and not choose the ones I don't want you to? Not very good, are they? How could I get you to pick the ones I want without telling you? How could I convince you to make my choices become your choices, but make you think that you decided?

That is easy. I could play a manipulative discipleship game. First, before you started the game, I would teach you that, although this may be your first time playing, I have played this game a lot. In fact, I have spent so much time in prayer and study that God now inspires me to know the best choices (for you). Then we would begin to play. After two choices, I would tell you that it is God who wants us to agree on each choice. This, I would tell you, is the kind of spiritual unity the Bible teaches. With this in mind, you would proceed with the remaining choices.

Suppose in those six choices, you only stumbled on one of the three items I did not want you to take. This is the only time I had to tell you that I did not agree with you. When you were on your last choice and you still hadn't picked item 5, I shared with you that God revealed to me the superiority of item 5. So you took it last. Five out of six times you got your choice, but you also benefited from my "divinely inspired wisdom" to make a good last selection.

You feel as though you are making up your own mind. You feel neither coerced nor controlled. In fact, you appreciated the help you got. In the end, however, I got what I wanted without your knowing it; and, of course, I was the one who said you had 12 choices and who directed you to select only six. I set up the rules of the game.

Abusive discipleship is played approximately the same way. Control over people is disguised as agreement with a discipler who, you are told, has your best interests at heart. Unlike the game, the choices are not trivial, but are more likely to be important (e.g., whom to marry, what vocation to pursue, and where to live). Unlike the game, however, abusive discipleship results in unnecessary fear, shame, and guilt—and, most importantly, the rules of abusive discipleship are not Biblical rules.

In his letter to the Colossians, Paul warns of the foolishness of man-made rules: "Such regulations indeed have an appearance of wisdom... but they lack any value in restraining sensual indulgence." The Apostle also admonishes us, "Do not let anyone judge you by what you eat or drink, or with regard to a religious festival, a New Moon or a Sabbath day" (Col. 2:8-23).

Leaders in most discipleship groups will admit that their rules are different than those in most churches. In truth, they feel they are closer to what an authentic Christian experience should be. I have heard many people compare the discipleship groups they were in to monastic orders or the army. Some disciplers even draw the comparison: "We are God's Green Berets!" When people are inducted into such orders or join the military, they know what they are getting into and know what the rules will be. Ask yourself: When did you agree to the rules? When did you find out what the rules were?

The rules of abusive discipleship are not evident in the beginning. What is initially obvious is a great display of personal attention, love, and caring. This is what people usually (and understandably) find so attractive about such groups. They will call you even when no one else does; they will invite you out to dinner; they will tell you that they care. They will also tell you that you can grow much faster spiritually by having a discipler who is wiser (than you) in the Lord. They will impress upon you all the wonderful benefits of being a part of such a program. They also will teach you that Jesus did this exact same thing with His disciples. You will be assigned a "buddy" to stand alongside, who will be your constant friend. It is often true that, with spiritual guidance, we can grow much faster. The problem is that in some discipleships, spiritual growth accelerates for a short yet seductive period before being restricted by controlling techniques.

As your relationship with the abusive discipler develops, you find out there are rules—actually more rules than you might have expected. By contrast, there won't be hidden rules in healthy discipleship. From the beginning, the non-abusive discipler will lay out what is expected from you without intentionally withholding certain rules or ideas.

Abusive disciplers expect you to:

➤ make considerable time in your schedule for them

➤ call them frequently to get advice

➤ meet with them often

➤ share with or confess your sins to them, and to be "transparent" to them in every area of your life

➤ trust them with all your most intimate secrets—even though they may have nothing to do with sin

➤ discuss even your non-moral decisions with them

➤ trust the advice your discipler gives you, and obey this discipler in every area of your life.

You may be led to believe that any violation of the discipler's rules can be a sin. This is part of the deceptive and hidden agenda built into the program. You begin to believe that it is actually sinful to not follow the rules after you have accepted the discipler as your buddy. After you become involved in a domineering program, you frequently discover it's considered sinful (or at least backsliding in your spiritual development) to break your commitment and end the relationship.

In a controlling discipleship, there are other ideas that are hidden from you. Aberrant discipleship teaches new meanings for such words as *obey, submit, die to self,* and *brokenness.* Their meanings are altered from the true Biblical understanding of these concepts. Abusive disciplers expand the meanings far beyond what the Bible teaches, to imply that anytime you don't want to accept the advice of a leader, you are likely not sufficiently *obedient, submissive, broken,* or *dying to self.* These non-Biblical definitions are usually concealed until the abusive disciplers feel you are trustworthy enough to be given their teachings in full.

ABUSIVE DISCIPLESHIPS MAKE IT A SIN NOT TO FOLLOW THEIR RULES!

The Bible offers us these examples of sin:

"the cravings of sinful man, the lust of his eyes and the boasting of what he has and does" (1 John 2:16)

"lovers of themselves, lovers of money, boastful, proud, abusive, disobedient to their parents, ungrateful, unholy, without love, unforgiving, slanderous, without self-control, brutal, not lover of the good, treacherous, rash, conceited, lovers of pleasure rather than lovers of God" (2 Tim. 3:2)

"bitterness, rage and anger, brawling, and slander, along with every form of malice" (Eph. 4:31) and "sexual immorality, impurity, lust, evil desires and greed" (Col. 3:5)

Romans 13:9 mentions "adultery, murder, stealing, coveting" as sins.

In abusive discipleships, sin is expanded to mean almost anything that the leaders don't like (e.g., challenging leaders' actions, not obeying leaders' advice, disagreeing with leaders, questioning leaders, or openly criticizing leaders).

The most common non-Biblical idea that is planted in members' minds by abusive groups is that they are rebellious, hard-hearted, or prideful when they decide not to follow the group's rules. Breaking a rule is usually taken to mean sinning against God; this is coercive because these dedicated Christians will force themselves to follow agendas they would otherwise refuse to accept.

An important, yet subtle, rule is:

You should wait until both you and your discipler agree before you actually make an important decision.

You are led to believe that you should get this confirmation so you will "know" that whatever you want to do is God's will. Actually it simply means getting permission from the discipler. Responsible disciplers will not ask this of you (they know from experience that they have advised people wrongly in the past). Occasionally the wise discipler does not "have peace" about a situation but he realizes that the disciple may be following the Lord's leading by not accepting advice. The abusive discipler presumes to know what's best for you. (Note: To "have peace" is a code phrase used by some groups and churches. It means that a person feels that God wills certain things and, thus, the person feels spiritual peace concerning these things.)

THE PROGRAM OF BONDAGE

The hidden agenda of abusive discipleship is that you should not make decisions without both you and your discipler feeling at peace about it. They claim this will ensure that you will make fewer mistakes on your Christian walk. At first this seems to make logical sense: more accountability, fewer mistakes. What you must realize, however, is that slavery may soon begin to develop. Once you agree to play this discipleship game, your discipler will be a major deciding factor in many of your choices because you come to believe that you are likely to be in sin if you act without the discipler's confirmation.

How nice of the discipler not to want you to make any mistakes in your new Christian walk. The discipler wants to help you. You probably feel grateful that someone cares about what you do in a world in which people often don't seem to care at all. This discipler may also say that he wants to make sure you find and follow God's perfect will, and that he is advanced enough to be able to help you with your decisions.

As long as all your decisions follow the discipler's agenda, you will get all the confirmation you could possibly want. You don't feel manipulated because you are making many decisions and are allowed to follow through. You see no control because your decisions either follow the path your discipler wants you to take, or the discipler may have no preference in a particular instance. When you veer off the "path," the controlling discipler may first try to subtly persuade you and, if that fails, *tell* you that you are in sin.

The non-abusive discipler, on the other hand, doesn't see you as less holy for rejecting advice in matters which do not deal with morals. There is no manipulation to make you feel guilt or sin for refusing to follow this type of advice. The abusive discipler does not expect you to always follow his advice either. But he is much more inclined to judge you as not humble, not broken (obedient), or not spiritual if you reject his advice in non-moral, or non-Scriptural matters. (Note: Non-moral matters are those which do not involve an issue of sin, such as selecting the color to use in painting the walls of your dining room, or whether to buy a two-door or a four-door car.)

There are terms a discipler may use to guide the disciple back onto the desired path:

➤ "I don't have peace about it"

➤ "I don't know if that is God's will"

➤ "Let's continue to seek God's will about that."

You are free to disagree if a non-controlling discipler uses one of these phrases. When they are used by an abusive discipler, however, these phrases are a kind of discipleship code that really means: *"NO, NO, and NO."*

The thrust of the program subtly implies—and you, as the disciple, believe—that you are probably in sin if you don't go along with whatever you are advised to do, regardless of whether or not the matter is a question of morals or Biblical mandates.

Did your discipler actually tell you "no"? Of course not. Isn't that sneaky? So sneaky in fact that disciples who are being controlled will nearly always swear they are *never* told what to do. Rather, they only receive *advice*. While this is often true, these victims don't realize that, under psychological pressure from their discipler, they may be making many decisions against their own God-given wisdom.

There are times, however, when sneaky is not enough and the controlling discipler needs to use a heavier hand (remember, we are not discussing *moral* advice). This is called "discipline." A disciple who refuses to yield will be chastened, rebuked, counseled, or will have some other Biblical-sounding word thrown in his face to get cooperation. This frequently involves being told he is *not submissive, not broken, not obedient,* or *not humble.* The disciple might be accused of being rebellious, *not dying to self, not trusting enough,* or *being hard-hearted.* This labeling game usually works remarkably well in abusive discipleships.

The result is that you are compelled not to change jobs, go to school, date, get married, or do other things without first clearing them with your discipler. If he or she doesn't "feel peace" about it, then you don't really have permission to do it and will probably feel guilty if you go against your discipler's opinion.

I invite you to ask yourself, "Would I have played this game if I had known all the rules?" If you had been told at the outset that to be a disciple meant to obey practically all the advice from your discipler in every area of your life, would you have become involved?

The Bible does assert that we must obey the laws of God in all areas of our life, but it is quite a jump from there to the belief that church or group leaders must be obeyed in every area of life.

"COMMITMENT MANIPULATION" TACTIC

There is good reason why abusive discipleships don't reveal the rules up front—they wouldn't get many recruits!

People are not exactly beating down the doors of monasteries that teach poverty, chastity, and obedience. Commitments like that take time to make. But, unlike monastic orders, abusive discipleships use a "commitment manipulation" tactic: getting people involved first and then introducing them to all the rules. Once people are committed and involved in something, they are much more likely to accept such new information.

I remember a college professor telling me that if a person signs an insurance policy but later finds out it says much more in the fine print than he knew about, that person would still agree to it because he had made the commitment. This is similar to an abusive discipleship. The new disciple doesn't realize the involvement in the beginning of a long-term and intense commitment, nor does he know all the commitments involved.

People get involved by participating and, as time passes, feel committed. Then, when they find out more of what is expected of them, they go along with it because they have already made a substantial emotional commitment. In some cases, they have also made a financial investment. They have signed on the bottom line and the discipleship will fill in the blanks as they go along.

There is a tendency to justify, and cling to, whatever you are already involved in. You must take time to look at *all* the information in this book before you push it aside. If you are currently participating in a group, I know it will be difficult for you to look at this information objectively. If a group can get you involved first, form your friendships, and gain your trust, then begin to lay one rule after another on you, you will more than likely accept them without argument.

I have faced controlling disciplers and asked them: "Why don't you tell your people up front what your discipleship is all about?" Sometimes they answer that the Lord doesn't lead them that way or that the people are still babes as Christians and would not be able to handle it. This is discipleship code. What it really means is that few would join if they knew beforehand all that would be expected of them. These disciplers are not hiding "deeper truths"—they are hiding manipulation.

Many legitimate organizations provide membership cards that

list the regulations of the organization. I don't know of any abusive discipleship groups that have membership cards; but if they did, they might read something like this:

DISCIPLESHIP MEMBERSHIP CARD

As a member, I agree to:

➢ Give up nearly all my personal time to the program...

➢ Open up completely and share everything about myself—not just my sins...

➢ Relinquish my privacy of thoughts, sinful or not...

➢ Be willing to give up my opinion if it conflicts with my discipler's, and accept his opinion as right...

➢ Believe that it is a sin not to trust my discipler's judgment...

➢ Obey all requests of my discipler...

...even if the request affects a decision such as not being allowed to announce my engagement until my discipler wants me to, not pick a wedding date until my discipler approves, to put off my wedding date until my discipler approves, to put off my wedding date until my discipler has peace about it. Obey my discipler in matters of dating and other relationships, changing jobs, going to college, moving, or whatever is requested of me. If I do not obey, then I accept whatever punishment my discipler believes appropriate. I will accept being called "rebellious," "hard-hearted," "not trusting," "uncommitted," "prideful," or whatever else my discipler thinks that I should be labeled. I will accept my discipler's opinions as the truth and feel terribly guilty for not obeying.

You should wonder why a group would want to conceal the way it really operates from newcomers or those on the outside. Jesus certainly did not operate this way. Furthermore, Jesus made it clear He did not teach something different to His inner circle than what He taught new members (John 18:20). Further in this book, you will find out more about why some discipleship groups follow a different practice toward their followers than Jesus did.

In a recent bulletin of a church that had discipleship, there was a special notation that the discipleship class was by *invitation only*! No other activity at this church had this requirement. I had to wonder what secret Bible knowledge has to be by invitation only. My guess is that they were teaching some ideas that were controversial to the average person. They were going to make sure that the only people they would teach would be those they thought could swallow this stuff behind closed doors. Their excuse is that some people aren't ready for their lessons yet, and only the discipleship leaders can tell when they are ready.

CHECKLIST
The Discipleship Game—Chapter 1

Check those that apply to your group:

❑ Did not get my fully informed consent before I joined

❑ Withheld certain teachings until I was more trusting

❑ Wanted my commitment as soon as possible

❑ Consistently makes new demands of me

❑ Did not tell me in the beginning of my involvement that anything less than total obedience was unacceptable

❑ Seems to create non-Biblical classes of sins (e.g., labeling people as "full of pride" if they don't agree with the discipler's decisions or advice)

❑ Leaders don't tell me "no," but instead ask me to "pray about it" and delay my decision

❑ See themselves as "more committed" to Jesus than those not in the discipleship

❑ Want me to refrain from making decisions without the discipler's concurrence

❑ Disciples are rebuked for actions that aren't really sinful but which merely differ from the leaders' opinions

❑ My leader/discipler makes no distinction between moral advice and non-moral advice

NOTE: If you have checked *any* boxes, it may indicate a misuse of Scripture and/or may represent the presence of abuse and excessive control.

Chapter 2

THE DISCIPLESHIP DISASTER

No one believes that their discipleship is abusive; it's always the other group. Look more closely; you may be surprised.

On Christmas Eve 1979, my parents dressed as Mr. and Mrs. Santa Claus. They rang sleigh bells and gave gifts to twin sisters and their parents. We had just met this family three days earlier.

Our involvement began when the twin daughters called home announcing they were both getting married. Concerned because of the unexpectedness and abruptness of this announcement, their mother asked if they loved the men they were to marry. Instead of giving the expected answer, they both responded by saying they wanted to marry them because it was God's Will. That's when their mother called me to ask if I would speak to her daughters before their double wedding (which was scheduled for the following week!).

When I finally was able to convince the twins that refusing their church leader's choice of husbands for them was not disobeying God's Will, they were so happy. They hadn't really wanted to marry these men anyway. As a matter of fact, they hadn't even wanted to hold hands with them!

Experiencing the joy of that family's happiness in their reunion was one of the most wonderful experiences in my life. It was this incident that prompted my initial research into abusive and controlling groups. What were they teaching? How could people be convinced to marry a person in whom they weren't interested? I began to find the answers as other parents called me for help.

The more people I worked with, the more I suspected that an unwarranted amount of control was being exerted over the individual lives of Christians in these groups. I was also disturbed

19

by the kinds of experiences that the parents related. They described radical and abnormal personality changes in their adult children—sons and daughters who stopped coming home to visit or calling on the phone; children who had lost interest in normal hobbies, social relationships, and even in lifelong friends. For the most part, it was not the new-found faith or commitment of their offspring that bothered the parents, but their perception that their children were losing normal and precious aspects of their personalities.

Many of these parents were upset because their adult children, with whom they had enjoyed a trusting and open relationship, were becoming evasive and guarded about their activities. When career, marriage, or vocational plans were discussed, their children (adults, actually) were now unable or unwilling to give clear answers. The parents felt emotionally cut off from their children.

I discovered that many times these disciples could not answer because they needed to check in with their discipler, not only about the kind of answer they could give, but whether they should give an answer to their parents at all. One mother said, "The immediate and total compliance of our son to heed the advice of the leaders was terrifying." This mother had always taught her son to make decisions and to think for himself. Now it seemed as if he were being told what to do in nearly every detail of his life. He couldn't even decide about coming home without discussing it with his discipler.

I saw common threads that linked the most destructive controlling groups together with controlling evangelical churches and abusive discipleship programs. That is how I came to the definition of an abusive group:

> *An abusive discipleship is a group that exerts coercive persuasion through systematic deception.*

Specifically, the types of coercion, deception, and beliefs found in these discipleships are:

➤ the belief that *we are superior* to all other churches; our message is superior as is our understanding of the Bible

➤ *a lack of tolerance for disagreement* with leadership

➤ *hidden agendas* as evidenced by withholding of information and concealing manipulation and exploitation that occur after disciples are more deeply involved

➤ *instilling a belief* that *disobeying certain requests* (which do not deal with Scripture morals or values) from the discipler is a sin.

Once a disciple has been convinced that it is sinful to disobey even a portion of non-moral advice from the discipler, the disciple will "voluntarily" follow the discipler's suggestions in order to avoid feelings of guilt. In essence, the disciple becomes a slave obedient to the discipler's advice.

Information concerning the leaders, which the group defines as negative, is suppressed by demeaning those disciples who speak out. This humiliation frequently is done by:

➤ imposing a standard by which disciples are often caused to feel guilty or ashamed

➤ continual judging of members' hearts or motives

➤ threatening to rebuke the "offending" disciple, sometimes even in public

➤ arbitrarily dismissing disciples or causing them to want to leave when the disciple merely disagrees with opinions of the leaders.

When a person can't freely share doubts about an important matter without the threat of expulsion or other negative repercussions, it can cause great inner struggles and leave one emotionally devastated.

Controlling groups usually withhold their additional meanings of the words *obey* and *submit*. These definitions typically are held back until the leaders see that you trust them enough to assure your acceptance of these new teachings. Controlling groups lower the disciple's defenses by distorting the highly important concepts of *commitment* and *trust*. These concepts are twisted by abusive discipleship groups to take on new meanings that the Bible doesn't support.

When abusive controllers deliberately withhold information, they may say: "You are not ready to be radically committed." In short, there is one set of teachings for beginners and a different set for the more committed. If you think, "My discipleship group doesn't use hidden agendas," I want you to look more closely. These mind games and hidden agendas are difficult to see initially.

SOME HISTORY...

This is not a new problem. In order to understand how we got here, you need to know something about the history of these groups.

Discipleship programs became popular because the culture had become permissive and Christians wanted to distance themselves from such ungodliness. Many were looking to dedicate their lives to God in a closer way. Discipleship leaders offered to help Christians grow fully through the ill-conceived concept of being held *more accountable*.

It was not necessarily because of evil men, who are generally blamed, that this corruption grew but mainly due to the non-Biblical teaching of what "being more accountable" supposedly meant. In practice, this teaching of "more accountability" frequently meant suppressing freedom of expression and action, and pressure to give up one's own convictions when these differed from those of the leaders. This, in turn, created mental anguish and moral dilemmas for many disciples. A Christian magazine reported in 1990 that:

> ...*the movement quickly became elitist, exclusive. Operating on the basis that everyone needs to be accountable to a pastor, "sheep" were assigned to various "shepherds"—many of whom were young, immature, sometimes arrogant and often proud of their new authority... Havoc followed and horror stories abounded. Families were sometimes forced to relocate from one city to another at the whim of a shepherd. Churches split... Mumford and Simpson in particular took the heat from the critics, who charged they dominated those under them... Critics cited numerous examples of "shepherds" who required their "sheep" to ask their permission before they dated, changed jobs or made major decisions.*[1]

The shepherding leaders claimed that they were teaching a renewed Biblical understanding of God's government, delegated authority, and covenant loyalty. But soon other national leaders opposed them. During a *700 Club* broadcast, Pat Robertson called Mumford, Simpson, and Prince "false teachers" and banned the shepherding leaders from appearing on any of his radio or television outlets.[2]

The conflict over the shepherding movement seemed to reach a turning point in 1990 when a Christian magazine quoted a prominent leader in the shepherding movement as saying:

> *Discipleship was wrong. I repent. I ask forgiveness... discipleship resulted in unhealthy submission resulting in perverse and un-Biblical obedience to human leaders... for the injury and*

shame, I repent with sorrow and ask for your forgiveness.[3]

This admission of unhealthy submission and non-Biblical obedience to human leaders shook the foundation of discipleship in America. Many leaders in this movement followed and repented of the abuses. Since that time, discipleship programs have been dropped by literally hundreds of thousands of people. The movement has continued to shrink as the abuses and the non-Scriptural base of some of the teachings are exposed. It spawned eggs, however, that continue to hatch even today.

After many years, the fruits of broken hearts, damaged psyches, and disillusioned spirits are becoming more and more evident. Several former leaders echo these same complaints and observations:

> *Pastors like myself have spent large amounts of time over the last fifteen years picking up the pieces of broken lives that resulted from distortion of truth by extreme teachings and destructive applications on discipleship, authority, and shepherding.*[4]

> *Victims of this movement are usually born-again Christians and are fundamentalist and evangelical in their orientation. The errors are covered in many different terms like delegated authority, covering, unquestioned submission, covenant, commitment to a fellowship, etc. ... Terms change from time to time. Submission may be called "commitment," "covenant relationship" or "divine order" in church government. Many times terms aren't used at all; it is the actions that tell you what is going on.*[5]

(Note: Appendix 2 gives a more detailed history of the discipleship movement.)

Since many leaders in the shepherding movement admitted doing wrong, various people who continue to use the same methods have begun to give different labels for the same actions. But once the wool is pulled from over your eyes, you can see that "labels" are misleading. It's the same game. Many call it discipleship, but some new groups (which are promoting similar errors) emphasize an excessive degree of "accountability." These groups insist that members become totally accountable to one or more leaders (or to the entire group) for nearly every action in their daily lives. To show you how different words are often used to disguise the abuses and excesses in these groups, here is a hypothetical conversation.[6]

Jay: I overheard you mention that your discipler is your authority. Does your church teach the shepherdship doctrine?

Ben: Oh, no. Our discipler is not submitted to those national leaders anymore. That was really a bad error. Lots of extremes.

Jay: But you were just talking about submitting to your discipler; that's a shepherdship term.

Ben: The shepherdship movement did have lots of truth. We kept all the good Scriptural ideas.

Jay: Which Scriptural truths are you talking about?

Ben: That our discipler is our delegated authority over our lives. We submit to him so that he can rebuke and correct us to maturity.

Jay: Does your discipler tell you what to do and make decisions for you?

Ben: No, not at all. We are taught to be led by "the Spirit." We go to our discipler for confirmation after we get our own leading.

Jay: What if you get an important leading and your discipler doesn't get a confirmation?

Ben: Then I would know that I was probably wrong. After all, he knows how to hear from God better because he is spiritually more mature. We need to trust and obey our leaders. God has set him over my life and will show him what is right for me. Certainly the church has confidence in my discipler or they wouldn't put him in authority over my life. The year before last, I thought God was leading me to go to Bible school but my pastor said I wasn't yet ready. I was to stay and be a disciple in his church for a little while longer.

Jay: How long have you been in this church?

Ben: Seven years.

Jay: You're 27 years old, love to minister to people, and you have a great teaching gift. Didn't it occur to you to question this leading? Maybe he just hates to let you leave his church?

Ben: I will admit that I was very upset and disappointed at first. But I don't want to be rebellious and question his motives because the Bible says, *"Touch not my anointed."* I certainly don't want to get on the wrong side of God by questioning my discipler. If I don't submit to him, my relationship with Jesus will suffer because I won't be accountable to anyone in authority. There is no telling what the devil might do to me if I get out from under my discipler's authority.

Jay: You say you're not involved in shepherding, yet everything you are doing is standard shepherdship doctrine. Those folks had to be under someone's covering. You need to be under authority. There is no difference in your actions. It looks like... you are being controlled by your discipler and not led by the Spirit.

Ben: Oh no, you must be mistaken. We just obey the Bible in our church. Our discipler says that some may think that we are in shepherdship, but what he teaches is not the same at all.

Jay: Several people have told me that they were labeled factious because their viewpoints were different from the leaders' and [that they] then were threatened with a public rebuke. That sounds like bondage to me.

Ben: Sometimes it is hard to take, but we need to be corrected and kept in line for our own good in order to grow spiritually.

Jay: Could you freely leave your church with the good will of the members and leaders?

Ben: I would never think of leaving my church for any reason unless my discipler felt it was from God. God set him over my life as my authority. I don't understand why you think that I am in bondage.

These are typical responses of those in denial. As you read the following chapters, you will see that much of discipleship today includes the same control and errors as the shepherding movement. Just how much of the error *your* discipleship carries will have to be weighed and evaluated on an individual basis.

Even though some large churches have abusive discipleship, excessive accountability, or abusive pastors within the community, the whole church might not be indoctrinated into the errors.

Like weeds, however, these abusive concepts keep popping up. Though the shepherding and discipling movement of the

1970s and 1980s seemed to be dying out in one area of the church, it now appears to be springing up in other areas. In March 1994, I attended a large Baptist church connected to the Southern Baptist Convention. To my surprise, inside this church they were teaching this same extreme obedience. The teacher said that people she counseled had to be willing to do whatever she requested. She labeled people as "not really wanting help" if they weren't willing to follow all of her requests.

Then I found this program was not isolated but was networking with many other mainline churches. After this experience, I knew it was time to warn others by clearly defining the problems of abusive discipleship. We must address the problem and expose these heretical and damaging teachings. Even though this book will be controversial for those of you who have this problem in your church, I would like to remind you what the late Dr. Walter Martin once said: *Controversy for the sake of truth is a divine command.* [7]

CHECKLIST
The Discipleship Disaster—Chapter 2

Check any that apply to you and/or your group:

❑ I feel somewhat distant from family

❑ My spontaneous decisions have diminished because I feel compelled to check with my discipler first

❑ I sometimes feel uneasy when talking with my family about my plans

❑ I'm not as close to my old friends as I used to be

❑ My church has more accountability than most other churches

❑ My spiritual growth depends upon following most all of my leader's requests

❑ I feel guilty when my desires don't match the will of those in authority

❑ I sometimes feel burned out and depressed when I have to suppress my own thoughts and desires to follow what my discipler thinks is better

❑ When my thoughts are different from my leaders', I feel as though my heart is going against God's Will for my life

❑ My leaders are better able to hear from God than I am

❑ I am sometimes labeled as "rebellious" when I am struggling with accepting their advice

NOTE: **If you have checked *any* boxes, it may indicate a misuse of Scripture and/or may represent the presence of abuse and excessive control.**

Chapter 3

AUTHORITY UNLIMITED

When we preach the message of Jesus, if some reject His message, then they are rejecting Jesus. We can't stretch that to mean that if our disciples reject our advice they are rejecting Jesus.

Touch not my anointed and do my prophets no harm! (Ps. 105:1 KJV)

Some discipleship groups interpret this verse to mean we should not question or say anything negative against our leaders. This interpretation squelches legitimate questions that might prevent potential errors.

Leaders who adopt this slant on Scripture become immune to accountability from their people. This is only one example of the ways in which abusive discipleship groups may use Bible verses. Also, passages are often taken out of context and their true meanings distorted. But these groups also correctly interpret many verses, which is why it is frequently so difficult to see exactly what they are doing.

John tells us that, in the body of Christ, we each have the anointing of God (1 John 2:20-27). This anointing does not apply only to the man behind the pulpit; we each have the anointing of God. The Holy Spirit is available to every one of us. We can be filled as we open ourselves and yield to God. It's not just some church leaders on earth whom God has set apart anointed. This particular concept is twisted and groundless.

A good leader should be honored and respected, but we are instructed to prove all things (1 Thess. 5:21 KJV and Amplified Bible). We are instructed to discern, examine, test, and prove (1 Cor. 14:29; 1 Thess. 5:21 NASB and Amplified Bible). In 1 Tim 3:10, deacons must be tested. According to Revelations 2:2, even those who call themselves Apostles should be tried. Jesus commends them because they tried those who called themselves Apostles and found they were false. In abusive discipleships, the mere fact that someone is a leader means that followers should never say anything critical about that leader.[8]

What a nice position—to be a leader when your flock feels that they can't criticize you without risking that they are going against God! Nice for the leader, but very dangerous for the flock.

The foundation of the discipleship movement is the *authority* of the discipler. What distinguishes discipleship relationships from the typical relationship between a pastor and the flock is that *the discipler is granted a significantly greater authority to guide the directions and decisions of the disciple.* Could this possibly be Biblical, that a young Christian layperson is granted power to oversee souls? It is not (see 1 Tim. 3:6, and James 3:1,2).

In an abusive discipleship, this heightened authority is combined with an insistence that disciples be submissive, obedient, trusting, and broken even in areas that do not deal with Scripture. It may be communicated directly through teaching or by the way a leader exercises authority over the disciple. The Bible holds that both the content of a leader's doctrine and the leader's *behavior* are important (1 Tim. 3:1-13; Tit. 1:5-11; 1 Pet. 5:2,3).

IMITATE, TRUST, BE LOYAL, AND HAVE FAITH IN LEADERS...OR GOD...OR BOTH?

What does the Bible say?

The more extreme controlling groups will stress one or more of these ideas to gain more control:

➢ Not only should you trust God but you need to trust your leaders

➢ Not only should you be loyal to God but you need to be loyal to your leaders

➢ Not only should you have faith in God but you need to have faith in your leaders

➢ Not only should you imitate Jesus but you need to imitate your leaders (human characteristics).

You won't find these ideas in the Bible, but, if a group wants to gain nearly unlimited authority over people, it is extremely important for that group to emphasize them. Even if your group only uses one of these ideas, it is time to analyze how it is misused and what the Bible really teaches about it. Of course, it is not wrong to have trust, faith, or loyalty in your leadership. It is wrong to teach that the Bible says this is expected of us. If your group labels people as sinners because they don't trust the leaders, don't have faith in them, don't have loyalty to them, or fail to imitate their human characteristics, then this is also contrary to Scripture.

Non-controlling churches generally follow more accurately the Scripture and only teach trusting in God, having faith in God, having loyalty to God, and imitating the life and virtues of Jesus or the virtues of Jesus in people.

Can you picture yourself in a non-controlling church and hearing the pastor preach that you should have faith and trust in him? I'm sure there would be complaints after the sermon. Many in the church would immediately wonder why the pastor wanted them to have faith or trust in him. It wasn't the pastor who died for us; it was Jesus. Yet, many discipleships erroneously teach trust in mortal leaders.

One argument that I hear is that "The Bible teaches us to obey and honor our leaders." This is true, but honor is not the same as loyalty, and obedience doesn't mean trust. We cannot play word games by interchanging these words at random. Honor, loyalty, trust, and obedience all have different meanings. We can honor a messenger, but not be loyal to him.

TRUST THE MESSAGE—THE MESSENGER HAS TO EARN TRUST

Jesus said:

The teachers of the law and the Pharisees sit in Moses' seat. So you must obey them and do everything they tell you. But do not do what they do, for they do not practice what they preach. They tie up heavy loads and put them on men's shoulders... (Matt. 23:2-4).

Jesus made it plain that we are to honor teachers of the law by listening to the Scriptures that they teach, which were handed down from Moses. Jesus wanted people to trust the *message* handed down from Moses.

LOYALTY TO THE TEACHER IS NOT A MUST

If Jesus didn't teach us to blindly trust the teachers, He certainly did not want blind loyalty given to them. Jesus never taught that men must have loyalty to His messengers because He knew that there would be wolves in His flock too. Jesus wanted loyalty to the teachings of God that were passed down through Moses. Jesus knew that teaching trust and loyalty to teachers would be dangerous because eventually there would be false teachers.

Immature Christians often make the mistake of losing their faith when a pastor in whom they have put their faith fails them. We hear many Christians say that their faith has crumbled because of a corrupt pastor. If their loyalty was to the *message of Jesus* rather than to their leader, these failures would have little effect on their faith. These immature Christians were not rooted in the word of God, but in their pastor.

If you have allegiance to your government, you don't change countries when you have a bad president. Your loyalty is to the principles upon which its Constitution is based. Controlling groups, however, expect you to have loyalty to them and their message.

Compare this to non-controlling groups that preach loyalty only to the message in order to protect you from being tossed about during a time of poor leadership. Think about it: wise leaders don't teach Christians to trust them, but only to trust the message of Jesus. If the group's leader falls from grace, members are less likely to lose their faith because that faith was not invested in the leader. Paul warned against being "followers of men" (1 Cor. 1-4).

SCRIPTURE "SLEIGHT-OF-HAND" TRICKS

The idea of trusting your group's leader, being loyal to that leader, and having faith in that leader may even sound like Biblical teachings after a while. However, you can't find a verse to back that idea, but you don't think about this because it is done so slyly. Major cult leaders—and now some mainline churches—use tricks like these to gain maximum control over their flocks.

I will give some examples of this kind of twisted teaching from an extremely controlling discipleship group. I am using an extreme example in order to clearly expose the methods used. You may think, "Well, our group never went to such an extreme with this teaching." Please don't allow yourself to be in denial this way. If your group's teaching places even a slight emphasis on trusting leaders, having faith in them, or being loyal to them, they have veered away from Scriptures.

Here is a typical twisted idea supposedly taken from the Bible, which you might be taught about imitating your discipler:

> *You should set your mind to be an exact replica, you should set your mind to be an exact imitation...*[9]

Do you ever find yourself thinking like this?

> *...it takes humility to be like another person exactly... I really need to imitate everything. The way he speaks, the way he preaches, the way he thinks, the way he acts.*[10]

It is true that we should want to imitate virtue in others, because they are exemplifying a Godly characteristic. The problem arises when "imitate me only as I imitate Christ's virtue" gets turned into "imitate me, your discipler." Then subtly the discipler, *not Christ*, becomes the focus. The imitation of Christ's virtue is fused with the idea of imitating the discipler's virtue and human characteristics. Subtle? Yes it is, and it makes robots of people.

In a somewhat less intense group I studied, a disciple mentioned he wanted to imitate his discipler. He made no distinction of which of his discipler's characteristics he was supposed to imitate. He wanted to be "just like him." This disciple couldn't hear how odd this sounded to me as a Christian.

Here is a typical twisted idea supposedly taken from the Bible, on trusting leaders:

> *...if we do not trust these people, we do not trust God.*[11] *[Implying that if I trust my discipler, I am in reality trusting God.]*

> *The people that you are discipling must believe... must trust that you are [out working] for God and their best interest... they must believe emphatically that your judgment is better than theirs... [they must] build a trust which allows you to guide and mold their lives.*[12]

Such positions are a dime a dozen in controlling groups. Once the idea is instilled that "we must give our leadership blind trust," then any discipler can easily get away with abuses.

Having faith in leaders is a non-Biblical principle taught in some abusive churches which say:

> *...distrust of the person God has put in your life is equal to distrusting God, and your faith in God is shown by your faith in*

your discipler.[13]

Loyalty to leaders is not a Biblical command, but it is sometimes taught in controlling groups which say something like this:

You seriously restrict any growth you might have if you, like Peter, oftentimes do not trust the people God has put into your life.

If you hold back your affection and loyalty, you maintain an independence that kills the learning spirit that you are to have in your quest to become like Jesus.[14]

LEAPS IN LOGIC TO GAIN CONTROL

Peter trusted Jesus as the Apostle began to walk on the water. When Peter was distracted and frightened by the wind and he started to sink, it is correct to say that his trust in Jesus failed. Some groups, though, make a big leap in logic when they teach their members that anytime we don't trust our leaders we are being just like Peter when he failed to trust Jesus.

Why do you think controlling groups equate the lack of trust in church leaders with a lack of trust in Jesus? Why do you think they teach that you are to look at your discipler like the Apostles looked at Jesus?

If you were a church leader, wouldn't it be wonderful if everyone in your congregation trusted and had faith in you equal to that which they have in Jesus? If you can instill that degree of loyalty in your parishioners, then you could dominate every aspect of their lives.

Abusive discipleships are built on the foundation of a non-Biblical premise that we are to trust our leaders as if they were Jesus himself. Think about it. Can you accept that you are committing the same sin as lacking trust in Jesus when you do not completely trust your discipler? Do you really believe that when you don't have complete faith in your discipler, you commit the same sin as if you lack faith in Jesus? Do you honestly feel that you are committing the same sin as lacking of loyalty to God when you don't have total loyalty to your discipler?

Since Jesus is God, these so-called sins amount to making your leaders nearly equal to God!

WHAT ABOUT MATTHEW 10:14, 15, and 40?

You might ask, "What about the Bible verses where Jesus says 'if they reject you then they are rejecting me'?"

To whom was Jesus speaking? To His Apostles. Jesus also told them to not take money or clothes with them. Who was Jesus telling to go to another city without money or extra clothes? Again, Jesus was talking specifically to His Apostles. It is important that we understand that Jesus was talking exclusively to the Apostles who were presenting His straightforward message and performing miracles.

Jesus wasn't talking about the Apostles' opinions. He did not say that anytime the Apostles' opinions were rejected, it was as if the faithful were rejecting Jesus. Jesus wasn't giving the Apostles authority over peoples' lives to direct them in every detail. Jesus did not say that every time a person refused the Apostles' advice, it could be said that they were rejecting Jesus. Here again is that Scripture "sleight of hand" of which I spoke earlier.

It is true that, when we preach the message of Jesus and some reject that message, they are rejecting Jesus. But don't stretch that to mean that whenever disciples refuse advice, they are rejecting Jesus. This perversion of Biblical truth is at the very foundation of controlling discipleships.

There are many ways of structuring authority outside the church, ranging from dictatorships to anarchy. Christian leaders are to serve, not to have domineering control over others (Matt. 20:25-28).

If someone has convinced you it is a sin not to trust your discipler or leaders, or a sin not to have faith in your discipler, they are adding falsely to the word of God. The people in David Koresh's group believed this way, and that is why many couldn't escape. They had been persuaded that a lack of faith in David Koresh was the same as not having faith or trust in Jesus. Unfortunately, these "Scripture games" are being played in some of our own churches.

THE LIMITS OF AUTHORITY

Let's start an exploration of authority in the Church on a mountain in Galilee. Matthew 28 records Jesus' teaching to his disciples before his ascension into heaven:

All authority in heaven and on earth has been given to me.

Jesus is certainly the one with all the authority. But He never said to his Apostles, "I am giving you all the authority that I have." Jesus gave them certain, specific, and limited authority.

This passage is a crucial text on authority, because it joins Jesus' authority to the church's task. We must ask what kind of authority Jesus entrusted to His disciples (and to us) to carry out the command He gave? Disciplers indicate that, in order to carry out the commission to "make disciples," leaders must have authority over them to guide them in their growth in Christ. These disciplers ask, "How can we teach them to obey everything Jesus commanded without authority?"

On the surface, this seems sensible; but it simply is not what Jesus taught.

A second important text on authority is included in all three of the synoptic Gospels. Matthew, who recorded Jesus' words on the mountain, also recorded these words to disciples that set the tone for authority within the church:

> *You know that the rulers of the Gentiles lord it over them, and their high officials exercise authority over them. Not so with you. Instead, whoever wants to become great among you must be your servant, and whoever wants to be first must be your slave just as the Son of Man did not come to be served, but to serve, and to give his life as a ransom for many* (Matt. 20:25-28).

Jesus is recorded in Luke 22:25-27 (NAB) as saying:

> *The kings of the Gentiles lord it over them and those in authority over them are addressed as Benefactors; but among you it shall not be so. Rather, let the greatest among you be as the youngest, and the leader as the servant. For who is greater, the one seated at the table or the one who serves? Is it not the one seated at the table? I am among you as the one who serves.*

Discipleships that encourage members to be accountable to leaders in every area of their lives are following the "Kings of the Gentiles" model. This is *not* Biblical accountability.

DELEGATED AUTHORITY WITH FEW LIMITS

Are you thinking that supervisors in the workplace have authority over others? What is wrong with that? At work, your delegated authority has guidelines. Supervisors can't stretch their delegated authority to other areas without someone stopping them and telling them that they have overstepped their boundaries. Can you imagine what would happen if the company president came to work and delegated his complete authority to your manager without sufficient guidelines?

Many groups delegate authority to disciplers far beyond the limits of the Biblically explained rights of Christian leaders. Some disciplers feel they are free to advise in every area of a person's life. Since many of these disciplers have been told that they are more spiritually mature, it makes sense to them that they should advise their disciples in every area. They may actually believe that they know what is best for their disciples. These disciplers haven't bothered to verify whether this kind of behavior is based on the Bible.

Some disciplers claim, as part of the basis for their behavior, that the eunuch in Acts 8:26-39 was discipled by Philip. They miss the fact that Philip spoke only one time to the eunuch, leading to his conversion. God apparently didn't want Philip to stick around, because he removed Philip right after the eunuch's baptism. No one was constantly there to whom the eunuch would have to continuously report. In fact, the Bible says the eunuch continued on his way home to Ethiopia.

Why didn't Philip think it was important enough to tell him about being accountable to someone so the eunuch wouldn't go back to a non-Christian country? Why don't we hear the Apostles stress being accountable to someone so their disciples could live a more committed life? Why? Because the Apostles didn't teach that. Yes, Jesus did command His Apostles to make disciples, but not the type being taught by today's abusive disciplers.

Byron Fike, a Minister for *The Church of Christ*, writes:

> *It has been argued that in Matt. 20:25-28 Jesus was not denying that men would possess authority in the church, rather that he was seeking to correct the abuse that such authority could create when given to men. Actually, just the opposite is true! The word translated "authority" in Matt. 20:25 and Mk. 10:42 is "katexousiazo." It is scarcely found in secular Greek literature and occurs only twice in the New Testament. In secular Greek the word was used to mean not the misuse of power, but its possession and exercise.*[15]

Jesus wasn't giving men authority over people in his church. He said they were to be the servants and slaves (Matt. 20:26, 27). Servants can't have authority over the people they serve or they are no longer servants. Jesus gave the Apostles authority to present His message but He did not tell them to place themselves above people by giving them advice about every area of their lives. Jesus even referred to them as slaves. Abusive discipleship has perverted the Gospel to make it sound like Jesus gave His leaders authority over peoples' lives.

ACCOUNTABILITY MAY BECOME SLAVERY

Unfortunately, some disciplers teach new Christians that the Bible says they must be accountable to their leaders *in every area of their lives*. New Christians invited into some of these discipleship programs can become slaves. God never intended this for His followers (Luke 11:46; 1 Thess. 2:7-12).

Christians searching the Scriptures for the kind of authority often exercised in abusive discipleships will be sadly disappointed or joyfully relieved, depending on whether they're using it or are a victim of it.

There are seven other words translated into "authority" in the NIV. None of these is used to refer to anyone in the church as having an authoritative position. Four times they are used to say one should *not* be in a position of authority.

Some have pointed to Titus 2:15 as a prooftext proving that Titus occupied an authoritative position. The text states: "These, then, are the things that you should teach. Encourage and rebuke with all authority. Do not let anyone despise you." The word translated as "authority" in this passage is "epitage." The lexical definition is "with all impressiveness." Titus is to speak authoritatively as he presents the message of Christ. Paul is not giving him [a position of authority to rule over the individual lives].[16]

What authority are leaders supposed to have? Their authority is defined by the narrow constraints of Scripture. They are to present and represent the Gospel of Christ. The Apostle Peter, who certainly had every right to claim an exalted position of authority, shared this perspective in Chapter 5 of his first letter (I Pet. 5:1-3) to the Church:

To the elders among you, I appeal as a fellow elder, a witness of

Christ's sufferings and one who also will share in the glory to be revealed: Be shepherds of God's flock that is under your care, serving as overseers—not because you must, but because you are willing, as God wants you to be; not greedy for money, but eager to serve; not lording it over those entrusted to you, but being examples to the flock.

Note that, in this short passage, Peter did not issue a command—he appealed to his followers. He made it clear that a proper shepherd goes before his flock, leading the way, not driving the flock from the rear! If you are convinced that the Bible teaches that every committed believer should be accountable to another person (which means spending lots of time with your discipler and going over many details of your life), you may have just given permission for another to run your life.

AUTHORITY IS IN THE MESSAGE—NOT THE MESSENGER

In regard to the apostolic message, which Paul preached with all authority, the Apostle himself says this:

Even if we, or an angel from heaven, should preach to you a Gospel contrary to that which we preached to you, let him be accursed (Gal. 1:8).

How could Paul say this if he believed his disciples needed to be submitted and broken to him?

Yet most abusive discipleships say, "Check me out, don't take my word for it." This is misleading, because many ideas they teach are not contradicted in the Bible. As a matter of fact, they aren't there at all! Demands to trust disciplers, accusations that openly criticizing leadership is sin, requirements of loyalty to leaders, demands for commitments not to miss meetings, etc.—none of these appear in the Bible. What we do see in the Bible is room for critical thinking and disagreement with leaders.

Spend a certain amount of time with your discipler, confess your sins to your discipler, spend one hour in the morning praying, do not miss a meeting, etc.—while it is true that these may be good disciplines, they become legalistic rules if they're used to make you feel as though you are sinning if you fail to follow them rigidly.

Many disciples have told me that they feel guilty when they don't do these things. You may even be told you don't have to follow the rules, but your leaders will make it obvious that they think you are falling short of what is required to be a follower of Christ if you don't. The pressure will always be there.

Leaders are to proclaim the Gospel by word and example. They have no authority to expect you to heed their advice for every personal move and decision—such as which person to marry, what kind of major to pursue in college, where to live, what job to have, how to dress, whether you should wash your hands before you eat, etc. In these things, you are under no obligation to obey your discipler. His or her opinions are just that—opinions. The problem is that too frequently disciplers label their disciples as rebellious or otherwise sinful because they refused non-Biblical advice.

YES—OBEY EVERY REASONABLE COMMAND BY LEGITIMATE AUTHORITY

Leaders have the responsibility to proclaim what is moral and ethical for believers. "We do need the guidance and counsel of others. Obedience to authority is an act of the highest reasoning."[17] We, as believers, should obey "every reasonable command of legitimate authority."[18] What do "reasonable" and "legitimate" mean? They mean not overstepping the boundaries of Scripture!

The problem is that some disciplers *do* overstep the boundaries of Scripture, thinking that they have the authority to make their disciples follow by accusing the disciple of sin. This abuse by disciplers can cause disciples to believe that they are in sin if they don't obey, even when the particular matter has nothing to do with Scripture.

It is the disciple's responsibility to determine how to respond. The disciples are only bound to obey under the pain of sin if the matter is scriptural.

Some abusive discipleships give the impression that you are to relate to your discipler like the Apostles related to Jesus. It is important to note that many disciplers have only been committed a short time themselves. Disciplers can be very young and inexperienced in counseling and may be laypersons with very little training. They frequently don't have to meet qualifications of church leadership. Ask yourself, "How can these disciplers have legitimate church authority qualified to oversee souls?"

It seems that the leadership of abusive discipleship groups ignore James's advice:

Not many of you should presume to be teachers, my brothers,
because we know that we who teach will be judged more strictly.
We all stumble in many ways. If anyone is never in fault in
what he says, he is a perfect man, able to keep his whole body in
check. (James 3:1, 2).

Is a true discipler not a teacher? A true discipler hears your
sins and gives you spiritual advice. You are induced to follow his
direction. He has much more authority over you than would a
mere layperson. Yes, the discipler is a teacher.

An abusive discipleship must have a lot of "bodies" to sustain
the program as all disciples need someone with whom they can
spend hours to go over their personal lives. As a result, they are
forced to use novices for teachers because a really qualified person
engaged in spiritual oversight like this can disciple only a few
persons, as this work is very time-consuming.

The Apostles converted 3,000 in one day (Acts 2:41). Each of
the original disciples was obviously responsible for the spiritual
direction of many new converts. It is obvious that these original
disciplers could not have spent the hours with each of these
thousands that today's abusive discipleship programs demand.

ARE ABUSIVE DISCIPLESHIPS RAISING NOVICES?

The Apostle Paul gives this criterion for overseers in the church:

He must not be a recent convert, or he may be conceited and fall
into the same judgment as the devil (I Tim. 3:6).

Satan fell when he presumed to be what he was not, and to
possess the authority that was not his. Those who lead must be
aware of a similar presumption. If your discipleship puts novices
in a position of responsibility over souls, then it is straying from
Scripture. Disciplers: if you have been a committed Christian for
only a short time, think twice before overseeing souls.

I learned from a Benedictine monastery that it has been a
tradition for centuries that the church fathers recognized that
persons would have to be members of the community for many
years to make certain they have a great deal of maturity before
being assigned to be spiritual directors of any Christian brothers or
sisters. Today, new discipleship programs give the same type of
authority to disciplers who have only been committed Christians

for a short time. Remember that Paul the Apostle had a reflection and growth period of three years after Jesus appeared to him before he began his full-fledged mission (Gal. 1:15-24).

APOSTLES DIDN'T COMMAND RESPECT

Scripture recognizes that even the Apostles were ordinary men who put their sandals on one foot at a time. These men did not command awe and respect—the message did. When Peter came to Cornelius with the message of the Gospel (Acts 10:26), Cornelius fell at his feet and Peter said, "Stand up. I am only a man myself."

Leadership in an abusive discipleship is all-encompassing. It flows like water into every nook and cranny of life. Abusive disciplers claim authority to direct disciples in areas of interpersonal relations, business, study, and even home-buying. Such wide authority is certainly beyond the model we find in the Scriptures. We can all agree that Jesus did give directives on morals and values that His followers were to obey. We never read in Scripture about Jesus spending hours going over all the Apostles' personal problems. In fact, when a man begged Jesus to direct him in such areas, Jesus commented, "Who made me a judge over you?" (Luke 12:14). Jesus refused.

Paul himself limited his authority when it came to matters in which the authority of the Gospel was not at stake. Of disagreements the Romans had over observation of holy days, Paul says, "Each one should be fully convinced in his own mind" (Rom. 14:5 NIV). There is plenty of room for individual decisions in the true Christian community; much more than you will find in abusive discipleships. Paul and Peter call those who go around poking into other people's business "busybodies," and that is what they are (2 Thess. 3:11; 1 Pet. 4:15 KJV).

There are former disciplers who are agonizing over advice they gave when they were put in positions of authority. They realize that they stopped some disciples (many of whom were dear friends) from accomplishing their dreams and lifelong goals because they gave wrong advice.

I've been told by some of these former disciplers that they thought it was best that many disciples (especially if the disciplers felt they had the potential) serve God full time in the discipleship ministries. So it was only natural that they saw going to medical school or other careers as giving God less than they felt these disciples should give. With this prevailing attitude, it is not surprising that many disciples find their jobs without meaning.

Many decide to become full-time ministers, not because God is calling them, but because dissatisfaction was implanted in them by the discipleship program.

Many former disciplers tell me that they were taught to be able to discern the right marriage partners in their groups. They advised disciples about the partners they approved. The disciplers would encourage some disciples not to date persons the discipler did not believe were potential leaders, and they certainly wouldn't encourage someone to date someone that was not being discipled.

These disciples regularly heeded the advice from their disciplers. Several former disciplers regret that engagements were called off because of their advice. It was only after they escaped the influence of the controlling group that they realized their advice may have been harmful. A former disciple said that she didn't date for six years, including her college years, because of her discipler's advice. Others were encouraged to date more because disciplers were trying to get certain people together.

Discipleships also teach a kind of submissiveness and obedience that is not found in the Bible. Passages from the New Testament may even be used to suggest that submissiveness is always a positive character trait. Some passages (e.g., Hebrews 13:17: "Obey your leaders and submit to their authority") are used with great effect. What God-fearing disciple wants to be found in rebellion against God's leaders? Yet, as we have already seen, the obedience called for here is limited to Scriptural authority. Paul encouraged his Corinthian brothers and sisters, "Follow my example, as I follow the example of Christ" (I Cor. 11:1). In abusive discipleship, this passage is understood to say: *Follow me, (the discipler) because I am a follower of Christ.*

SUBMIT DOESN'T MEAN "JUST DO IT".

The actual meaning of Hebrews 13:17 is far less daunting and much more practical. The word used here for "submit" is *hupeiko*. W. E. Vine's *Expository Dictionary of Biblical Words* defines "hupeiko" as "to retire, or withdraw." The sense is one of "yielding" or "keeping out of the way" rather than "following an order."

The author of Hebrews is actually saying, "Don't hinder or

obstruct the leaders in doing their jobs, because they have to give an account to the Lord." When we understand "submit" in this way, the rest of the verse makes sense: "Obey them so that their work will be a joy, not a burden, for that would be of no advantage to you."

There is another Greek word that translated means "obey." *Peitharcheo* is found in Acts 5:29: "We must obey (peitharcheo) God, not man." It is interesting to note that this Greek word is used in reference to obedience to magistrates (or those in authority). It is never used when the Scriptures tell us to obey our church leaders. We must do what God asks, but we need to weigh and evaluate when others ask us to obey them.

> *You should be aware that there is no word for "authority" in Hebrews 13:17 in the Greek text. Neither is "authority" found in the translations of the RSV, NASV, NEB, KJV, ASV, or NKJV.*

> *A casual reading of Hebrews 13:17 may give the impression that pastors are to rule over the sheep, but brief word study in a concordance and an expository dictionary will disclose that this is incorrect. The word "obey" used here is from the Greek "peitho." It is in the passive middle voice so that the obedience suggested is submission to authority but results from persuasion. It's not "you'd better!" but, "here's the light and here's the darkness." It's not obedience taught by a rod. This passage is more correctly read: "Be taught or persuaded by those who lead and be pliable, for your teachers watch for your souls, as they must give account of WHAT THEY TAUGHT YOU." Not of what you did but of what they taught you.*

> *Many controlling groups give the impression that, if somehow you are not falling into line, then the leaders will have to answer to God for your failure. It is as if they are saying: "You've got to work with me because I've got to stand before God for you. So you have to listen to what I'm telling you."*

> *Sadly, this controlling idea has become reality for thousands in the family of God. You should understand that the meaning of these Greek words translated as "obey" and "rule" doesn't mean leaders are to rule over our lives, but only that we must keep a sweet teachable attitude toward them.*[19]

Some disciplers will focus on a verse like Titus 3:1-2: "Remind the people to be subject to rulers and authorities, to be obedient, to be ready to do whatever is good, to slander no one, to be peaceable and considerate, and to show true humility towards all men."

It is easy to equate the idea of "speaking evil" with saying *anything* negative. The translation of Titus 3:1-2 above (i.e., "slander no one") is better understood by those who speak modern English. There is a big difference between slander and disagreement. We are not to spread false information, but if our leaders are not following the ways of God, we are free to respectfully disagree. But, as you have seen, in some discipleships there is pressure not to disagree. Paul (1 Tim. 5:19, 20) indicates that church leaders can be rebuked, and Paul allows us to disagree without being called factious (1 Cor. 14:29).

Compliance is another characteristic of abusive discipleship. Submission is equated with compliance with leaders; disagreement and dissent are rarely tolerated. Disciples who speak critically about leaders are frequently labeled as rebellious, divisive, factious, or slanderous. For you to be counted as a slanderer in an abusive discipleship, your words don't have to mean anything false or malicious. In these groups, slander can mean anything negative that is said about the leadership. In a discipleship employing this kind of coercion, "factious" and "divisive" actually mean that your opinion differs from that of the leaders.

Think about it: If you were the leader and you convinced your congregation to believe that almost any criticism of you should be labeled as divisive, factious, slanderous, or something else sinful, then you could squelch nearly all criticism of yourself.

The Scripture associates obedience with "good enterprises" or "honest work," not blindly doing something with which (in good conscience) we cannot agree. The Bible limits our subjection and obedience to work that is for a good end. We cannot be commanded to do bad work.

A TWIST ON OBEDIENCE

"Selective focusing" is a technique of emphasizing one part of an idea over another until we lose the true meaning of what was meant by the original idea (politicians are notorious for doing this). This is also done in groups that twist Scripture. In abusive discipleships, selective focusing is applied to the words "obey" and "submit." To see how this technique works, let's examine part of a message from a discipler from the Boston Church of Christ:

We become like Jesus when we accept authority... Jesus submitted not only to the Father; but to sinful man as well. He totally submitted, even when He was wronged, and He was obedient to an unjust, ungodly death on a cross... Our trust is based not on the righteousness of the person in authority but on the power of God to take care of godly, submissive people... Jesus taught submission to authority. "The teachers of the law and the Pharisees sit in Moses' seat. So you must obey them and do everything they tell you" (Matt. 23:2, 3). Jesus rebuked abusive authority but He did not accept this as an excuse for disobedience.[20]

The idea planted in a member's mind through this teaching is: "I must obey all in authority completely if I am to be a disciple of Christ!" This is a logical conclusion if we accept that the Scripture really teaches this. But this discipler apparently forgot the basic principal of interpreting the Scripture, which is that we must take all the Scriptures together for complete understanding of the Bible. We must balance Jesus' words in the Gospel with His actions and the Apostles' words to that same leadership in Acts: "We must obey God rather than men" (Acts 5:29). Sometimes we should follow authority and sometimes we should not. The deciding factor is the mandate of Scripture, not the demands of human beings. Such perspectives are easily lost when "selective focusing" is used.

Jesus said:

The teachers of the law and the Pharisees sit in Moses' seat. So you must obey them and do everything they tell you. But do not do what they do, for they do not practice what they preach. They tie up heavy loads and put them on men's shoulders... (Matt. 23:2-4).

Does this Greek word for "obey" mean "comply with each command that the Pharisees request"? Does "do everything they tell you" mean every area of your life? What did Jesus mean? We can examine Jesus' own behavior to find out.

JESUS REFUSED TO OBEY RELIGIOUS AUTHORITY

When Jesus healed on the Sabbath, He refused to obey the Jewish leaders (John 5; Luke 13:10-17). Another time Jesus' Apostles were picking some heads of grain on the Sabbath, an activity the Pharisees said was unlawful. Jesus turned to the Pharisees and blasted them saying, "The Sabbath was made for man, not man for the Sabbath. So the Son of Man is Lord even of the Sabbath" (Mark

2:27). Jesus again refuted the Pharisees and "teachers of the law" ("church" authorities) when they demanded to know why His Apostles failed to wash their hands before they ate (Matt. 15:1-9). On another occasion (Luke 13:15), Jesus called the synagogue rulers hypocritical for putting their own man-made rules before God's commands. Again, religious leaders were overstepping the boundaries of Scripture.

Jesus never said that we are to obey our leaders in everything. He qualified what He meant by "obey" in action and words. We are to obey leaders in those things that are passed down from Moses. When Jesus said, "Do everything that they tell you to do," He didn't mean in every area of life, just in those areas covered by Scripture.

Yet, there are discipleships who demand complete accountability. They lay this heavy burden on you—just the thing against which Jesus preached. Think about it. Jesus wouldn't even let religious authorities require His Apostles to wash their hands, yet many disciplers teach that we should "just be flexible and obey" in all aspects of life. They think that it is "being broken and humbled" to become a doormat for leaders.

ABUSIVE DISCIPLERS SAY, "IF IT DOESN'T CONTRADICT, THEN BE FLEXIBLE AND OBEY"

Disciplers should say, "You don't have to obey my instructions unless they are a Biblical mandate." But the manipulative disciplers imply, "You have to obey unless I contradict Scripture." Isn't this a nice out? Disciplers can give a lot of advice that doesn't contradict Scripture. If you follow this theory, you will probably feel pressure to accept most of their advice.

In the diagram on the following page, the "Non-Moral or Non-Biblical Advice" area represents all those activities of life that do not contain moral elements (e.g., going to school, buying a house, etc.). The two smaller segments represent areas that are directly related to the Bible. The chart is designed to illustrate how a "non-Biblical disciple" might feel highly inclined to obey a high percentage of advice from the discipler (i.e., the "Non-Moral" and the "Non-Biblical Mandates"), because of the warped teaching.

The Biblical Disciple

This disciple is highly inclined to obey all Biblical mandates, but not necessarily the non-moral or non-Biblical advice offered by his discipler. This disciple is *not* highly inclined to feel that it is sinful to reject his discipler's non-Moral or non-Biblical advice.

The Biblical disciple would be strongly inclined to obey only 20 percent of "Biblical Mandates" without feeling that he or she is disobeying God. There is little or no pressure to accept advice from a non-manipulative discipler outside this 20 percent range.

The Non-Biblical Disciple

This disciple is highly inclined to obey most advice offered by his discipler, unless it clearly goes against the Scriptures. This disciple will be highly inclined to think that he is *in sin* for rejecting his discipler's non-Moral or non-Biblical advice.

Of course, disciplers will rarely ask disciples to rob a bank or lie for them, which would be "Advice Against Scripture" (clearly evil). But when an abused disciple disputes a request by his discipler to do something that falls into the "Non-Moral or Non-Biblical" areas, he will often feel he is disobeying God when he refuses the discipler's advice. This leaves only a small range of activity ("Advice Against Scripture") in which the disciple can feel certain he is not disobeying God when he disputes the advice of his discipler.

In reality, the abused disciple doesn't have much room to reject advice from his discipler without being made to feel he is failing in humility or being sinful. Although there are a few such occasions, they are far more common in non-manipulative spiritual direction. In non-manipulative spiritual direction, the Biblical disciple realizes that strict adherence is only required in the areas of Biblical mandates, and his discipler knows that he does not have the right to expect compliance with his advice in private non-Biblical affairs.

It could be a worthy sacrifice to God, however, to accept some advice that you don't like. For example, you may be asked to fast three times a week. It would not be sinful if you failed at this task, but it might be beneficial to make the sacrifice. In abusive discipleship, it would usually be looked upon as sinful if you didn't fast when told to do so. This is a major difference between non-abusive and abusive discipleship programs.

Disciples defending their disciplers have told me they would not obey anything that contradicts Scripture. This is dangerous thinking and, besides, it misses the point. The abusive discipler does not usually tell victims to go contrary to Scripture. Compare this to a non-controlling discipler who would not pressure you to obey anything that was in conflict with your conscience. Under such a discipler, you are free to reject a broad range of advice without feeling guilty.

Controlled disciples would probably say the discipler only wants them to pray and get God's leading on non-moral advice. However, they feel pressure to agree because they are taught that:

➢ their discipler probably knows what is best for them

➢ going against advice probably indicates a lack of humility, teachableness, brokenness, etc.

➢ their discipler has more maturity than they do

➢ going against the discipler's advice may be going against God

they need to obey disciplers, not just in Biblical mandates, but in all areas of life.

Believing all of this "extra stuff" puts a lot of pressure on the individual to go along with almost all advice, which can cause a person to be very controlled.

Eventually, it comes down to questions of such fine detail that if their discipler asks them to wash their hands before they eat, would they accept this? They probably would. Washing one's hands doesn't contradict Scripture, so they would pray about this even though Jesus balked at such rules (Matt. 15:1-9). Jesus didn't need to even pray about it to get God's leading on this type of activity. It was not handed down in Scripture from Moses and He wasn't going to obey or let His disciples think that they were in sin for not accepting man-made rules!

REJECTING ADVICE ISN'T SIN

Failing to wash your hands doesn't contradict anything from the seat of Moses. Is there something intrinsically wrong with asking someone to wash their hands? No. It sounds like good, healthy instructions, although this is referring to a religious ceremony. Why did Jesus refuse such rules? Because the rules were made equal to, or more important than, the Commandments of God.

Beware of discipleships that call it a sin to fail to keep their man-made rules (e.g., you need to open up to your discipler; be loyal to leaders; trust your leader; missing meetings is sinful). The thrust of much discipleship is that frequently it is seen as sin to refuse advice from the person to whom disciples are accountable. This defies Scripture. What do you think Jesus would say to disciplers who do this?

Has your discipler labeled you for being in sin because you didn't want to come to activities planned by the discipleship, such as Bible meetings, because you failed to accept advice, or because you didn't attend some church functions? Disciplers who do this commit the same sin as the Pharisees. They are telling you it is a sin to go against advice. Even healthy advice like washing your hands or going to more church meetings is nothing more than a suggestion. If you feel guilty when you don't do these things, look at your situation carefully. This is probably an artificial sin for which you should feel no guilt.

One disciple told me he had made a commitment to the group, and that is why it was sinful not to go to meetings. It wasn't a matter of the discipler's advice, he insisted.

Wait a minute! Who asked for this kind of commitment in the first place? The discipler! So the discipler instills in you that not being fully accountable (in this case, failing to come to every meeting) is a sin. This is the same thing that angered Jesus with the Pharisees. You want to go to the meetings? Fine. But it isn't morally wrong not to go.

HOW TO REMEDY A DISCIPLESHIP THAT IS CONTROLLING

Your discipleship program needs to say:
> ➤ it is not a sin if you don't want to share personal information with your discipler
> ➤ it is not a sin to reject any non-moral advice
> ➤ it is not a sin to distrust your discipler
> ➤ it is not a sin to miss discipleship meetings.

If you are the leader, keep the Biblical parts of your discipleship and discard the non-Biblical. You don't necessarily have to call off your meetings or Bible studies; just don't make them mandatory under pain of sin. Don't tie your disciples into a stiff commitment to your group. If your disciples decide to miss some meetings, that should be their option.

SUBMISSION—ALTERED MEANING

Too many Christians are being taught that if one is submitted, one should not care what the leadership does since God placed them in authority. Leaders are accountable to God. This, of course, is the kind of obedience displayed by the followers of Jim Jones and David Koresh, and it flies in the face of what the Scripture counsels: *"Test everything. Hold on to the good"* (1 Thess. 5:21; see also 1 Cor. 14:29).

The Bible teaches that we are to die to sin (Rom. 6:2-11; 1 Peter 2:24), while abusive discipleships teach that we should die to our sense of logic as to what is right and wrong and simply follow orders. Their misinterpretation is that "dying to self" means "obeying the will of the discipler"—in essence making the will of the discipler equal to the will of the Father. Not only could we find ourselves going against our conscience if we obey leaders in areas of opinion, we could be ignoring the will of God.

I brought up the concept of "dying to self" to one Baptist theologian. He told me, with signs of great frustration, that "dying to self" is not a Biblical idea. We are not to die to ourselves, just to our sinful ways, he explained. It infuriated this Bible scholar that these new ideas were being forced into the Bible.

Since discipleships warped this idea, I will use the term anyway. If we are to keep this phrase in our vocabulary, we must give it a correct Biblical definition.

A Principle of Abusive Discipleship

Dying to self = Giving up for God your own ideas, desires, ambitions, and obeying your discipler even when your heart tells you not to.

A Principle of Good Discipleship

Dying to self = Giving up for God your own sinful ideas, desires, and ambitions.

In an abusive discipleship, if the discipler's will doesn't match God's, you will be following the will of a mortal being instead of God's.

Good discipleships are critically different. Their principle requires you to follow the will of God, even when it is different from the will of your discipler.

When Jesus talks about denying yourself (Matt. 16:24; Mark 8:34; Luke 9:23), the context explains what He is talking about. He tells us to be willing to face persecution and death from enemies for being His follower. We are told not to be ashamed of Jesus in order to avoid persecution. Therefore, don't deny Jesus in order to save yourself from ridicule or death. This has nothing to do with obeying the casual or whimsical command of a human leader.

I often hear, "My leader lets me disagree with him and make my own decisions." All disciplers do that to some degree. That is not my complaint. I am not talking about those occasions when your discipler allows you to disagree or permits you to make decisions against his advice without negative repercussions. I am talking about the times when the discipler makes it clear that you are not living up to Christian standards because you are not obeying the rules or accepting advice.

Most abusive discipleships will let you disagree at times and not label you as being in sin. When they decide it *is* a sin to disagree with them, however, then you'd better change your mind or they will accuse you of "not dying to self," or some other sin.

Answer the following question: *Which one is the abusive discipler?*

A: The discipler who readily labels you as being in sin for not obeying when he decides you should follow his advice, or

B: The discipler who doesn't accuse you of being in sin if you reject his advice because it is just that—*advice.*

Of course, "A" is the answer. Don't forget that controlling disciplers will, at times, allow you to not follow their advice without negative repercussions. That can keep you from seeing the control. If total compliance were always demanded, you would see the problem. So just because you make some decisions on your own and can disagree to an extent, it doesn't mean your discipleship is guaranteed to be non-abusive. The discipler is not justified in labeling you as "going against God's moral law" (which is saying that you are in sin) if you go against the discipler's opinion.

"LIVING FOR GOD" AND "OBEYING LEADERS" ARE SYNONYMOUS IN ABUSIVE DISCIPLESHIPS

In the Biblical understanding, Jesus said, "Deny yourself... and follow me." He did not intend for a human being to stand in His place. A mere mortal cannot see into our hearts and tell us if playing the piano is living for God or glorifying ourselves. Only we can determine that. True, we should strip ourselves of all self-seeking, as we need to prefer God to ourselves.

Literally hundreds of Christians through the centuries have written about offering up all desires, goals, and ambitions to God so as not to be self-seeking. This is not to say that it is wrong to have our ambitions, goals, and desires, as long as they are not self-seeking.

Abusive discipleships promote the idea that living for God and obeying the discipler are nearly synonymous. In monastic orders, the members take vows of obedience to their superiors, yet these superiors don't expect their followers to act contrary to conscience. Monastic orders allow much more room for disagreement than do abusive discipleships. You must realize that disobeying a leader can actually be doing God's will.

WHERE'S THE ROOM FOR YOUR CONSCIENCE?

The director of spiritual development at Prince of Peace Monastery, Fr. Basil Mattingly, O.S.B, said that he may point out an action that could be prideful, but he can't make a firm judgment. The individual must decide in his own heart if something is prideful or self-seeking. Fr. Mattingly doesn't accuse someone in his order of being hard-hearted or proud because, he says, "Only the individual can see his heart." He leaves it up to the person to decide.

In abusive discipleship, you are *told* that you are factious, proud, or that you have a bad heart. Once they've marked you, there's little chance that you can decide yourself. For, if you complain that they've judged you wrongly, the controlling discipler is likely to rebuke you for what he calls "an unteachable attitude"—meaning that you refuse to accept how he has labeled your heart. You're in a no-win situation.

The thrust of abusive discipleship is that you need to have someone between you and God confirming that your decisions are God's will. Abusive disciplers claim this will ensure that you will be more accountable to God, but actually you are more accountable to a mortal being. You are convinced the discipler knows what is best for you. You think your discipler can better tell you if your ambitions, goals, and desires are for the glory of God, or for yourself. Abusive discipleships twist many Scriptures to cause you to believe in this type of accountability.

I am not saying that you should ignore advice from your spiritual director. I am saying that non-controlling spiritual directors won't view you as unteachable for rejecting their advice in areas of opinion, nor will they commonly label you as sinful for disagreeing.

OBEDIENCE IS GODLY—SO WHEN DO WE OBEY?

Freedom exists through discipline and through obedience to God. Many disciplers apparently think only they know the right way of obedience. What they teach, however, is deception. Though these disciplers teach "dying totally to self," they then turn it around and require obedience to themselves.

If you are to be free, then you must know when to obey. There are moral requirements to be met before we obey. Ask yourself: "Is this authority legitimate? Is it reasonable?" Do the "authorities" stay within the boundaries prescribed for their station in life? For example, can your pastor ask you to mow his grass? Yes, but you aren't disobedient to God if you don't do it. It is not sinful to reject this request because it is out of your pastor's jurisdiction.

Legitimate authority usually won't take advantage of you or cause you to feel guilt if you decide not to comply with these types of requests. Watch out when leaders make it a sin not to follow requests that are outside the boundaries of Scripture.

PUBLIC REBUKING FOR A DIFFERENT OPINION

I was recently threatened with being publicly rebuked for disagreeing with the actions of leadership in a matter unrelated to morality or the Bible. In Scripture, we see leaders publicly rebuked because they misled their flock, but we don't see laypersons publicly rebuked for personal sins, or for holding opinions that differ from those of the leaders. In abusive discipleships, leaders feel they have the right to publicly rebuke you merely for your opposing opinion, especially if they correct you and still you refuse to agree with them.

Abusive disciplers think any sin you commit gives them the right to publicly rebuke you. They make little distinction whether your "transgression" is a grave matter or just a differing opinion. Many times, the opinion for which the person gets rebuked is not sinful at all, but, because it differs from the leadership's opinion, they claim it is sinful.

Leaders will less likely become controllers if they are not allowed to rebuke someone just because they happen to disagree. When a discipler believes he can rebuke disciples for anything he considers a sin, he is now a danger to his flock—he is abusive.

The incident that brought forth these thoughts was one involving a discipler with whom I disagreed about the frivolous rules concerning single adults in an apartment complex. I was threatened with public rebuke; I tried to persuade this discipler that the Scripture does not give him the right to rebuke me publicly for simply a difference of opinion. The discipler replied that, since my opinion was wrong, I was in sin. Since he had first told me in private that I was wrong, he believed the Bible gave him permission to rebuke me publicly, since I persisted in my position.

I tried to convince him that he was wrong in threatening me with public humiliation because of a disagreement. This discipler could not see that his false belief wrongly allowed him unlimited authority to intimidate me.

CHECKLIST
Authority Unlimited—Chapter 3

Check those that apply to you and/or your group:

❑ Goes beyond Scripture when it gives authority to leaders

❑ Uses verses such as "Touch not my anointed" to imply we can't criticize leaders without being critical of God

❑ Emphasizes trusting leaders, having faith in leaders, imitating leaders, and/or being loyal to them

❑ Occasionally assert that refusal to obey leaders' opinions in personal matters is sin

❑ Stresses that leaders are servants; but, in practice, allows leaders to use public or private rebuke for differences of opinion

❑ Implies, or even teaches, that we should trust our discipler as the Apostles trusted Jesus

❑ Classifies almost all criticism of leaders as slanderous or malicious

❑ Selectively focuses on the idea that Jesus endured under abusive authority by being crucified wrongfully, implying that we should obey even questionable advice from leaders to prove our brokenness

❑ Ignores Scriptures that describe how Jesus refused to obey certain religious leaders

❑ Implies that we need to be accountable to a discipler in every area of our life, even those not in the area of Scripture

❑ Teaches that, if advice from leaders doesn't contradict Scripture, then we need to be flexible and obey

NOTE: If you have checked *any* boxes, it may indicate a misuse of Scripture and/or may represent the presence of abuse and excessive control.

Chapter 4

BEYOND ACCOUNTABILITY

*When a group influences its members to trust in the
leaders and discourages criticism of the leadership, it
creates a lethal combination! Errors can be overlooked
and leaders can get away with almost anything.*

"Jan" was in prison. In her disciple's notebook, she wrote:

*I want to share Jesus with others, but I don't want them to be in
prison with me.*

Jan's prison had no walls. She was constantly baby-sitting for
the married couples in her group, and her presence was required
for so many church-related activities that she had little time for
herself or for the nursing school she wanted to attend. Jan could
not fully understand why the guidance of her leaders left her in
such a situation. She only knew she felt imprisoned. Although her
situation was extremely oppressive, Jan sensed she could not
question the leaders or say anything negative against the people
she viewed as "God's anointed."

**Abusive discipleship is a prison of the mind which can
imprison the body to accept the will of the group.**

When leaders deem control essential, whether in a Bible group
or a national government, they do not allow you to disagree with
their decisions. In abusive discipleships, questioning the leadership is as bad, if not worse, than adultery or murder. Almost
anything else can be forgiven and forgotten. Questioning leaders,
however, can bring painful consequences. It can mean demotion if
you are in leadership, or ostracism if you are a newer member.
You may even be asked to leave (or ignored to the point that you
will want to leave).

In abusive discipleships, we repeatedly see two things considered extremely important: (1) control of criticism and negative feedback; and (2) teaching people to obey even when they don't feel right about it because "the discipler knows best."

Just think about it. Pretend you are a leader of a group (any kind of group), and you have convinced your members that it is wrong to say anything negative about you (or, if they have something negative to say, they should only come directly to you so you can "correct" their wrong thinking). Also, they should be willing to obey you even when their goals, desires, or wishes conflict with your requests. Wouldn't you be able to get away with anything?

"Oh," you may say, "but I don't see that in my group."

Maybe that is because you and the others just go with the flow and therefore haven't provoked your leaders into asserting their authority. Perhaps the people who might question the leadership have already been forced out or suppressed. For these reasons, you may not see this control.

Test your program. Challenge your leaders when you don't agree with something they are telling you to do. Observe how you are treated. Express some negative comments (not gossip, but something you know is true), and observe what happens.

In a group that doesn't rein in negative comments, good leaders will permit questioning and allow others to hear of the concerns. They will sit down and calmly discuss issues without making a big deal out of them.

Leaders of groups that want power will label almost any challenge to their authority as *questioning* or *causing dissension or division*. They may say they have to "discern the motive or heart" of the individual before they will allow questioning to continue. They really believe they can judge your heart.

In mainline churches, we are not taught that all doubts about, or criticism of, leadership are sinful. In discipleships that control, we are conditioned to assume automatically that certain types of challenging questions, doubts, and critical thoughts concerning leadership are sinful. We are encouraged to think that when these situations arise, we don't need to analyze them to see whether they are legitimate. Once we have reached this level of indoctrination, it rarely crosses our minds that our leaders are doing something wrong. At this point, we have become putty in their hands.

Let's take a closer look at why we start to suppress, systematically, certain doubts, questions, and criticisms in a controlling group. There are techniques that will lead us into this mind trap. These techniques are very subtle. They work without our awareness of what is going on. Over a period of time, subtle mind games slowly wear us down. We are taught this new information under the guise of Biblical teachings, causing us to condition our own minds to reject doubts about our leaders and not to question their leadership.

Our minds more easily fall into this trap if we first:

➤ want to follow principles that will please God

➤ are convinced the Bible teaches us that we should not doubt or criticize leadership.

Abusive disciplers often say, "I'm not telling anyone how they are to think. I don't control anybody. They make up their own minds." There is an element of truth in this statement, but ask yourself: "Who is defining what constitutes doubts or what kind of doubts are deemed sinful? Who is avoiding certain negative questions? Who sometimes refuses to meet with someone who has challenging questions? Who is labeling members as prideful, factious, or divisive, for voicing healthy criticisms of leaders? Who is asking people to leave when they don't agree with the leaders? Who is judging the heart of the person who questions leadership?"

Who? The abusive discipler, of course.

So, if your discipleship puts a new slant on certain ideas (e.g., "doubts or challenging questions are sinful"), then you will repress or suppress these thoughts without the discipleship standing directly over you. This is a subtle way the discipleship uses to control your thoughts. Leaders were the ones who persuaded you to believe that criticism of leadership is probably slanderous, factious, or divisive. Eventually, you will automatically reject healthy criticism whenever it comes to mind.

Imagine that you are a teacher. You want to influence the class to never think a critical thought about you. You produce reason upon reason why students should be loyal and trusting of teachers. Then you convince your class that it is a principle of God not to have any negative thoughts about teachers. If you can make your students jump through all of these mental hoops, you can teach false ideas, and many students will swallow them without objection because they were conditioned to trust, be loyal, and not be critical of teachers.

TRUST IS EXPLOITED

Trust is an important word. Our Christian fellowship is a community of those who trust God. Yet the Bible does not tell us that we must trust leaders. Rather, leaders must continually prove themselves trustworthy (1 Cor. 4:1,2) [NASB]. A lot is made of trust of the leadership in abusive discipleships and most controlling groups. Some programs indicate that, if we are not totally trusting in our discipler, we are hard-hearted and rebellious, and that we are in sin.

The following statements are taken from prayer request lists published by an Atlanta discipleship group:

➤ *"John" repents of not seeking his discipler's advice and not thinking like his discipler*

➤ *"Mark" repents of being closed with discipler and distrusting God and his discipler*

➤ *"Joan" repents of not dreaming, not having visions and of relying on herself more than her discipler*

➤ *"Fred" repents of distrusting his discipler*

➤ *"Susan" repents of distrusting God and the people in her life*

➤ *"Anne" repents of independence and distrusting God, her husband, and her discipler*

➤ *"Mary" confesses she has distrusted God by not allowing her discipler to work in her life this past week and repents of being quietly stubborn and thinking she has a "better way"*

➤ *"Sally" repents of giving up too easily, depending on her own abilities, and not giving her heart to her discipler.*[21]

If you have never been in a controlling Bible group, you are probably saying; "Wow, I can't believe they confess these things!" If you have been conditioned to believe that this is "right thinking," this list probably has little impact on you.

Let me assure you that the guilty feelings expressed above are not due to real sin. The feelings spring from an artificial sin.

When I checked the word "trust" in my Bible concordance, I was surprised to find the word is never used in reference to church leaders. Nowhere does the Bible tell us to trust our church leaders. In abusive discipleship programs, "trust" is frequently stressed, and sometimes there are teachings on this non-Biblical idea. I find it interesting that the Apostles never exhorted their converts or disciples to trust *them*.

In my concordance, I found the word "trust" in Scriptures, used contrary to the idea of trust in people. Jeremiah 9:4 says: "Beware of your friends; do not trust your brothers." Micah 7:5 reads: "Do not trust a neighbor; put no confidence in a friend." When a discipleship program harps on trusting the leadership, they are distorting the meaning of a Biblical word that is precious to believers.

Over a period of time, church leaders may earn our trust and respect by their example. It would be proper and prudent to place a certain amount of trust in them. Yet, we should still evaluate their teachings and be ready to speak out against wrongdoing, to protect the leaders from continuing in error. We have a responsibility from God to condemn wrong teaching. To misuse "trust" by applying it to our leaders may seem harmless, but it opens the door to a dangerous method of control. Churches that are not trying to unduly influence the thinking of their members will not misuse "trust" in this way because, to do so, is adding to the word of God.

If we are taught to trust totally and are discouraged from criticizing leaders openly, then we lose the ability to think critically. That is why it is unhealthy to stray from Scripture and teach trusting our leaders. If our leaders don't want us to be critical of their actions when they are doing something wrong, then we shouldn't follow these leaders. They are supposed to be servants, not dictators. Leaders need to have humility in order to be able to accept honest criticism.

UNITY MEANS CONSTANCY OF PURPOSE

Another powerfully exploited word is "unity." Ephesians 4:3 says: "Make every effort to keep the unity of the Spirit through the bond of peace." Controlling Bible groups will make serious efforts to embed "unity" in the minds of their members, meaning they should change their views to whatever happens to be the current "group think." In the Scriptures, "unity" means "constancy of purpose" (Col. 3:14). The Apostles often had differences, but they still kept a constancy of purpose. For example, the inclusion of Gentiles was strongly debated in the early church. Just like the Apostles, we can have opposing views and still have one purpose.

The Bible also mentions a disagreement between Paul and Barnabas over Mark (Acts 15:36-41). The passage indicates that the disagreement was so sharp that Paul and Barnabas split up and traveled separately. This does not mean that their unity was broken. They still had constancy of purpose (spreading the Gospel). They just found it was better to work separately—and God blessed them both.

Ephesians 4:4-6 also talks about what makes us unified; it is "one hope... one Lord, one faith, one baptism; one God and Father of all, who is over all and through all and in all." This certainly is not saying that we must agree with our leaders on non-moral issues or support all their actions to be unified in Christ. Yet in the abusive groups, you often hear such comments as, "You need to be in unity with the body." Again, this is often about non-Biblical issues.

In abusive groups, you can be considered out of the Body of Christ for a trivial matter. For example, if you don't agree that the group should purchase property, or you don't agree to participate in church activities, you could be labeled "out of unity" with the Body of Christ. As long as you don't agree when the leaders think you should, you can be told that you are out of "unity."

Here is a concise understanding of Non-Biblical and Biblical Unity:

NON-BIBLICAL UNITY

Agreement with leaders and actively participating in all group activities.

BIBLICAL UNITY

Is not an earthly bond. It is a commitment to Christ, His values, virtues, love, and mercy. You may disagree with leaders; you are not expected to participate in loads of church activity.

The mere argument that you should be in unity tells you that the facts are not as important as agreeing. When a group stresses unity instead of the facts, watch out. They are asking you to mindlessly accept their opinions. The facts should be the reason why you make the right choice whether you agree or disagree.

Here is a teaching from a discipleship:

...even if he calls you to do something that disobeys your conscience, you still have an obligation to study it out and prayerfully change your opinion so you can be totally unified.[22]

As you study this, you will find it ridiculous to presume that two people can't have different opinions and still be united in purpose. How many times have you and your best friend disagreed about an issue but still believed in your friendship? In more extreme discipleships, members must be unified in thought or they can be asked to leave!

Recently I heard of an extremely controlling elders' group that decided everyone had to be in agreement before they would make major decisions. This makes it difficult for the few people who would like to have their own opinion and not have to agree on everything completely. Pressured by the rule that no decisions can be made without a unanimous vote, members (unless they feel like battling it out) give into the pressure to vote with the majority. Since most don't want to be looked upon as out of unity and perhaps unspiritual, they give in and go along with the group-think.

If your group has this strange controlling rule, consider eliminating it. Try something less demanding than all-or-nothing (e.g., a two-thirds vote). One dissenter among you may be the only one who is right, yet this person might not be strong enough to stand alone. Allowing some dissension on an issue might possibly bring in God's will. Leaders need to give humble consideration to voices that differ.

INCORRECT USE OF THE WORD "JUDGE"

"Judge" is another word that is thrown around, and takes on new meanings, in some manipulative groups. When these groups want you to be quiet about what you see as errors in leadership, they tell you, "You shouldn't judge." *Do not judge, or you too will be judged* (Matt. 7:1) is often quoted from Scripture. You will find many places in the Bible that speak about reproving someone who does wrong, but you must understand that there is a great difference between reproving and judging.

This is just another word game to make you think that judging what is wrong with leaders is, in itself, wrong. You will notice that when you judge these disciplers in a positive light, you will never hear them shout, "Judge not!"

Let's analyze this incorrect use of Matthew 7:1. If it means we cannot evaluate the actions of others, then Paul would not have said he has already passed judgment on the one who was being an immoral brother (1 Cor. 5:3). Then (1 Cor. 11:31) we read that if we judged ourselves, we would not come under judgment. At first, this seems rather confusing. We can judge ourselves, but we must be extremely cautious when we judge others because we cannot see their hearts or motives.

Can we judge or not? Scripture gives us evidence we can "judge righteously" but we should avoid "passing judgment" (condemning). In a positive sense, "to judge" means to carefully assess a situation and come to a right conclusion.

On the other hand, we must be very careful about making judgments about other people in things that do not concern us. This idea of a person's accountability for his actions before God is brought out in Romans 14:4: *Who are you to judge someone else's servant? To his own master he stands or falls. And he will stand, for the Lord is able to make him stand.* We are supposed to realize that we should not worry about the speck in our brother's eye while there is a log jammed in our own (Matt. 7:1-5).

Another passage that abusive discipleship misconstrues in order to suppress public criticism is Matthew 18:15: *If your brother sins against you, go and tell him his fault, between you and him alone...*[23] This Scripture was used against me when I was checking for balance in a discipleship program in a mainline church. I sent a letter to the leader of the program expressing some concerns. This is the response I received from him:

> *It grieves me that you would be so concerned about whether or not I am being Biblical in my teaching, yet exhibit a complete disregard for whether or not you are being Biblical in how you address these concerns. In Matt. 18, Christ makes it clear that if your brother offends, you are to "go and reprove him in private." In the Greek it literally reads "between you and him alone." In other words, if you go to anyone before or in addition to your brother, it is sin. You did not come to me in private. Instead, you have talked with numerous others in violation of the clear teaching of Christ. From the number of people I have talked with who you have maligned me to, I can only guess how many there are out there you have spoken with who have not come to me.*[24]

He failed to recognize the context of this passage from Matthew. It deals primarily with a member of the flock—not one in a leadership position who goes astray or commits sin. He ignored, or failed to recognize, other Scripture passages that specifically deal with leaders who err and sin.

This leader wasn't interested in possible problems with his discipleship. Rather, he was concerned that, by my discussing questions with another person, I was not being Biblical. He even wanted me to go to anyone with whom I had spoken and retract my words. According to him, this conformed to the Bible. Isolating a Scripture passage can lead to serious misuse of Scripture, to a distortion of God's design, and to mistreatment of God's people.

A strong principle used by the controlling discipleships is that you must go straight to, and only to, the leader when you have a criticism. If you don't, you probably will be blasted just as I was. If you do go to him alone, you will probably get blasted anyway for at least one or more of the reasons I pointed out earlier. If your discipleship thinks this is the only right way to handle criticism of a leader, your environment is being controlled. This causes you to push aside your reasonable concerns, because you have been led to believe this criticism is probably evil.

This Scriptural passage (i.e., Matt. 18:15) has been misapplied. It actually pertains to serious problems between two individuals that will involve the whole church if the person persists in doing wrong.

The Bible specifies:

➤ Sin against a person, seek personal redress
➤ Sin against the congregation, seek congregational redress.

Paul brings out this second, and much neglected, side of redress when he writes to Timothy:

Never entertain an accusation against an Elder[25] unless there are two or three witnesses to accuse him.[26] Those who continue in sin, rebuke in the presence of all.[27]

Here we find a different standard being applied to leaders. They are protected from personal vendettas by requiring the testimony of several, but the redress is public. Ironically, in abusive discipleship groups, it is the followers who are subjected to public rebuke for personal sins, rather than the leaders for sins against their flock.

It is important to ask yourself, how do two or three witnesses hear an accusation against an elder or any leader unless it is first discussed among members? Logically, you have to have permission to talk with members in order to find out if there are witnesses. In abusive discipleships, you are not to discuss problems about leadership with others, but go directly in private to the leader alone. We are told, however, that we shouldn't accuse an elder unless there are two or three witnesses. How can leaders make this requirement conform with their demand for private discussion? Obviously we have to discuss the leader's conduct with others to find two or three confirmed testimonies in order to ascertain the truth.

Other passages of Scripture give us additional examples of how we can address incorrect teaching.

In Acts 11, Peter is criticized publicly by circumcised believers over the issue of his doctrine calling for uncircumcised Gentiles to be included in the church. According to controlling discipleship, this verse should be overlooked, as this is not the way they want you to confront an important teacher!

In Chattanooga, a prominent mainline church had an intense discipleship program where I asked two ladies working at the front desk, "Why don't you ever use Acts 11 or Galations 2:14 as a way to handle a Scriptural complaint or problem with a leader?" They told me, "The early Christian church should never have handled it that way. *It was wrong.*" Then one of them said, "The church then was in transition, so we can't use those Scriptures." I was amazed by this rationalization. These groups always seem to be inventing new ideas so they don't have to accept certain parts of the Word of God.

Those New Testament men did not go in private to Peter. They must not have had that loyalty teaching either, because they seemed to feel that it was okay to think that Peter could be wrong and even to challenge him publicly. The idea that they needed to "just be flexible and obey" must not have been instilled in them or they would have agreed with Peter. Instead, they debated the issue in the open.

Teachers should seek public criticism to keep themselves in line. If the public challenge is wrong, then the truth will hold up on its own. Leaders need not fear criticism unless they are the kind who demand extreme control.

Read what Paul says to Timothy (i.e., a *third party*) about Hymenaeus and Philetus (2 Tim. 2:17). Paul says that their words "are like cancer." If the matter had been kept private, the church members may have stayed confused on the issue. In Gal. 2:14-21, Paul confronts Peter and others in front of everyone. He had no qualms about speaking aloud what was wrong. We have a moral obligation to speak when our Christian leaders have gone astray. That is not to say that going to our leaders in private is the wrong way to handle a problem. In this case, however, Peter's fault was public, seen by all of the members of the church. Therefore, it had to be addressed in public, before the entire congregation.

What if, in the early church, there had been a policy that someone with a complaint must go to Peter in private? Peter may have not agreed that there was a problem. By the time the two of them talked it all out, took witnesses, and then went before the entire church, it could easily have been too late. The damage may already have been done, and a number of other church members could have been misled, and perhaps could have strayed from the true Christian path, while those private discussions were taking place. Peter may have been able to intimidate Paul in private discussion by telling Paul that he was low man on the totem pole and needed to be flexible, teachable, humble, and obedient. (Well, that's doubtful considering Paul's personality, but Peter could have intimidated you or me!)

This is what happens in controlling groups or cults when you go to the leaders in private. You are convinced that you need to be humble and obey the leaders. In these groups, isolated confrontation of leaders by a layperson is dangerous.

If we want to be Biblical and only handle things as the New Testament Christians did, the Bible tells us that such disagreements may be public. In most cases, the leaders were called on the carpet in front of everyone. *That's* what the Bible tells us to do.

Leaders need feedback to keep them accountable. If they can easily discredit and ignore people who question or criticize a program, they can continue controlling. If they can suppress criticism by telling someone that they are being negative—and, therefore, in sin—they can shrug off accountability. There is no one to keep them honest except their yes-men, who are conditioned to be trusting, loyal, and uncritical of them.

Doubt and criticism may also be linked with slander or gossip. Read Titus 3:2: "Slander no one" or James 4:11: "Brothers, do not slander one another." These are true Biblical principles. But controlling Bible groups may trick you into believing that, when you think something negative of leadership, it is "slander" or "gossip."

Let's take a look at the word "slander" in the Bible. Englishman[28] translates the word in Titus (3:2) as "to speak evil of one." This is used in reference to those people who find fault with others, spreading derogatory information about anyone whose back is turned. It is true that we must not speak maliciously.

Does this mean that, when leadership is in the wrong, we cannot speak the truth in front of everyone? No. But if you are in an abusive discipleship, you might say, "Yes!" When the Apostle Peter was called down in public for refusing to eat with the Gentiles, no one suggested it was slanderous to speak out against leadership. Abusive groups want you to feel that it is slanderous to criticize them or their leadership publicly. Slander is not the same as speaking truthful facts, even when those facts aren't favorable toward the leadership of the group.

Once leaders have convinced you that anything negative about leadership is slander or gossip, you will suppress such thoughts. Then leaders can get away with abuses and build greater control of the flock. If no one can question leaders' activities without thinking "I am guilty of sin" for voicing a negative opinion, it sure makes it easy to control the flock with few objections.

Note to leaders: You will be much more effective if you allow criticism openly, with no public negative repercussions to those who disagree with you.

If your group harps on "not doubting," "not slandering," and "dying to self," you should see a red flag. Look more closely and you may find that their definitions of these terms veer away from the Biblical ideal. You may find that the group's leadership is trying to condition you to avoid thinking critically and objectively about their teachings and practices. You should step back and take a hard look at your group, for there may be a lot of other problems!

CHECKLIST
Beyond Accountability—Chapter 4

Check those that apply to your group:

- ❏ Controls negative feedback of leaders
- ❏ Equates doubts and criticism of leadership as sin
- ❏ Teaches people to obey even when it doesn't feel right
- ❏ Emphasizes such ideas as "dying to self" in a non-Scriptural manner
- ❏ Subtly redefines the meanings of words
- ❏ Seems to repeat certain Biblical words almost to the exclusion of other Biblical principles
- ❏ Members confess being sorry for not trusting their discipler
- ❏ Teaches "unity" as meaning members' opinions should match those of the group
- ❏ Members must meet in private with leaders when pointing out errors

NOTE: If you have checked *any* boxes, it may indicate a misuse of Scripture and/or may represent the presence of abuse and excessive control.

Chapter 5

THE LANGUAGE OF ENSLAVEMENT

The disciple can be steered by mere suggestion and by manipulating the meanings of words. The cumulative effect of repeatedly rejecting one's own desires and the continual pressure to conform causes severe emotional problems.

A non-Biblical definition of authority opens the door to abusive discipleship. This takes place, in part, through a distortion of language. Biblical terms may be subtly redefined to have different meanings and applications than the original Scriptural intent. As the meaning of the language is changed, disciples begin to think and behave in new ways. These changes allow a discipler to have excessive influence on the disciple's everyday decisions.

In an earlier chapter, we discussed some Biblical words whose meanings were altered to allow leaders to escape accountability. I have compiled a glossary of some other words and verses frequently distorted, redefined, or misapplied by abusive discipleship groups. As you read them, perhaps you can think of how these are used in your group.

STRUGGLE

Originally, if a person was said to be "struggling," it may have meant not wanting to keep the commandments of God. Today, in controlling groups, if you simply don't agree with a leader's opinions, you may be described as "struggling."

In a non-abusive discipleship, you wouldn't have to struggle when rejecting advice because there isn't much pressure to accept ordinary advice. If you are struggling with accepting your discipler's opinion that is contrary to your own judgment, then the discipler has likely become a subtle spiritual dictator in that area of your life. There will be times when he doesn't mind if you don't follow his advice, but I am speaking about those times when he says you are not following God's will because you do not accept his opinion. At those times, you will suffer repercussions if you fail to agree with the discipler.

In the abusive discipleship, there are subtle pressures brought about by the implication that if you don't agree with your discipler, you likely aren't humble or broken. You really aren't free to choose, since there is intense psychological pressure to pick one path over another.

When I challenged a discipler about his particular group, he responded by saying I was causing him to struggle and have doubts as a result of my information. Doubt and struggle meant that he was questioning what his leaders were telling him. Still, in his mind, it was clear that the group was comprised of totally committed Christian believers, and he felt God was leading their group more directly than any other Christians he knew. Under these conditions, having serious doubts about his leaders meant doubting his own faith in God.

Could you possibly have this bias? If I suggested that you might doubt what you have learned from your discipleship teacher, would you give credence to what I said or would you refuse to listen? People who are not willing to listen and discuss their concerns outside of their own group are admitting they have closed their minds. This is very dangerous. This is what destructively controlling groups try to get their members to do when questioned about their group.

It is very important for you to seek advice from outside your church group, since the opinions of leaders in a strictly controlling church almost always echo one another.

I know from personal experience that struggling is a painful process, especially when you fear you might be turning your back on God. You need to know that you have the freedom to think negatively (or positively) without feeling sinful. Once you find out that Scripture does not say that it is sinful to criticize leaders, you'll no longer feel guilty. You'll no longer struggle against yourself. Your inner turmoil will be greatly reduced.

ADVICE

What is advice? It is counsel you can accept or reject. In coercive discipleships, there is pressure to routinely accept advice. Frequently, in abusive discipleships, getting "advice" is excessively encouraged. Certain kinds of advice may not be refused without painful repercussions. These repercussions may be punishment by the leaders, although more often it is in the form of self-induced guilt. If you decline to accept advice and are punished or made to feel guilty, it is no longer advice—it is an order or a command.

Perhaps you say, "I don't accept all the advice of my discipler." You may think this proves you are not being controlled. How wrong you may be! Carefully examine the advice you reject. Think of the times you had to struggle to accept the advice of your discipler. If you force yourself at times to accept the advice of your discipler, it may be because you are trying to accept his or her opinion contrary to what your own conscience is telling you. You may have convinced yourself that this is "dying to self."

Remember when you felt guilty about refusing the advice of your discipler? Write down these events and discuss them with a trusted person from outside your discipling group. Maybe you should not have felt guilt, or perhaps it wasn't really mandatory to struggle because it was nothing more than the opinion you were rejecting. It's not necessary to accept your discipler's opinion. You are not obligated to accept human opinion. You are only obligated to what is Scripturally based (Acts 5:29, Rom. 14) and mandated by God. In this system, however, you may begin to feel you are not committed if you reject the discipler's direction. This is not direction or counsel—this is bondage!

Do you frequently feel you are not doing God's will when you go against your discipler's advice? If you suffer as a result of rejecting advice, you are probably being coerced. If you made a decision you feel would have been different in the absence of your leader's disagreement, your will is probably being constrained. If you changed your direction solely because your discipler held an opinion contrary to yours, you may be in great danger. Although you think you are freely accepting advice, you may actually be under great psychological pressure to move in the direction set by your discipler. Your decisions are being unduly influenced. You are accepting your discipler's ideas as your own. You are being held in "mental slavery"—and it may affect your mental health.

SELF-INDUCED GUILT AND "ARTIFICIAL SIN"

"Rachel" loved to pile cream cheese on her bagel but the authority who lived in the house with her said that was gluttony. Rachel sometimes would sneak a bagel and cream cheese. But, while it tasted wonderful, the feelings of guilt were there, too. While you may regard this as trivial, it is not. An accumulation of minor manipulations exerts constant pressure to conform to someone else's expectations. This can lower your self-esteem (that sense of self-worth that arises from the knowledge that you are God's child), diminish self-confidence, and eventually lead to serious emotional problems.

Who but the individual is to judge whether something is gluttony? In abusive discipleships, the leaders make that judgment. Leaders often question your personal habits just to see if they can find some possible cause for judging you. Is your leader qualified and justified to give such personal direction? Leaders should, of course, teach about the principle of gluttony, but pressuring you to diet, suggesting what to eat, etc., is beyond Scriptural boundaries. You must be allowed to live by your own conscience. Leaders must follow the restrictions of Scripture as did the Apostles. You don't hear Paul saying, "If you eat two plates full of food, you are a glutton!" Instead, Paul taught the principles and left it to the individuals to decide if they were sinning.

ADVICE WITH REPERCUSSIONS

If Rachel were caught eating more cream cheese than her discipler thinks she should, she might be rebuked. If Rachel persisted in her "rebelliousness" because she wouldn't stay away from the cream cheese, she may be rebuked in front of other disciples. You may think this sounds outrageous. It is.

Suppose we are dealing with real sin. Wouldn't public reprimand be allowable? No, it would not!

Take "Katie" who was falling for one of her aerobic instructors. Her discipler, "Sally," took note. Because Sally felt Katie's "lust" had to be stopped, Sally gave her a list of rules: Katie was told not to go to the center, not to call that good-looking instructor, etc. Sally was playing God, taking away Katie's free will by these demands supposedly meant to keep her from sinning. Some discipleships twist Scriptures to make you think that your discipler has this right. Maybe they think they are showing they really care for you by laying down the law and forcing you to be a good Christian. They are, quite simply, misguided.

As a leader, Sally has the right to express her concerns and to show where the Bible spells out that Katie should not have lustful feelings and should avoid the occasion of sin; but this is Sally's limit. This is where abusive discipleships overstep their Scriptural boundaries, thinking they have the right to enforce correct behavior. Do we see Jesus giving an ultimatum even to Judas?

If Katie were actually committing a sin, according to Scripture, Sally has the right and obligation to warn her. Scripture shows us that Jesus always rejected sin, but showed compassion to sinners. Sally's rules and punishments are not acceptable. Some coercive discipleship methods call for interrogation, confrontation, and accountability in the belief that they are making Christians live right. To the contrary—this is reminiscent of the medieval inquisitions.

Abusive discipleships also teach the principle of cutting off sinners, quoting narrowly from the Scriptures to make certain passages seem as though they are saying that's how you handle sinners in the church. This may be correct for actual persistent, serious sins, but many of the so-called sins these groups are focused on are artificial sins.

PERVERSION OF THE GOSPEL

The Bible doesn't give us the right to lay on restrictions in order to make someone do good. The idea that we must force our disciples to meet our standards, or reject them for their immaturity or weaknesses, comes from twisted Scriptures.

One verse often misused is 1 Corinthians 5:9: *I have written you in my letter not to associate with sexually immoral people.* Paul was referring to a man who had actually committed adultery with his father's wife and who was continuing this affair—an outrage even by non-Christian standards. Behavior of this type could not be tolerated by church authorities. Paul goes on to say: *You must not associate with anyone who calls himself a brother but is sexually immoral or greedy, an idolater or a slanderer, a drunkard or a swindler. With such a man do not even eat.* He continues: *Expel the wicked man from among you.* (1 Cor. 5:11, 13). But non-Christians with these problems need to be reached out to and saved, which can't be done if you don't associate with them. Paul's letter dealt with clear and specific problems—leaders must take this into account when trying to apply his words to present circumstances in their groups.

Abusive discipleship groups are experts at using these one-liners out of context, misapplying them to any sign of weakness in members. If a father is an alcoholic, these disciples might feel justified in refusing to go home and eat with him. Likewise, they would feel justified in cutting off a friend who loses his temper, slanders someone, or who is caught up in greed for worldly goods.

Is "confronting all sin" loving? Non-controlling churches allow much more room for error. Controlling churches are eager to confront sin whenever and wherever possible, regardless of how small the sin. In abusive discipleships, there is much more emphasis on confronting the sinner than on patience or mercy. When this balance is lost, we find disciplers interrogating Christians. They believe churches that don't confront don't care about the sin in their members' lives. They see themselves as caring about your sin. They will change your ungodly ways once you are inside where they will demand you to repent. They see this as truly loving, but they go far beyond what is taught to us in Scripture.

NEW CONVERTS

A new convert is someone who has just become a Christian, right? Not always. In abusive discipleships, a new convert is usually someone who has just entered into a discipling relationship with the group. Such people may be considered new converts even if they have been Christians for many years. As I began to understand the mind-set (the group's distorted concepts induced not only by their teachings but also their practices and methods that form their new view of reality) of destructive discipleship programs, I realized that people who are beginning in discipleships are looked on as less spiritually advanced. This wasn't taught, but it was clearly understood. New members are not usually judged like this in other churches. Prior to the beginnings of discipleship influence, it was almost unthinkable to judge new members this way.

The problem seems to be that virtue and maturity are connected not to the quality or length of one's walk with Christ, but to the level that one attains in the discipling pyramid. Ironically, mature individuals who have been Christians for many years, but are new to the discipleship program, become disciples assigned to relatively young believers. These disciplers, by virtue of their conformity to the discipleship system, have more authoritative positions. The less mature discipler is then in a position to give advice and counsel to the more mature believer.

BAD HEART

The traditional meaning for "bad heart" was evil in the heart (i.e., such things as jealousy, impure thoughts, etc.). In controlling discipleship groups, a bad heart also means that you don't readily accept advice, or you don't trust your discipler, or you question leadership.

According to Scripture, one is never labeled as having a bad heart for questioning leadership, or not accepting the opinions of leadership. This use of the term "bad heart" has the effect of molding behavior by negative labeling, and by making many things "sinful" that the Bible does not consider sinful.

When a discipler tells you that you have a bad heart, it is a weapon of control. One particular disciple, who is also a medical doctor, tells how his image of a person was affected when this person was labeled bad-hearted by the leader:

> *I had not met much with Jim or talked to him for a long time. It is hard to describe how horrible a picture of Jim was left in my mind. If he didn't have horns, it would be because he was wearing a hat. His name carried the same dark weight as Judas Iscariot. Looking back, I was naive; I did not understand the power of the conditioning to which the leadership had subjected us. A few special meetings, and we all believed terrible things about a man who did not have a chance to defend himself. "That is not like me!" I say, but I believed strongly that Jim had an evil heart.*[29]

If an authoritative leader describes someone as bad when he or she is not, the one accused is thus misrepresented. Since that's the only side of the story heard, you tend to believe it. In this case, Jim was labeled as really evil when in reality he was not evil at all. This technique is typical of brainwashing techniques historically used in totalitarian systems.

Disciplers cannot read the hearts of men. In fact, Scripture tells us that only God sees our hearts. In abusive groups, however, disciplers are given new criteria from the program's directors that causes them to believe that criticism or rejecting advice can mean a bad heart. It is a judgment they have been falsely taught and encouraged to make.

Life is more complex than this. Leaders must make a thorough search of a person's ideas instead of making quick labels and drawing shallow conclusions. If the discipleship environment narrows thinking, simplistic answers may be offered so you don't have to think with much depth. If a person refuses advice from a discipler, he or she may be labeled rebellious. If a person distrusts leadership's actions, then he or she may be labeled divisive. If a person isn't cooperating with authority, he or she may be labeled prideful or unteachable.

As I investigated one discipleship group, the leadership became uneasy with my challenging questions and began to attack my motives. They tried to pressure me by saying not only was I not allowing the Holy Spirit to lead, but that I was "leading the Holy Spirit." This was interesting! Since they couldn't decide exactly what I was doing that was wrong, they made up their minds that "leading the Holy Spirit" was my sin. Obviously they knew exactly how the Holy Spirit would guide me, and I did not appear to be following.

The truth was, they did not like what I was saying. They wanted me to be quiet. They wanted to control my actions. Instead of directly telling me I could not speak out, they tried to intimidate me by telling me I was in sin by not allowing the Holy Spirit to guide me. I wasn't about to fold under these pressure tactics.

Their next move was to label my motives. They told me I had "ulterior motives to control," and that, too, was my sin. They were even more adamant about silencing me, because their mind games were not working. Next they threatened to ask me to leave if I persisted in questioning the leader's opinion. These pressure tactics are effectively used with those unfamiliar with controlling discipleship methods. They are such powerful mechanisms that even I, as an informed professional, felt a lot of pressure to comply.

If you have been subjected to—and struggled with—these same condemnations and accusations because you doubted or disagreed with leaders' opinions or because you didn't accept advice, it is very likely that a labeling game was being played. These labels effectively coerce people to comply with the leader's demands.

BROKENNESS

Scripturally, "brokenness" means to be pliable in God's hands and describes a person's relationship to God. Through life experiences that have convinced us God's ways and wisdom are greater than ours, we become teachable to the ways of God. In abusive programs, it is used to mean "the more accepting we are of advice and direction from the discipler, the more broken we are to God." You put immense pressure on yourself if you believe you are more broken to God if you accept more of your discipler's advice! This can compel you to accept advice that goes against your best judgment. Depending upon the degree of control the discipler exerts, this false definition of brokenness leads many disciples to feel they are not controlled; indeed, they are the ones who are forcing themselves to accept the discipler's advice.

CARNALITY

In most Christian churches, "carnality" refers to the sinful desire for bodily pleasures. Abusive groups broaden the meaning to include anything their members want that conflicts with the desire of the leaders. One member went to his disciplers saying he wanted to go to a certain seminary and, as a result, could no longer be on their staff. He was told that he was being a "carnal man." In the minds of these leaders, the question was not whether he should go to the seminary, but does he agree with our plans for him. Their response was based entirely on the fact that this Christian should agree with the leaders' plans for him.

FORSAKING FELLOWSHIP

A disciple told me his group strongly taught members not to "forsake the fellowshipping of the Saints" (Heb. 10:25). He felt he could never leave that group because they were the only believers who had the "fullness of truth" and, if he left, he would be forsaking fellowship with the saints. He recalls:

> *I remember once, after we had left our group, feeling a pang of guilt when I ran across the verse in Hebrews, "Do not neglect to meet together, as is the habit of some." I had not attended community meetings. Of course I had to remind myself that this verse did not apply to the People of Praise but to the real church.*[30]

There are many verses that can be misused to keep persons locked into a group, even though they would like to leave. Your group might not have used these particular verses, but think of what you may have been taught along these lines. Are you possibly a victim of this form of coercion?

IF ONE IS RIGHT AND TWO IS WRONG—IS THAT A CHOICE?

After you've swallowed the teaching that "we are more broken and humble if we embrace our discipler's advice," the choices are limited:

1. you can be a virtuous person by accepting the direction of your discipler without question, or

2. you can refuse the discipler's advice and likely feel guilty about it.

As you can see, you do not really have a choice once you believe in this false teaching.

Contrast this situation with the teaching of a discipler who doesn't control or manipulate your decisions. This discipler won't make you feel as though you are faced with making one choice over the other. You are free to accept or debate your discipler's advice with no subtle pressure pushing in one direction or the other.

UNEQUAL CHOICE GAMES

I show you two pairs of shoes, pointing out that one pair is new and just your size, and that the other pair has some small holes in the bottoms and is too large for you. I tell you to freely select whichever pair you want (obviously not a choice between equals). This is the nature of the game so often played in abusive discipleships.

Abusive groups color the options to bias you toward selecting what they want you to choose. The technique is very subtle. They cause you to see one choice as God's will and one as not, subtly narrowing your choices. The Pharisees and Herodians tried to do this to Jesus when they asked Him if it was right to pay taxes to Caesar or not. The implication was that there were only two mutually exclusive choices, but Jesus refused to play this either-or game (Matt. 22:15-22).

How many pairs of shoes were there to choose from? The person who gave you a choice not only colored the choice (by pointing out bad things about one pair), but also limited your choice to only two pairs. Perhaps it wasn't necessary to choose *any* pair! If disciplers artificially limit the choices offered, disciples may not understand that the choice is not entirely free. The disciples usually think choices are without influence; but, in reality, they are being walked through a maze with the discipler presenting pre-selected choices.

The Biblical Concept of Brokenness

DOING WHATEVER GOD WANTS

The Non-Biblical Discipleship Concept of Brokenness

DOING WHATEVER GOD WANTS + FOLLOWING THE ADVICE OF THE DISCIPLER

Non-controlling discipleships teach you to follow a general principle, then it is left up to you to make the final decisions. In controlling groups, however, you are normally expected to accept lots of advice to prove that you are a humbled being. In fact, if you need lots of advice, it may be that your group has reduced you to a state of dependent childhood—where you no longer can stand on your own two feet but feel you need their ideas in order to find God's Perfect Will.

It is often difficult for us to know exactly what God wants. Our understanding is subjective. When you are trying to hear God's voice, but are still uncertain—and your discipler is saying, *"This* is probably God's Will"—it is likely that you will go along.

In an abusive discipleship, you may be following God's will. If you do not agree with your discipler's opinion, however, you likely will be viewed as not doing what God wants.

Assume that one of the holiest men on earth joined a discipleship program such as the one I am describing. Suppose this man decided to go against the advice of his discipler because he felt

God wanted him to go in a different direction. It is likely that our holy man would be viewed as rebellious, not broken, and prideful for following his own will instead of the discipler's directions or suggestions. In abusive discipleship, even if you are the holiest person on earth, the leaders will not believe it unless you are following lots of their advice.

"Commitment" in abusive or controlling programs also means loyalty to the program and its leaders. People in abusive discipleship programs who are totally committed are compelled to follow advice much more often than members of groups whose programs don't use these techniques.

Many of the disciples in controlling groups will do almost anything, go almost anywhere, and obey almost everything their leaders suggest to them.

Former disciples state that they saw disciplers as more committed than Christians outside their programs. It didn't matter if the person outside the discipleship strictly kept the laws of God, was kind, loving, and compassionate. They would usually see this person as less committed than one with fewer Christian attributes who was submitted to a discipler.

DOUBT

Doubt is a word that causes negative feelings in many disciples. Did these disciples have such a strong emotional response to the word "doubt" before their discipleship? Most of the former disciples I interviewed said this response was formed during their participation in the discipleship program.

Why is doubt made to be a negative in these discipleship groups? Is it because the Bible condemns doubt? We might think so when we read passages such as:

...but when he asks, he must believe and not doubt, because he who doubts is like a wave of the sea, blown and tossed by the wind (James 1:6).

Well, who wants to be like that? "Of course doubt is bad," you might say.

But wait! Notice that *this* doubt is limited to doubting God, not doubting fallible leaders.

Jesus accepted the doubts of another person (Mark 9:24). Some Apostles still doubted on the mountain, but Jesus issued His commission to them anyway (Matt. 28:17-20). Thomas doubted Christ's resurrection, and Jesus graciously appeared in order to satisfy his skepticism. Jesus did not condemn the doubting Thomas (John 20).

Doubt, in the theological sense, has to do with basic doctrinal issues. In areas of "non-revealed" truth, doubt is a God-given capacity that warns us that we should test things to ascertain their truth. How can we know what is true in life if we believe everything we are told? Doubt is healthy. Doubt can be a matter of conscience. We feel doubt when we are involved in things we know may be morally wrong. Can the Holy Spirit put doubt in our minds about something? Of course, especially in matters of faith, morals, or sin.

People in abusive discipleships are not taught to think that the Holy Spirit might induce doubt about the group. *Doubt about the group is almost always wrong, and is almost always sin.* Any thought or feeling about the group that can be labeled as doubt triggers an automatic negative response in these disciples. The disciples are likely to feel guilt even before they analyze the situation to see if it is truly sinful. Disciples who suppress doubt will be held up to the group as "teachable, humble, and/or broken." Accepting this belief makes you the perfect programmed disciple. All a discipler has to say is, "That's doubt!" The disciple will then dismiss the thought.

Does your group have a lot of teachings concerning doubt? Is there no distinction made between healthy doubt and doubting God? Is doubt almost always equated with sin in your mind? If so, you have probably been conditioned to suppress negative ideas about the group, leaders, or their teachings. These may have been healthy doubts. You need to evaluate each doubt (not just from the group's point of view) to determine if it really is sinful.

Such misguided teachings actually eliminate doubt as a useful tool of the Holy Spirit, block critical inquiry, and compromise good decision making.

If leaders can impress upon you that all doubt is sin, then they can twist a few more verses to say that distrusting your discipler's advice is sin. This concludes that you should not raise questions which show doubts about the discipler's advice.

If you believe that honest criticism of leaders is a sin, your range of thought and action is narrowed. If you are told by your leaders that someone is divisive and you are conditioned to trust leadership, you will most likely believe that accusation to be true. You probably wouldn't investigate or speak to the accused person in an effort to discover the truth. If you believe you should trust leaders implicitly, you are less likely to take independent action to challenge their teachings, nor will you be as able as you once were to comfortably think about the possibility that your leadership might be wrong.

This limitation on your actions will hamper your creative thinking skills and limit your perspective. You will likely use your innovative thinking skills to weigh and evaluate only areas of activity against which your leaders have not conditioned you.

One disciple with whom I was working was told it was sin for him to comment negatively on something a member of his group told him, or about the teachings of one of the group's disciplers. If you asked "Mark" about anything else, he was happy to give his opinion; but he felt that he could not comment critically on anything that was being taught by his own leader unless he heard it with his own ears.

His discipler's reasoning was that the information Mark had received may have been incorrect, and that the person who told him about this may have misquoted the teacher. Therefore, it would be a sin to comment on it. Mark was told he would be spreading non-truths about one of the group's disciplers, so he was not to say anything about this secondhand information.

Even though Mark was a leader, his belief that it might be sinful to "comment negatively on something he had not *personally* heard from another leader" kept Mark from discussing the issue. He would not even suggest that we discuss this with the discipler, because he was inhibited by fear of going against a higher-up leader in the group. Therefore, Mark chose to abandon his right to discuss what was being taught by a teacher in his group. Mark's freedom to think and act has now been restricted. (Note: Mark would not be restricted in voicing praise!)

There is another trick used by controllers to stifle criticism or questioning of the group's teachers. The person who has a negative thought can't get validation from other leaders because of the teaching "You must not comment on secondhand infor-mation." Even new members who have not yet been conditioned are trapped in this situation because no one else will validate their negative opinion.

If you can be led to connect words such as "doubt" to something that is always negative and sinful, this can cause you to avoid exploring the issues when your leaders label them as doubt, and dismiss them.

When trying to free the minds of victims caught up in a destructive group, I put a great deal of effort into showing them the error of automatically equating doubt with sin. If I fail to accomplish this, the victims may not permit themselves to have any negative thoughts about their group. They will not be able to consider the possibility that the group may be a destructive movement or controlling discipleship; the victims will stay deceived and remain entrapped.

DOUBTING GOD IS A SIN

Yes, the Bible says doubting God is a sin, but you must not substitute the word "leader" for God. Discipleships that teach this are making an enormously egotistical mistake! This is one of the many scripture tricks you come across in evaluating discipling groups. Disciplers begin by teaching the pure Biblical idea that doubting God is sinful, and then quietly drop in the false lesson that "when you doubt our leaders, you are doubting God." This is a pretty sneaky trick.

Labeling a thought as doubt—which is equal to sin—stops your mind from thinking critically about your situation. You don't have to think deeply about your real problems; your discipler can quickly classify it as doubt which will cause you to reject your feelings. This is the "language of non-thought."[31] Your range of thought and action has been greatly narrowed. You are being controlled through elimination of valid doubts, which may well be informative and could help you make objective evaluations.

Deeply programmed disciples are subject to a form of instant amnesia. A discipler who fears that questioning might show the cracks in his twisted Scripture has only to say, "That is doubt." Click! The disciple's mind shuts out the question because the *disciple doesn't want to commit a sin.* That's how it works—much as the stage hypnotist's trigger-word puts his subject into a state of unconsciousness, the discipler has trigger words, too.

DISCIPLE, DISCIPLESHIP, FOLLOWER—WHAT DO THEY MEAN?

I found a small booklet that contains this false definition of discipleship:

> *...discipleship means being a follower, imitating the example of the leader. For example, the word Christian means "Christ-like," and living up to that name should be the goal of every believer. It also means putting the wishes of the leader above your own, making your desires subservient to his.*[32]

This is *not* what following Jesus Christ is all about. Following Christ means dying to our evil wishes and desires, and following what God lays on our hearts, even if it is contrary to a leader's wishes.

Many in the discipleship movement follow this false principle from the booklet. This is a glaring mistake and a defect in the very foundation of many discipleship programs. These groups believe you are to imitate and follow their leaders, putting another person's wishes above your own. Unbelievable as it may sound to those who know Scripture, many discipleship programs teach this.

Originally, discipleship meant a process of learning to follow the example of Christ and becoming obedient to His teachings. With the new and twisted definition, discipleship now means follow the leader.

I have been told of countless instances of missed career opportunities because a disciple didn't want to move away from their discipler, or because accepting that opportunity ran counter to the discipler's advice. In another twist, but with the same repercussions, disciples have given up jobs because a discipler was moving and they followed so they could still be discipled by him.

An unhealthy attachment seems to develop. Many former disciples complain about failing to finish college or missing an opportunity to go to medical school because of their discipler's advice. Others regret calling off engagements on the advice of disciplers. Some didn't go home for family reunions and other important events because their disciplers advised against seeing the family.

The list of abuse is endless. Not only do the victims (the disciples) suffer, but so do family members and friends outside the discipleship program. When we follow Christ, we are on the right path. But when we imitate and become subservient to a discipler in all areas of our life, we are headed for trouble.

FALLING AWAY

Falling away is a scary idea, and the last thing faithful believers want to do. How is this term used in your group? Often, in abusive discipleship groups, falling away does not mean that someone has abandoned Christ, but that they have only left the group or rejected the system. Most of these people who fell away did not abandon Christ, fall into pagan unbelief, or pursue a lifestyle of immorality (although such stories are sometimes circulated). In abusive discipleships, "falling away" is a label used to camouflage the real issue.

What is the reality of the situation? It may be that you just don't want to go along with some program that tries to see every problem as an "attitude problem." You may simply be fed up with accepting an immature discipler's advice, or you are just tired of disciplers trying to make you feel guilty when you reject advice. You may be ready to leave your discipleship group because you are frustrated when any criticism of leaders results in being called down or told that you "have a bad heart."

This trick of saying that someone fell away, when actually they just left the group, deflects attention from the leader accused of wrongdoing to the disciple making the accusation. The truth is that this labeling technique is a tactic for gaining control. What healthy Christian community says that someone fell away if they simply left due to a disagreement, or could not work peacefully with their discipler? None that I know. But I know many abusive discipleship groups that slap this label on dissenters.

Traditionally, falling away means turning away from Christ's commandments. Jesus said, "If you love me, you will keep my commandments" (John 14:15). If you drop out of the discipleship, you will probably be seen as falling away from your commitment to Jesus even if you keep His Commandments. Why is that? The reason is simple—disciplers believe they have the most authentic Christian way. If people don't follow their way, then they are falling away from the truth. Is this attitude Biblical? No.

When Jesus' disciples came to Him and told Him they had stopped a man casting out demons in Jesus' name because he was not part of the discipleship program, Jesus said, "Do not stop him. No one who does a miracle in my name can in the next moment say anything bad about me, for whoever is not against us is for us. I tell you the truth, anyone who gives you a cup of water in my name because you belong to Christ will certainly not lose his reward" (Mark 9:38-41).

Jesus had a much larger idea of following and faithfulness than His disciples did. He knew that the essence of commitment was commitment to Him. Today's abusive discipleships are making the same mistake those original disciples did while they were yet immature.

INDEPENDENT

Try this test right now. Write on a piece of paper the word "independent." Write other words you associate with this word. If you labeled someone in your group "independent," would you see that as positive or negative? Describe the characteristics that a person would have if your group labeled him independent.

If you are reading this book with others, share the words that everyone has associated with "independent." Is there a significant difference in the way each of you perceives this word? If you are in a controlled environment, you likely saw "independent" in a negative light. If there are others not in a controlled environment, they probably saw the word in a positive light.

Is it a bad thing to be independent? Not if you are raising children. You want them to grow up to make decisions on their own, keep their own place, and eventually stop bringing their dirty laundry home. But the word "independence" has a negative connotation in controlling groups. It is understood that your decisions should almost always be weighed by your discipler. This will keep you from independent decisions and, eventually, you probably will come to believe you are "missing God's Will" without this guidance. The end result is to make you regress to an infantile state.

Interestingly, independence is neither sinful nor virtuous in the Biblical context. Paul, for example, was very independent but also completely dependent on God. Another person may be independent but not keeping God's commandments. Sin and independence are not inextricably related.

OBEY and SUBMIT

"Obey" and "submit" are two more words often twisted by abusive discipleships. In abusive discipleships, the chief virtue is not love, but obedience. Obedience in abusive discipleships can be honored even when a leader gives wrong advice. One of the many Bible stories that is used to convince disciples to obey and submit to even bad advice is that of Abraham, Sarah, and Pharaoh (Gen. 12:10-20). Abraham asked his wife, Sarah, to lie to the Egyptians and say that she was his sister. Abraham was afraid the Egyptians might have him killed because Sarah was so beautiful. As a result of the lie, Sarah was taken into Pharaoh's palace and Abraham was treated well. Because of the lie, however, God inflicted diseases on the Egyptians and the lie was revealed.

It is said in some discipleships that because Sarah submitted to Abraham, God protected her and blessed her. The implication is that if you follow the advice of your discipler—even if he or she is wrong—God will protect and bless you. This is surely warped thinking. The Bible does not tell us that Abraham and Sarah were without failing or sin. If there is a clear lesson in Abraham's lies, it is that we may sin and God may punish, but He will always forgive us if we truly repent.

One time I worked with a person who admitted that his discipler was corrupt. "How can you follow someone like that?" I asked him. His response was, "According to 1 Samuel, God will remove bad leadership." This disciple thought he needed to obey his bad leader until God removed this discipler. I did remind him that David fled to the wilderness to escape his wicked ruler. The truth is, we can rationalize anything from Scripture if we twist the words far enough.

Another example of Scripture-twisting used in respect to obedience or submission is Romans 13:1-3:

> *Everyone must submit himself to the governing authorities, for there is no authority except that which God has established. The authorities that exist have been established by God. Consequently, he who rebels against the authority is rebelling against what God has instituted, and those who do so will bring judgment on themselves. For rulers hold no terror for those who do right, but for those who do wrong. Do you want to be free from fear of the one in authority? Then do what is right and he will commend you.*

First, most Biblical scholars seem to agree that this passage is about civil government. It is misapplied when used in regard to church leaders. We have already discussed Jesus' distinction between church leaders and other leaders.

Second, notice the words "for rulers hold no terror for those who do right, but for those who do wrong." This passage only refers to *good* government, because those who do right under good government have no fear of the rulers. Under corrupt leaders, there *is* fear of doing what truly is right. The early Christians experienced the terror of bad government and were thrown to the lions because they did what was right. Many good people feared their rulers.

If a government we believe to be good asks us to do something we know is wrong, Paul says that we are to "do what is right" (Rom. 13:3). This implies that, even when we are submitted to legitimate authority, we are only to obey what is right and just.

To gain a Biblical understanding of "obey," we will do a short word study in the Greek of the New Testament, because there are several Greek words all translated "obey" in our English Bibles. When we read words in the Bible, we have to understand that they originally had different ranges of meanings for the early Christians. For example, we might be tempted to understand every use of "lord" in the Scriptures as denoting a figure of great authority, but sometimes "lord" is simply a term of respect (e.g., "sir"). In studying the Bible, therefore, we must try to understand words though their original Scriptural context and definitions. When these meanings are changed, or when a definition is imposed on words they did not originally have, distortion of language occurs.

The first Greek word in the Vine's Dictionary for "obey" is *hupakouo* which means "to listen, attend." It is used 21 times in the New Testament. "To listen" surely doesn't sound like our modern idea of "obey." This word is used in 1 Peter 3:6: "like Sarah, who obeyed Abraham and called him her master. You are her daughters if you do what is right and do not give way to fear." The Biblical writers would not have found it necessary to qualify "obey" if it just meant doing what Abraham asked. The Bible makes it clear that Sarah was not to do whatever Abraham asked but "what is right." So Sarah listened to Abraham and did what was right. This is very important because many discipleships feel that Sarah should have obeyed Abraham's every request even if it was wrong.

From this passage, we see that Sarah could have refused Abraham's request to lie to the King, and still be seen as an obedient wife because, according to this definition of obey, refusing a request that was wrong Biblically cannot be labeled rebellious or disobedient.

The second Greek word for "obey" is *peitho*, which means to "persuade, to win over," and in the passive and middle voices, "to be persuaded, to listen to." Again, this is not our modern understanding of "obey." In another place, *peitho* is translated "obey" in Hebrews 13:17: "Obey your leaders and submit to their authority." (I could find only two versions that insert the word "authority," the New International and the J. B. Phillips; it is not found in the Greek text, which can cause more confusion.) Here, "obey" means to "listen to your leaders and if they win you by persuasion then yield to this advice." This is much different than the sense of "absolute obedience" that is often poured into this passage. Furthermore, in Hebrews 13:17, Jesus and his disciples clearly taught that leaders were to serve their followers, not *dominate* them (Matt. 20:25-28; Lk. 22:25-27; 1 Pet. 5:3).

The third Greek word, *peitharcheo*, most closely resembles our modern English understanding of "obey." It is used only four times in the New Testament! It appears in Acts 5:29: "But Peter and the Apostles answered and said, 'We must obey God rather than men.'" In the Vine's Dictionary, *peitharcheo* is translated, "to obey one in authority." You will find this term in Titus 3:1: "Put them in mind to be subject to principalities and powers, to obey magistrates, to be ready to do every good work." Here again, "obey" is qualified: we obey to be ready for only good work! The context implies that we don't obey magistrates when they ask us to do something evil or against our conscience.

Many members of controlling groups tell me they don't accept all their leaders' advice so they feel they are not being controlled. I usually ask these people to think about their feelings when advice causes them to "struggle" because it conflicts with what they want to do. They usually have a feeling that they might not be living up to God's will if they reject the advice. In a normal relationship with a spiritual director, you should have freedom to disagree with your discipler without being highly inclined to feel that you are not doing God's will if you don't follow the advice.

You might ask, "What if following their advice over my will *is* God's will?" Think this through carefully; discuss it with an outsider. Let's say your discipler advised you not to go to a seminary and you want to go. How can you tell if his advice is God's will? Well, after you pray about it and discuss it with others you trust from outside your group and your heart still feels compelled, you should follow the message that God has laid on your heart. You may think: "What if my heart is selfish, not humble, and it just wants to do its own thing which is go to a seminary and I should take the advice of my discipler and go against my desire?" That's the problem—so much of the time you have been told things are selfish desires, when they really weren't. How can you know what is true and what has been instilled by your discipler?

Try this technique: make a list of the reasons that you would like, for example, to go to a seminary:

- ➤ Did you say you wanted to go to satisfy your own ego?
- ➤ Did you list "To have an important position of authority in society"?
- ➤ Did you write down, "Because I want people to recognize me as a holy person"?

If these are not the reasons, then recognize that it is not for selfish purposes. Your discipler is wrong. It is as simple as that.

Some have disagreed with their discipler without feeling guilt. It is true that there are going to be times when the discipler allows you to have your own way, even when the discipler feels that you are in sin. Opinions are opinions and Biblical mandates are Biblical mandates. If we feel pressured to conform to disciplers' opinions, unnecessary internal struggles arise.

The discipler usually has the unfounded notion that conscience is a "selfish desire" and, by contrast, his advice is "spirit-led." After a disciple accepts this belief, he will usually go against his own opinions and follow the leader in order to keep from feeling guilt.

SELFISH

Many times, in abusive discipleship, "selfish" is used to label disciples who are not conforming to the group's or the leader's will. Many of these disciples would hardly ever question their discipler's judgment. If their discipler said that their motive was selfish, they would repent from whatever they were wanting to do. Using "selfish" to label followers whenever they do not conform is a great controlling mechanism.

"Sharon" said her discipler told her that she never really cared about anybody in her whole life, that she just used people. Sharon immediately repented, believing the words of her discipler to be true. Sharon wanted to be broken and teachable. She believed her discipler had a right to judge her like this. This discipler was, in Sharon's confused mind, an "arbiter of truth."

In controlling discipleships, selfish also can mean that disciples want to carry out their own desires instead of the discipler's. It may have nothing to do with truly being selfish. I have had former disciples tell me that they were accused of being selfish for wanting to go to college, wanting to learn to play guitar, wanting a good tennis racket, and even wanting to visit family instead of staying for a church function. Sometimes the discipler is right and the disciple is being selfish in the Biblical sense. It is difficult for a disciple to know when the discipler is wrong when it is the discipler who has occasionally helped the disciple see actual faults.

These controlling non-Biblical ideas, once implanted, will cause disciples to follow along through the maze with little deviation from the desires of the discipler.

"Doug" played guitar for a dying woman. His discipler questioned his motive for playing. It was suggested by the leader that Doug had a selfish motive. He felt terrible about this. After Doug left this discipling relationship, he eventually realized that his motive for wanting to sing and play for a dying woman was not selfish. He discovered he had readily believed the judgments from his pastor about his heart's motives. Doug is now free to follow the desires God truly places in his heart.

Loading words with emotional impact can give the discipler more influence over the lives of disciples. If a certain word elicits strong negative or positive feelings and is linked to an idea, then disciples most likely will respond in the way the leadership wants. Former disciples say that, prior to group influence, they did not have an emotional response to words like "commitment," "obey," "rebellious," "doubt," "selfish," and "independent."

WORDS THAT GIVE AN EMOTIONAL RESPONSE

I was talking to two disciplers one day. One of them said, "The Bible can answer every question." That sounded a little odd to me and I asked if that were a true statement. They both replied vehemently, *"The Bible can answer every question!"* The intensity of their words was so great that I quietly backed away, and did not try to reason with them.

Both had probably been subjected to a teaching that the Bible answers every question. I imagine they were taught this by someone in authority and they were conditioned to trust what their leaders taught them, unless it was contradicted by the Bible. I know the Bible can't teach me accounting, nor is it intended to answer questions concerning good driving techniques. But these guys were spouting this misinformation so intensely that I could not even discuss it with them. The Bible does answer many questions on how to behave toward one another, but it doesn't always give specifics. No, it doesn't answer every question.

One group used "awesome" as an emotional-trigger word. I must have heard it 25 times during one of the discipler's talks. Another term they used was "back burner" when referring to people they'd contacted three times and who still did not show an interest in coming to church. When you heard "back burner" in this group, you were being led to think of someone who simply wasn't interested in being committed to Christ.

How can you tell if words or ideas are being altered in these ways? Are there certain words that cause you to feel more intensely? What is the subject? Is there a certain word that puts you in ecstasy that didn't before your group involvement? Try out these words and ideas on others not in your environment to see if they stand the test of validity outside your group.

Many common words or phrases are loaded with feeling or altered in meaning. Just a few of these twisted concepts and words are listed below. Circle the words for which your group has altered the meaning from the way they are meant in the Bible. Add other words that are manipulated in your group. You might have a hard time thinking of words. Instead, think of the words that were more frequently used than in other churches you've attended—these have likely been manipulated.

Make three columns. In one column, write how your group defined the following words and phrases, in the next column write the Biblical usage of each, and in the last column, describe your emotional reaction to hearing them:

STRUGGLING, TRUST, OBEY, COMMITMENT, SUBMIT, OBEDIENCE, SELFISH, CARNAL MAN, DYING TO SELF, BROKENNESS, JESUS IS LORD, FAITH, REBELLIOUS, BAD HEART, QUESTIONING, HARD-HEARTED, SIN, DOUBT, LED BY

THE SPIRIT, FALLING AWAY, UNITY, NOT OPEN,
INDEPENDENCE, DIVISIVE, FACTIOUS, DIVISION, BEING OF
ONE MIND, SURRENDER, ACCOUNTABLE, PERSECUTION,
SLANDER, WORRY, FEAR, UNEQUALLY YOKED, VIRTUE,
ADVICE, CRITICISM, DENYING CHRIST, CHRISTIAN,
COMMITTED FOLLOWER, SELF-CONFIDENCE, BEING PROUD
OF ACCOMPLISHMENTS, AND HUMAN PERSPECTIVE.

CHECKLIST
The Language of Enslavement—Chapter 5

Check those that apply to you and/or your group:

❏ Labels me as "struggling" when I don't want to follow my discipler's advice

❏ I feel pressure not to reject my discipler's advice

❏ Teaches that the Bible says to stay away from those "fallen away"

❏ Often rejects the sinner along with the sin

❏ Wants me to confront nearly every sin in others

❏ Does not emphasize overlooking weakness in others

❏ New people in my discipleship program are viewed as newly committed to Christ regardless of their knowledge or Christian maturity

❏ Leaders categorize disciples as having a bad heart when these individuals are only offering healthy criticism of the leaders

❏ "Brokenness" means "willingly giving up your desires and following the directions of the leaders"

❏ Total commitment is rarely possible without a discipler

❏ I find that many things are now sinful, when I didn't before

❏ Puts down my family in subtle ways

❏ I feel an urge to imitate my leader in every way possible

❏ Puts down my former church or former members

❏ I would be falling away from God or regressing spiritually if I quit the program

❏ "Following Christ" means giving up all personal wishes, desires, and goals

NOTE: If you have checked *any* boxes, it may indicate a misuse of Scripture and/or may represent the presence of abuse and excessive control.

Chapter 6

WHOSE WILL IS IT?

If Christians believe that God will give them a direct command for every detail of their life, then they don't have to think for themselves anymore. They just have to listen to God and jump when they get the order.

I heard a head discipler remark that we didn't really have a choice of whether to eat pancakes or waffles for breakfast. If we are listening, he argued, God will tell us every move to make.

This statement reflects a belief in some destructive groups that God will tell you what to do in every area of your life if only you are listening. Such an idea would seem to arise from the honest desire to do God's will and not one's own. But this statement was more extreme than even I'd heard before. It is the kind of dangerous "black and white" thinking that is found in some discipleships. This kind of thinking may sometimes be based upon the false assumption that your desire and God's will are always opposed—and, therefore, if you desire something, it is probably contrary to God's will.

This same discipler taught that we will never find God's way when we are "not settled" in our heart to do what God wants. Again, this is another black and white statement.

Assuredly, you will find God's will more often if you settle in your heart to do what God wants. To say we will never find God's way when we are "not settled" puts limits on God. *"I was found by those who did not seek me. I revealed myself to those who did not ask for me!"* (Is. 65:1,2; quoted by Paul in Rom. 10:20,21). If God is big enough to reveal himself to those who don't ask, he certainly can reveal his will even if you are not settled in your heart to follow it.

Also disciplers may tell you that your way is never God's way; this is a manipulation that causes you to be more vulnerable to

97

disciplers' suggestions. The implication here is that, if you don't know God's way with certainty (as *they* seem to), you need their guidance.

ONE MIND CAN BE INFLUENCED BY GOD OR EVIL

Many manipulative groups apparently want to make you think that the mind has two parts: one which God inspires and one which is human nature. The human part is always, according to them, operating contrary to God's will.

Some groups make a distinction between the mind and the spirit, suggesting that the mind can be deceived, but God will speak to our spirit. These groups teach their disciples to believe that once we commit ourselves to Christ, we must completely turn from all our former desires, goals, and ways of thinking. They teach that we must find a new way to live based not on simple reasoning, but on discerning God's Will.

We can be easily confused if we believe that we can't use our own minds (minds that God gave us) to find His Will. It is equally perplexing to think that our simple human reasoning is always contrary to God's Will. How are you supposed to figure all this out? Discipleship! Discipleship groups characteristically assure you that if you have a "covering of authority" (theirs, of course), you will find God's Perfect Will.

The authors of one book declare that if you are sincerely listening, you can "hear God speak" and "know God's Will" for every move in your lives as clearly as did Moses, Abraham, and Noah.[33] You may find this book in your local church because it has sold over one million copies. This book does teach Christians to be wary of their own thoughts and to more diligently seek the will of God. Unfortunately, there are also many false ideas planted alongside these good principles.

The authors quote John 8:47: "He who belongs to God hears what God says. The reason you do not hear is that you do not belong to God." Then they ask, "What does John 8:47 have to say about a person who does not hear what God says?"[34] The answer they expect you to give, based on this out-of-context quote, is: "You do not belong to God if you don't hear what God says."

There would be no problem with this answer if your definition of "hearing from God" wasn't distorted. This book harps on the idea that "hearing from God" means getting your orders from God as clearly as did Abraham and Noah for every detail of your life. But the Biblical idea of "hearing from God" normally doesn't mean this direct kind of hearing. When Jesus said, "Everyone who is of the truth hears my voice" (John 18:37), He meant that those upholding the commandments of God were paying attention to his voice. He did not mean that we would all hear Him speaking to us as clearly as did Moses, Abraham, and Noah.

I do ask Jesus to bless my work and direct my thoughts, but I don't demand that God speak to me as He did to Jonah (although I would count it a great blessing if he did). Like every Christian, I have sometimes wished that God would dictate every move I should make. The fact is, God gave us freedom. Within that wide range of freedom there are many choices, within moral limits, that are within God's Perfect Will.

God gave a few people such as Noah, Abraham, Moses, and Isaiah direct revelation, but to claim that God will speak to everyone this way is heresy. God used these individuals to lead His people and for special missions. If God gave all His children direct revelation, then all denominations wouldn't be continually contradicting one another. The truth is, sometimes God does show us clearly and sometimes He doesn't.

Those who propagate this narrow understanding of "hearing God speak" repeatedly tell you that, when God speaks to you, you must know that it is God as clearly as did Moses. You must know what God says, even as Noah did, and you must know what to do in response just as did Abraham.[35] These authors claim, "If you have trouble hearing God speak [like this], you are in trouble at the very heart of your Christian experience."[36]

If you find this teaching attractive, let me warn you: At times you will think you know God is telling you what to do and then (sometimes years later) you will realize it wasn't God. This does not mean that you are in trouble at the very heart of your Christian experience. Demanding this kind of direct assurance and guidance from God may cause you unnecessary guilt. (One husband complained how his wife became alarmed thinking he "didn't belong to God" because he could not say that he heard God this clearly.)

What test can you make to assure that you belong to God? Is it hearing a directive that you attribute to God? No, the real test is made by reading the entire passage in John 8:31-53. If you hold to

Jesus' teaching, then you know you are listening to God and hearing him. If we love each other, we are hearing from God and we can be assured that we belong to Him.

A discipler asked me if God told me to mail a certain letter I had written. I replied that I felt it was the right thing to do, but I couldn't say God told me to do it. Since I couldn't say that it was God telling me what to do, the discipler inferred that something was wrong with my relationship to God. The fruits that our lives bear, not our claim that God is speaking to us, tell if we are following God's Will.

"Doug," a former discipler, explains how hard it was for him "to hear God speak":

> I had to distinguish which voice was of the Lord and which was my mind's or the devil's. Now that I learned in this new Christianity that God would always tell me what to do, I certainly was listening to all my thoughts. I'd hear, "Go to Pittsburgh" and I would think "That's crazy. I'm in school down here in Tennessee. Maybe it is God because I don't want to do it..."

> I felt forced into using the language of the others. "Sarah" (another member) would say that "The Lord had me visit John today or the Lord showed me this." I used to say, "I am going to see Sarah." Then I always said, "The Lord had me visit Sarah today."

> I also felt uncomfortable that everyone was saying what the Lord showed them. I couldn't be sure what the Lord showed me, and what was my own inclinations, so I felt it was best not to put everything on the Lord. After a while, I felt terrific pressure to think of something that the Lord was showing me. It may not have been the Lord but I felt so much pressure to find something that the Lord showed me that I did find something. Now I realize that, in regular English language before this group, I would have said, "This is what I learned today." Then I always said, "The Lord showed me this or taught me that." Maybe it was the Lord or maybe it wasn't. Being away from it all now, I feel free and I'm not being pressured into figuring it all out.

Doug continued:

> I remember one time in college when my discipler made me feel very guilty. I was learning to cook, being away from home for the first time. I bought a ham for dinner. I put it on a few

minutes before dinner not realizing that it would not be done for hours. When my discipler came over, he questioned me, "Doug, did the Lord tell you to do this?" I felt terrible hearing these words. It was now obvious [realizing how long this ham would actually need to cook] that I surely wasn't hearing from the Lord. It was times like these that made me so uncertain that I was hearing from the Lord that I would ask for more advice so I wouldn't be missing the Lord's will!

FEAR OF MISSING GOD'S WILL

Because of the thrust of controlling groups to make one seek God's direction for every detail of one's life, disciples become afraid they may be "missing" God's Will. Some disciples actually feel a kind of terror. They are afraid they might not hear God, which leads them to even greater dependency on advice from the discipler. It was planted in their minds that they would hear clearly from God and should not make decisions through their rational thinking. One former victim said it reached the point where she was so afraid of "missing it" that she always relied on a teaching or someone "older in the Lord" to tell her what to do.

As noble as this all-or-nothing way of thinking about God's will sounds, it is not Scriptural. For example, Romans 14:6 says: "Whoever observes the day, observes it for the Lord. Also whoever eats, eats for the Lord, since he gives thanks to God; while whoever abstains, abstains for the Lord and gives thanks to God." In matters that do not concern the moral guidelines of Scripture, we are free to do whatever we want, so long as we do it for the Lord.

Jesus was upset with the Pharisees because they thought they knew God's Will for just about everything and they complained because his disciples didn't wash their hands before they ate. Jesus made it clear that it wasn't the riturals that made a man clean. It wasn't the things on the outside that made a man dirty. It was the heart that Jesus was concerned about (Matt. 15:1-20). Keeping ourselves pure in thought and keeping our heart clean from evil is what Jesus demanded. In abusive discipleship, however, we are told that we should expect God to tell us every move we should make, even whether it is His Will that we should eat pancakes or waffles.

If you accept the teaching of many abusive leaders that God's will allows only one choice for each action in your life, then there is virtually no freedom for the devoted Christian.

DRIVING YOURSELF NUTS

Sometimes I find people engaged in this kind of "magical thinking": If you had only continuously listened to God for every decision of your life, then certain bad things wouldn't have happened. For example, a discipler might imply that if you really listened to God about buying that car, you wouldn't have bought a "lemon." Have you ever heard of believers bragging how God got them a parking place? We should certainly thank God for everything; there is nothing wrong with that. But would you be upset to find out in a survey that non-believers find good parking spaces just as often as believers? Does that mean if we don't get the parking space that we did not have enough faith? In some groups, that is actually what they believe.

What does traditional Biblical Christianity say about these things? All trials should be embraced with patience and acceptance for Christ's sake. Problems are permitted for our best interests (James 1:2-4; Rom. 5:3-5; and 2 Cor. 4:16-18). All disappointments, misunderstandings, and contradictions should be met with resignation and patience, for our sanctification. We won't know until we reach heaven why many seemingly bad things happen. Yes, we can ask God to teach us the reason for whatever is bothering us; and, in His wisdom, He may grant our wish. At other times, we may not be given the answer in this life; it is up to God.

I was once like many disciplers, thinking that I knew with certainty why God allowed things to happen in my life. I would pray about it and think I was being given insight. Most of the time, I thought I had the right answer. Looking back, I can now see I was often deceiving myself. Yes, God is always shaping our lives with our surroundings. Yes, God is getting us ready to come home and sanctifying us by the events of our lives. Throughout the Bible, we see that misfortune and suffering happen to good people; but, in time, God brings good out of evil (Rom. 8:18-39).

Under hypnosis, you can be convinced that a bee is on your nose. You can see it and feel it, even though it isn't really there. This deception can be so powerful that, if you are told that the bee has stung, a reddened swelling may appear and you will feel pain. Similarly, if someone convinces you that God will give you a command for everything you do in life, even to the tiniest detail, you will imagine that you hear commands from God. That doesn't mean that God is really directing you. It only means that your mind imagines it to be true.

THE ARROGANCE OF RIGHTEOUSNESS

Maybe these trials happen as a result of human errors, maybe not. No one can be certain. However, if you have the self-righteous attitude that you know and more diligently follow God's will for every detail of your life than other Christians, you are deceived! This belief produces arrogance and reeks with superiority clearly sensed by outsiders. The disciplers we have been discussing are unaware they exhibit these traits.

When I thought I understood clearly why trials happened, I also reeked with a self-confidence that antagonized people outside my group. I had no idea that I displayed any arrogance at all. I just knew that I was more committed and that I understood better than all these other people why certain things happened in our lives.

Today I don't pretend to know. God's reasons are far beyond the capabilities of our weak human understanding. He allows people trials—sometimes to help them, sometimes to show them their sin, sometimes to give them a chance for some merit that they might receive in Heaven for all eternity. Now I understand that I cannot judge others based on tragedies that befall them.

Many Christians understand that God is not going to give them a direct command for every detail of their life. If God would just do this, we wouldn't have to think for ourselves. Good Christians still ask Jesus for guidance the whole day long and, in faith, believe He gives that guidance through natural human reasoning and impulses.

"Jody" was in a discipleship group at a small private university in Tennessee. She graduated with honors, but instead of looking for a job, she and four friends all felt God was calling them back to this university. Since this is a tiny college town with few job opportunities, Jody's father (a college professor and a student of the Bible) felt that it was obvious the discipleship leader's will was the driving factor in his daughter's decision. During that summer at home, her father made no progress in showing her how irrational her choice was, and one week before Jody was scheduled to return to the group, I was called into the case.

Fortunately, Jody's discipler hadn't yet begun to teach his students that they didn't have to obey their parents. So, when her dad told her to get into the car when they were coming to see me, she grudgingly obeyed. Three days later, Jody was free of the undue influence of her group and realized how strangely she had been thinking. She did not go back to the group. (Note: We succeeded equally well in two more cases before this particular discipler began to instruct his group that they were not to obey their parents!)

HOW DO YOU FREE YOURSELF FROM THIS DECEPTION?

➤ Don't force God into a time limit. You can pray to God for direction but He will move on His own time. It is good to ask God for guidance, but God may work through the mind He gave you to exert His influence. God does not dictate your every move; otherwise, He would not have given us free will.

➤ Don't put God in a box. Have boundless hope that He will answer, but don't insist that the answer be a passage of Scripture. God may inspire you in other ways (e.g., with enthusiasm).

➤ Don't attribute every thought to God. Yes, God will answer; but the answer may not be the exact thoughts that are in your mind.

➤ Don't demand direct revelation from God for every decision of your life. Yes, the Apostles were given the special gift of direct revelation when they wrote the Bible, the inspired word of God. However, if we all received direct revelation regularly, then we could all add to the Bible daily.

➤ Don't let people pressure you by asking you what you think God is telling you to do. This question puts a lot of psychological pressure on you. If you can't come up with an idea, you feel guilty; you may fear that something is wrong with your spiritual life. If you announce that you are doing what God told you to do, it makes it more difficult to back out later.

OVERRIDING LOGIC AND REASONING

The reasoning and logic skills given you by God can help you detect deceit and trickery, but there are methods that will override these skills. These psychological processes can deceive you and make you believe things that are not true.

For example, "authority figures" can be used to override

reasoning and logic skills as demonstrated by an eminent hypnotherapist. He explains how the use of authority figures can lead both individuals and entire groups to accept a totally false program to such an extent that it actually affects them physically as well as intellectually. I have taken the liberty of excerpting from, and paraphrasing, this long lecture.

> *Let's convince a group of people that, at a certain moment, they are going to lose control over all the muscles in their bodies. This will happen at the moment when they receive an injection. The actual injection is harmless—it could be distilled water or a Vitamin B shot. The injection has no effect; it is merely a time signal telling them when they will lose control.*
>
> *Our subjects are a group of new recruits arriving at the Marine Corps training camp. They are away from home for the first time and have not yet made new friends. We are going to convince them that, at a certain time, they will fall into an "altered state." We will do this by means of a series of lectures about a new "wonder drug." This wonder drug, they will be told, gives immunity to most tropical diseases. Due to its very high cost and limited availability, it has not been announced to the general population, and is given only to members of the military.*
>
> *The lecturer is an actor; he wears the uniform of a high-ranking officer in the Medical Corps. He describes the new drug's benefits, and warns that it has one side-effect: For about 15 minutes after being injected, they will not be able to stand, speak, open their eyes… they will not be able to move a muscle in their arms or legs.*
>
> *After the lecture, the troops will be told to pack their gear because many of them will be transferred to another section immediately after their shots. This is done as an excuse for separating those who respond properly from those who do not respond to our suggestions. We want to send those who respond well back to the barracks to mingle with the next batch of incoming recruits. Those who have been through the experience, and responded as we want them to, will boast to the new group: "When I got that shot, I fell right on my nose and so will you!"*
>
> *People love to talk about their experiences and this will predispose the new guys to respond even better.*
>
> *They line up for their shots. Unbeknownst to them, the first four*

guys in line are actors. Imagine your feelings as you stand in line and watch the first four guys flop down on the floor! After the fourth man, the rest will be told that they will be getting their shots privately. They will think this is to keep them from seeing everyone lose control, but it is really so that we can quickly send those who do not lose control out the back door and onto a bus for transfer to another platoon. Those who react strongly and lose all control will be sent back to the barracks as noted above, to "infect" the incoming troops with their conviction that the "wonder drug" does exactly as we told them.[37]

The essential elements in this experiment are:

➢ Creation of an authority-figure in the person of someone whom the recruits feel they must trust

➢ Separation of recruits (the weeding out of the undesirables) who respond from those who fail to respond (thus avoiding any perception of doubt)

➢ The use of those who do respond in order to precondition new recruits even before we begin to try to control them (an appeal to "real experience" as opposed to simply our words)

➢ Creation of an environment that removes the recruits' morale supports while at the same time subjecting them to stresses of several kinds (thereby making it almost impossible for them to think rationally about what is happening to them).

Under these conditions, many of the recruits will succumb even though they are intelligent and not predisposed to conditioning. As time goes on, the percentage of those who respond "correctly" to our conditioning will increase as new recruits are exposed to increasingly convinced "experienced" members.

Perhaps you think that those with proper religious training can't be conned into a controlling church or discipleship that teaches false doctrine? They can, because of the four points discussed above. After being subjected to these manipulations, many sincere and intelligent persons do not realize that they are being misled until it is too late.

Abusive discipleships set up victims for compliance just as these Marines were. It is impressed upon new members that this discipler hears from God better than they do. So the discipler is regarded as an authority figure. With that in mind, the member is likely to believe this "authority's" suggestions, especially since they are taught that it is sinful not to trust them. Anyone who doesn't comply is quickly weeded out. The combination of these techniques combined with others described in this book will gain extreme compliance from most anyone, even the strong-willed critical thinkers.

ERODING YOUR SELF-CONFIDENCE

Disciplers who tell you there is one Perfect Will of God for everything in your life are playing a manipulative game. First, they will convince you that they know God's Perfect Will better than you do. Next, they let you know what they think God is saying for your life. If it doesn't match with what you think, they will likely undermine your belief that you can know what God wants at least as well as your discipler does. Then you will likely accept most of their advice because obviously you aren't hearing clearly from God. You are expected to conclude that, if you were hearing clearly from God, your desires would be confirmed by matching your discipler's advice.

You will then be convinced they can hear God when you can't. This will usually lead you to go to them for an excessive amount of advice. At this point, your discipler has gained undue influence over you.

TRICKING YOU INTO DYING COMPLETELY

Once a group can convince you that God's Perfect Will for your life is that you need to die to all your desires, wants, goals, and thoughts (not just your evil desires, wants, goals, thoughts), then you will be stripped of everything that is you. You then have to rely on the group for help.

Here is a solid definition of "dying to self" written by a theologian of international repute:

> ..."dying to self" means the right use of human emotions and desires. They are to be followed insofar as they help us to fulfill God's Holy Will, and they are to be controlled insofar as they hinder us from doing so.[38]

Don't you dare let anybody con you into believing that you need to die to all your attitudes, ways of thinking, desires, or goals! This is not the self-surrender about which the Apostles spoke. Trying to reach this goal will cause you to be putty in somebody's hands. This teaching is a ploy used by most destructive cult leaders (an ethical spiritual director won't give you a simplistic idea of what it means to "die to self"). Die *only* to your sinful ways.

Disciplers—listen up! Telling people to chuck all their ideas so leaders can dump God's ideas into their heads is a con game. A non-manipulating discipler won't issue these false blanket statements to his disciples.

Abusive discipleship groups preach a "separatist" doctrine:

➤ My wants are always separate from what God wants for me.

➤ My desires are always separate from what God desires for me.

➤ My goals are always separate from God's goals for me.

➤ My will is always separate from God's will for me.

CHECKLIST
Whose Will Is It?—Chapter 6

Check those that apply to you and/or your group:

❑ I believe God will give me direct revelations for every detail of my life, if only I am listening

❑ I believe human reasoning and personal desires are always contrary to God's Will

❑ I am concerned that I am missing God's Will

❑ If we ask, God will always reveal why things happen

❑ The leaders can hear God better than I can

❑ I know I must die completely to my will

❑ My mind can be deceived, but my heart cannot

NOTE: **If you have checked *any* boxes, it may indicate a misuse of Scripture and/or may represent the presence of abuse and excessive control.**

Chapter 7

CONTROL IN BLACK AND WHITE

Part of the effect of abusive discipleship is to create a world where the motivating factors are so powerful that people will conform to the exploitive expectations of the leaders.

"Why don't they just leave?" You might ask this question if you are looking at an abusive group from the outside, or if you have never experienced a systematically controlled environment. It is difficult to believe that a healthy, thinking person cannot just pack up and walk out. It is easier to conclude those who are involved in such groups as these are weak-willed people. This is similar to the way in which many people still have a difficult time understanding why a battered woman doesn't just leave the man who abuses her.

Of course, if someone came up and started beating you, you would do your best to get away. The web that entangles battered victims, however, is woven in stages, one strand at a time, gradually compelling the victim to remain. In the same way, disciples of abusive discipleship groups are hemmed in by powerfully motivating forces, both positive and negative. Part of the effect of abusive discipleship is to create a world where these motivations are so powerful that followers will conform to the exploitative expectations of the leaders.

NARROWING THE GRAY

A person with normal moral sensibilities sees some things as wrong, some things as right, and the rest in an ambiguously "gray area." The first chart on the next page represents this normal range of moral sensibility. The second chart represents a mind inclined to a "black and white" understanding of morality, where very little is ambiguous. The development of control in abusive discipleship groups relies on attacks on this "gray area." When people are subjected to emotionally charged teachings on a wide variety of subjects that are actually "morally neutral," they begin to move those subjects from the gray area into the black or white areas.

Examples of Moral Objectivity

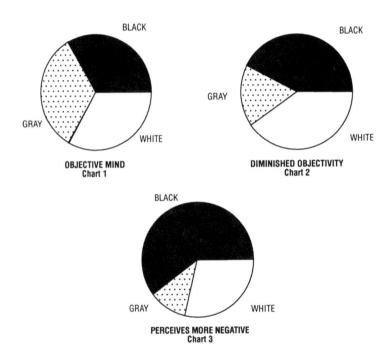

OBJECTIVE MIND
Chart 1

DIMINISHED OBJECTIVITY
Chart 2

PERCEIVES MORE NEGATIVE
Chart 3

The third chart shows the end result of this process—a very black and white viewpoint of morality. The more a group can influence disciples to narrow the gray area, the more significant are the areas where guilt can be produced in those disciples, and the more intense is the control that results.

Abusive groups, however, do not stop there. Inevitably, more items from the gray area end up in the black area than in the white. That's because narrowing the field of desirable or neutral behavior options makes it easier to control people. In the third chart, notice that the person has a more negative outlook on life with this particular black and white thinking. Almost everything is either good or bad, but evil seems to predominate. The more you are persuaded to narrow that gray area, the more your objectivity is skewed, and the more you perceive and judge reality in accord with the program directors.

PAINTING BLACK—"Imbalanced Teaching Trick"

By concentrating on negatives (e.g., sin and evil), your view of reality can be distorted. This is reinforced by negative feedback from people whom you trust (e.g., teachers, spiritual directors, group leaders). The result is a world view much different than before your involvement with the group. You rationalize that you really are seeing the truth and credit these people with opening your eyes. You would find that many of your new, seemingly solid beliefs would crumble if put to the test in the real world.

Under my guidance, "Lynn" had been studying much of the material which now makes up this book. After days of working to understand the teachings of her brother's discipling group, she exclaimed in frustration, "I just can't believe it. I've heard countless sermons on sin and evil but I haven't yet heard one on love." I checked—the word "love" appears in the Bible 590 times, the word "sin" is used only about half as often. Lynn had observed this discrepancy without my pointing it out.

What are the common themes in your group? Look for an imbalance of teachings. That's not to say all groups use this ploy, because some have much more balance in their teachings. In this particular discipleship group, however, there didn't seem to be many teachings on love, forgiveness, joy, kindness, or peace. My research—and the testimony of many others—reveals that abusive discipleships put excessive emphasis on teachings concerning criticism, commitment, doubt, falling away, submission, sin, and being saved.

CONTROLLING INFORMATION BY OVERLOOKING BAD NEWS

Some groups make a big deal out of the number of new baptisms for the month. There is a real "pep rally" mentality to pump up the members to get new recruits. They brag about the number of baptisms; but you'll seldom hear them discuss the fact that they may be losing old members as fast as they baptize new ones.

The reason these groups don't speak about turnover is that their general membership might question why so many old members no longer attend. Members might begin to question the group's superiority. Leaders want the group to look good. They don't want to expose any of their weaknesses.

The Apostles didn't make things appear better than they were. When there were problems in the church, they spoke about it openly and wrote it down for all to know. Coercive discipleship groups (when speaking about themselves) would rather have you dwell only on the bright side of affairs and ignore the negative. Churches that try to minimize the negative will likely "slam" those members who point out any problem. If that doesn't work, they may publicly rebuke them; and if that doesn't shut up the critics, there is always expulsion.

YOU ARE LOCKED IN PSYCHOLOGICALLY

The leaders of one manipulative church have members believing that the Bible teaches, "One has to count the cost of becoming a Christian when being baptized." In the broader Biblical sense, this is true. In this particular case, however, "count the cost" is a loaded term meaning, very specifically, revealing your entire past, recounting everything you ever did wrong—down to the very last detail. According to this church, the baptism is not valid unless the new member does this. If an unfortunate member should later recall some sinful detail (accidentally left unconfessed), then he or she must be re-baptized. If one has a poor memory, this could become a lifelong ritual!

These teachings redefine the definition of baptism. Having been thus indoctrinated, new members think they know what a genuine baptism is. Combine this with an exposure to more limited excerpts from Scriptures twisted to "prove" that no other church has a genuine baptism, and those new members are likely to conclude that their original baptism wasn't valid. What can they do under these conditions, except ask to be re-baptized into this church? This is not to say that disciplers ever actually told them that their original baptism was invalid. After exposure to these skewed teachings, they will "get the idea" on their own.

Consider the implications: "No other church has a valid baptism." All the discipleship has to do is convince new members that they are only following the Bible, and by interpreting some text about baptism differently than other churches do, then suddenly it seems only they have a valid Christian baptism.

If you come to believe that only your church has a genuine baptism, do you think you could leave and go to another church? You feel locked in. You believe that you have no other choice. In order to free yourself, you need to study baptism without the influence of biased leaders. You need to inquire into other churches to find out why their baptism is Biblical. Then, in good conscience, you can seek another church without feeling that you are turning your back on God.

These groups can also lock you in psychologically by teaching that there are only one or two ways to live a Christian life and that everyone's primary mission in life should be living that way. They regard anything different as short of God's Will. For example, there are groups that have a strong emphasis on evangelism—winning people to their group.

I've met with disciples who said that they had reservations about public evangelism in the streets, but their discipleship made them feel that they were not obeying Christ if they didn't do it. Some of these Christians felt guilty because it was implied that they did not love God if they felt uneasy walking up to strangers to talk about Jesus. Others were told that they were not being bold for Jesus. This humiliation of disciples is often used to psychologically force them to choose to cooperate.

Using Matthew 28:19 (i.e., where Jesus commanded His 11 disciples "to go and make disciples"), "Rachel's" leader had convinced her that it meant she should approach strangers on campus and talk to them about Jesus. He convinced her to believe that, if she didn't do this, she wasn't committed to Christ. So Rachel forced herself to participate in street evangelization and found herself in a continual state of inner turmoil as a result.

By having your attention focused on a narrow passage of Scripture, you can be deceived into thinking that being a witness for Christ means public preaching or confronting strangers and reciting the gospel. But there are other ways also to win people to Christ and make disciples. For example, Jesus said, "Let your Light shine before men in such a way that they may see your good works and glorify your Father who is in Heaven" (Matt. 5:16 - NASB).

God has given us different gifts for doing various good works. Ephesians 4:11 says: "It was he who gave some to be Apostles, some to be prophets, some to be evangelists, and some to be pastors and teachers."

Christians can witness for Christ through their particular gift, even if that gift is not evangelism. Take, for example, the gifts of serving and mercy which are listed among others in Romans 12:4-8. One with the gift of serving can meet the physical and material needs of others. This kind of Christian can be a great witness to his neighbor just by helping him voluntarily with some project or doing a particular job. One with the gift of mercy has the ability to show sympathy and empathize with people who are in misery and comfort them. This kind of Christian can be a wonderful witness when the need arises. If one of these is your gift, you can use it to open opportunities for you to speak about the love of Jesus and what he has done for you.

Take note of Paul's instruction (1 Thess. 4:11), which to us may seem irrelevant to the field of evangelism: "Make it your ambition to lead a quiet life, to mind your own business, and to work with your hands, just as we told you, so that your daily life may win the respect of outsiders and so that you will not be dependent on anybody." We see that our witness may not be public preaching, but in how we speak and act in our everyday conversation.

Over the course of my work with Rachel and many other disciples, I have pointed out that Jesus' words in Matthew 28:19 cannot be applied to everyone. Jesus was specifically talking to the 11 Apostles when He issued this command to go make disciples by baptizing and teaching.

It is illogical to conclude that Jesus is commanding every Christian to teach because of what James 3:1 says: "Not many of you presume to be teachers" because you "who teach will be judged more strictly." Paul corroborates this in 1 Corinthians 12:29 when he asks: *Are all teachers?* Paul makes it clear in the context, the answer is no.

When Rachel began to understand the gift of teaching or evangelizing is not for everyone, she wept tears of relief. No longer did she have to force herself to street evangelize, nor feel guilty for being taught that she really did not love Jesus for not wanting to do this.

If you have been convinced that the command in Matthew 28:19 is for every Christian, how can you explain the fact that not all Christians are required to baptize? The command to baptize is in the same sentence. Can you claim that only half of the command is for you? Most Christians who claim that Matthew 28:19 is for everyone never baptize anyone. It is illogical to claim that part of the command is spoken to all Christians yet the other part of the command is not.

Christians have different gifts and callings; all are not called to baptize, teach, or evangelize.

TEACHINGS THAT MOLD MINDS

We have seen how some specific group teachings can produce a narrowing of the gray areas for disciples. But this narrowing can also be produced through a consistent use of language that pushes the disciple toward the tendency to see life mostly in terms of absolutes—either "totally good or totally evil."

It is certainly not wrong to ponder the idea of knowing God's Will, but the concept gives some teachers a lot of material they can use to narrow significantly their disciples' frames of reference.

One of the first things I usually notice from people with the mind-set of these controlling groups is an abnormally frequent usage of certain words (e.g., only, must, never, and always). These are important words that, in a manipulative group, can narrow the members' views of life. In order to gain control, many absolute statements (which have the effect of establishing rules that must be followed in daily life) are usually made about "living the Christian life." The result of such statements is to set a trap of guilt, fear, and shame for those who transgress these non-Biblical rules that controlling leaders define.

For example, consider the following two sentences:

They were ONLY partially obedient, which isn't being obedient at all... Partial obedience is not obedience.[39]

The author of this statement is discussing 1 Samuel 15, where Saul didn't carry out all of God's command. The author quotes: "He (Saul) has turned back from following Me, and has not carried out My commands" (verse 11). God was specifically pointing out what Saul didn't do. The author generalizes this example to include *all believers.* I have heard this author comment many times that "if we torture the Bible long enough, we can get it to confess to anything." I believe that's what he's doing here. It can be a dangerous precedent to draw conclusions from a historical narrative in the Old Testament without some supporting doctrinal teaching elsewhere in the Bible.

Remember, disciples are constantly kept off balance by not knowing which advice they can reject without negative repercussions. They do not realize it, but they are constantly trying to figure this out. They may not consciously ask, but on some level they are thinking: "Is this advice that I must accept so my discipler will view me as humble or teachable, or simply the discipler's idea that can be ignored without risking a 'chewing out?'" The need to decide about so many often unimportant matters combined with the feeling that failure to obey everything is not obedience at all makes these disciples exceptionally compliant to their disciplers' every whim.

There are no Christians on Earth who totally obey God. We have not attained perfection. Still we must all strive hard for perfection; but, if God tells you to pick up "all the Manna which fell in the desert" and you miss one crumb, are you not obedient at all?

If a healthy Christian takes on this new belief, he will begin to lose sight of those morally gray areas and lose sight of God's mercy and grace. He will begin to think more in terms of black and white. The Christian's mind likely will assume that anytime he fails to "obey God" in any matter, he is not obedient to God at all. He is missing God's Will completely. He is totally bad. He doesn't even have to think about it. Nothing is morally neutral or "gray." In everything he does, he sees himself either as totally obedient to God or as a totally disobedient sinner.

Let's re-examine one "all-or-nothing statement" from this same book:

You'll never find God's will until you settle in your heart that you want to do it; whatever it is.[40]

The author could have said, "We are more likely assured of finding God's Will when we make a commitment to do whatever God asks of us." While that would be a true statement, the author wants us to think in black and white—with no alternatives. He says you can never find God's Will if you don't make that commitment. He forgets about willful Jacob, unwilling Moses, hard-headed Jonah, and reluctant Peter. These men were reluctant followers of God, but God's Will was done in their lives—sometimes against their will!

WATCH OUT FOR BLANKET STATEMENTS

Blanket statements can also mold disciples into a more black-and-white mind-set. Sweeping statements don't have to include such words as "only," "never," "must," or "always." Still they are statements that portray the world in all-encompassing, absolute terms.

For Christians, there are sweeping statements that are true:

God is Love. (Always. Forever. Everywhere.)

We live by faith. (True from beginning to end.)

Not everything Christian is so absolute, until interpreted by people like this who write:

...it is wrong and it is sin to decide by not making a decision.[41]

This is a blanket statement of how we are to perceive any situation in our lives when we refuse to make a decision: It is always sin. Plain and simple. You don't have to evaluate the situation, you can take his word for it that you're in sin. Such statements further narrow that "gray area" so that you don't have to use your critical thinking abilities. If, once you have accepted this teaching, and you can't make a decision—then you are in sin. Is it possible that, by *not* making a decision, we may actually be doing God's Will? Could God be that big?

GOD WILL NOT GIVE YOU AN OPTION—NO ALTERNATIVES

The black-and-white mentality is more solidly impressed in your mind by implanting the idea that God will leave you no option if you are serving His will. Typical examples are found in the book, *Experiencing God.*[42] They imply God isn't big enough to allow you two or more equally good choices in His will. God has only one thing for you to do each moment and you better be listening and doing it or you are out of His will.

Actually things aren't so black and white. God may allow you four choices and you can do any one of them while trusting Jesus, being in His presence, and acting in conformance with the guidance of the Holy Spirit. The activity we are doing is less important than doing it with love and asking Jesus to guide our thoughts, words, and actions (1 Cor. 13:1-3).

For example, a teen's mother may leave the house for the day and her only request is that the child be good. The teenager may do anything he or she wants, as long as it is not "bad." There will be other times when the mother asks her child to clean the house. Even in this case, our young person has the freedom to choose to clean the bathroom first or last, just as long as the job is done. It is not the details of how and when, but the fact that the work is done to the best of his or her ability that counts with mom.

Sometimes a parent makes a special request and is especially happy if the child performs this task well. If somehow the child could not fulfill the special request, it doesn't necessarily mean that the youngster went against the parent's admonition to "be good."

I believe that loving parents of this kind are modeled on God's own love and reflect His image for our edification. We in turn should strive to be loving and obedient children.

Other parents are domineering, as is the case with many discipleships. These parents demand every task be done a certain way, in a certain order, and at a certain time. This book's teaching of God's demands, contrary to Scripture, calls forth a picture of such a domineering parent. God says He wants us to be good and to do good works for our neighbor. We can freely choose how to accomplish this with the resourceful minds that He gave us. But, according to these authors, we don't have this free will if we are serving God.

They say:

> *The people of God at this church had a need for a leader. As they prayed, they sensed that God put me there purposely to meet that need. I, too, saw the need and realized God could use me there. As a servant of Jesus Christ, I did not have an option to say no.*[43] *[Emphasis added]*

They seem to be saying that God does not give you options or alternatives. Then they promise their readers that, if they do exactly what God tells them, they will "never have a sense of emptiness or lack of purpose."[44] They appear to be describing a God who permits only one task for us to do moment by moment. By this statement, these writers are promising that, if you obey, you will always be instantly rewarded.

Can you see that this belief has the effect of diminishing "gray areas" in your life? If you did not have this belief ingrained, you would likely search for the reasons why you feel an emptiness or lack of purpose. After being programmed with this belief, you no longer have to think about it—this book tells you that you feel this way because you are not following God's Will perfectly. These writers are telling us that, if we feel a sense of emptiness, we must be disobeying God and we must be in sin!

Unfortunately, even the holiest of men sometimes feel emptiness. God does not always make them happy even though they are following His Will. This simple answer does not solve all of life's problems.

The damnable practice of teaching that these inadequate feelings are always the result of our failure to "hear God speak" can drive a Christian to despair. Why? Because this can cause us to feel that we are always to blame for our feelings of emptines—feelings we have been taught we should never have if we are obeying God.

We always have a purpose, but that does not mean we will always feel this purpose. When God decides to let you feel a purpose in life to encourage you, be thankful, but don't delude yourself that these happy feelings will be permanent as long as you perfectly choose God's Will. This misguided belief can also drive you into the pits of depression when those good feelings stop, because you think this loss means you are not hearing God speak. Then you may feel this means you don't belong to God. What unnecessary guilt this belief can create!

Another lie is that you can always know how God wants you to respond. At the end of each short study section from *Experiencing God*, the authors ask, "What does God want you to do in response to today's study?"[45] It would be better if they said, "How do you think God might want you to respond to this lesson?" Otherwise the disciple might be putting words "into God's mouth" by saying how God wants him or her to respond.

The authors would be justified in saying, "If God gives you a response to today's study, write it down." Instead, their question teaches the false idea that God must immediately provide you with a response. *God is not under some kind of obligation to give you any feelings, sentiments, or thoughts!*

God may give us insights if He chooses. Christians can read a lesson without receiving an insight or distinct thought from God. If they don't hear God's voice, it doesn't mean that they will never hear from God or that they are not listening. God does not have to meet this book's schedule so that you will immediately have a response.

Another problem occurs when Christians feel embarrassed if they can't think of anything that God is telling them. Christians commonly feel intimidated, or that they must be spiritually lacking, because the question implies that everyone else is "hearing from God" on cue.

When Christians try to hear God speak at every moment, their minds may reach into their imagination and pull out something. They then ascribe to God whatever thoughts they might have. This self-delusion begins because of the fear that they may not belong to God if they don't hear something. This is the worst kind of coercion, because few will recognize that it is happening to them.

ANTI-INTELLECT TEACHINGS

Abusive churches often use "Anti-Intellect" teachings to disorient members. For example, some teach: "...your mind (your intellect) is evil." Others quote Paul's comment: "...knowledge puffs up" (I Cor. 8:1). (Seen in context, Paul was dealing with a problem having to do with eating food that had been "sacrificed to idols," and correcting some at Corinth who still thought that there were many gods.) It is true that knowledge can breed conceit; this is why we must always exercise humility, recognizing our human frailty.

Look out for different phrases that attempt to achieve the same results by undermining your convictions. For example: "Your old self is keeping you from fully experiencing the 'new truth.' Your 'old concepts' are dragging you down." Another example is found in *Experiencing God* where the authors warn: "looking at the circumstances from a human perspective" is self-centered. God created our human minds; He shows us things through our human intellects. You can ask God to show you His perspective but what God shows you is still filtered through your human intellect. What we must do is assure that we are in harmony with God's Will by using our human perspective to weigh and evaluate. It is the unthinking self that must be rejected so that we will make sure our actions and decisions are aligned with the Divine Will.

Members who are convinced that their intellects are evil or all their human perspectives self-centered are forced to rely more on the group's guidance, because they cannot trust their own thoughts. Accepting this belief leads members to accept the group's views to a much greater degree. If members cannot trust their own thoughts, then in good conscience they must reject what they are thinking. You can see that this is a clever move because members are more likely to give up their personal convictions, leaving them empty and vulnerable to the group's and the leader's ideas without it being "forced on them."

DEMOLISHING HUMAN CHARACTERISTICS

Leaders can also unduly influence members by teaching that human characteristics are evil. Any element of human nature may be subjected to this distortion; a good example is found in *Experiencing God.* The authors list these characteristics as being self-centered: self-confidence, depending on self, depending on one's own abilities, affirming self, life focused on self, being proud of self, and self-accomplishments. It is how we use these human characteristics that makes them good or bad. Self-confidence, for instance, is good if it makes you bold in a worthy cause; it is evil when it leads you to walk over others uncaringly. Other human characteristics can also be employed either lovingly or wrongly. Controlling leaders who use teachings of this type are attempting to create in their followers a general feeling that these human characteristics are always sinful; this encourages higher compliance to the leader's suggestions. You will see how this is accomplished in the following examples.

Suppose that you are a terrific drummer, and you often play the drums at your group's activities. You know that you are talented and skilled, but the head discipler doesn't think you should be getting all of that attention, so you are told: "You're displaying self-confidence when playing the drums!" Your distorted understanding of self-confidence may cause you to stop playing the drums. In reality, you may be doing good, not evil; the real problem may be the leader's jealousy of your ability.

Another group member plays basketball, leaving little time for church activities. The leader wants a higher attendance at these activities so he warns this member: "You are showing pride in your ability to play basketball." Having learned that "being proud of self-accomplishments" is always sinful, our basketball player drops off the team. Since the member has free time, he ends up coming to more church activities and following the hidden agenda of the leader.

One woman is very shy, and cannot bring herself to work in street evangelization with the group. The group leader informs her that shyness is self-centeredness. The woman in shame repents of this "sin" of being self-centered but she still can't bring herself to evangelize with her group. This young woman's shyness is used against her which puts her under an unbearable strain. Over a period of time, the guilt wears on her to the point that she forces herself to evangelize on the street.

There is a much greater compliance from disciples who have been ingrained with these false teachings although the leader's desired action isn't always brought about by these tactics.

With an understanding of the "Demolishing Human Characteristics" trick, you can see how it can happen that parents complain that their adult children are being controlled by their church leaders, while the young people cry, "No one is telling me what to do!" Skillful manipulators do not have to employ direct commands to control; they use misdirection and distortion of ideas to instill self-doubt. This encourages (almost forces) the victims to let go of their ideas and to replace their critical thinking with the group's or the leader's ideas.

I CAN DO ANYTHING GOD CAN DO

Another false idea in *Experiencing God*, which also helps confuse readers, is the statement, "With God working through me, I can do anything God can do."[46] This sounds stupid when you analyze it. The truth is that God gave humans limited powers over the elements of creation, but we *cannot* "do anything God can do."[47] Do you think I'm taking these words too literally? You should know that many "New Ager's" believe exactly that.

The authors also assure us that "Aided by the Spirit, we can understand all things."[48] Jesus did tell the Apostles that the Holy Spirit would lead them to all truth, but He didn't say they would understand all things. The Leading of the Holy Spirit will not make us omniscient (knowing all things).

One leader of young Christians said if she could change this sentence to read: "With God working through me, I can do anything that God wants me to do," she could accept that. I could, too, but this book, *Experiencing God*, doesn't say that. I agree that, aided by God, we can understand many things. Stated this way, it is no longer a black-and-white teaching.

Of course, this book does get some beneficial results. Readers gain an awareness of ways in which God can speak to them. Intertwined, however, is that false promise that all can hear God as clearly as did Moses, Abraham, and Noah. Top this off by telling disciples that, with Him working through them, they can "do anything God can do,"[49] you are guaranteed to fire up, at least for a short while, any human being.

POSITIVE CONFESSION IN A VARIED FORM

Through the years I have encountered many controlling groups that utilize "positive confession" (i.e., the belief that God will always heal you or will always do what you want if you verbalize it with faith). I will not cover this subject in depth because there are good books on the topic (in Appendix 1, I recommend some of these). I have found the confession principles (e.g., you must be specific in your prayer and you must not repeat your prayer, as this would indicate that you didn't have faith) subtly altered in discipleships.

I was studying a discipleship that taught that it didn't believe in "positive confession." However, the group stressed the principles of positive confession (e.g., "It is not Biblical to keep on insisting when we pray"; "We must be specific when we pray"; "Real prayer means praying specifically"; "You don't need to repeat prayers because that proves you don't have faith"). I have a personal letter from a leader in which he explained, "God may not think you are serious and won't answer [if you repeat your prayers]."

With these attitudes ingrained, people will likely believe very strongly that they have to pray specifically and that they shouldn't be persistent. In the faith movement, they say that you really are demonstrating to God that you don't have faith if you have to keep asking. This is a positive confession principle and not a Biblical idea at all.

So here is another example of black-and-white thinking, when petitioning God:

REAL PRAYER = SPECIFIC REQUESTS

FALSE PRAYER = GENERAL REQUESTS

According to their teaching, there is no in-between; either prayer is real or it isn't. But I do not personally believe that God turns a deaf ear when you don't pray "just right." Ask yourself, "What exactly does a merciful, loving God do with a non-specific prayer—dump it?" God is big enough to compensate if you don't pray just right. Another discipler told me that you had to be specific only when petitioning God, but it was okay to pray generally. This is still incorrect.

If a group can subvert your ideas about prayer in this manner, then when you encounter Christians in "general" prayer (at least, petitioning prayers) in another church you are apt to look down on them. Both forms of prayer are Biblical; but, because you've been persuaded to accept the view that general prayer isn't real prayer, you judge this other church group as "not praying." You will remain mired in this restrictive framework until you realize your group deceived you.

To attempt to undo this discipler's thinking, I challenged him with the Bible passages in which a widow kept bothering a judge and begging him to do her justice against an adversary. After a long time, the judge gave in to her request, not because of justice but because of her persistence (Luke 18: 1-8). The widow was *persistent* and that's what paid off. The Bible tells us that God wants us to persist. Romans 1:9 and 10 states: "without ceasing I make mention of you always in my prayers" (AV).

Teaching that we must only make specific prayers imposes limits on God's actions. Consider the fact that we have only a human mind, and perhaps a confused one at that. How could we specifically ask God for help since often we do not know what is best for us? Would it not be wiser to leave it to God to answer the prayer in His own way? His way is infinitely wise and good and we certainly can trust His wisdom and love. In other words, it is okay to pray "specifically" and it is also okay to pray "generally."

This idea of not being persistent in prayer was backed up by a discipler who quoted Matthew 6:7: "But when ye pray, use not vain *repetitions*, as the heathen [do]: for they think they shall be heard for their much speaking" (KJV). It is not the repetition about which Jesus was complaining, but the *vain* repetition. This text is Jesus' warning to those who pile up a lot of words in long-winded prayers.

Any prayer that engages our heart and our mind in sincere communication with God cannot be considered "babbling." Our loving persistence honors God greatly. If we don't pray with our hearts and our minds, however, we are just babbling, no matter how many or how few words we say.

EVERY LITTLE BIT PUTS YOU DEEPER INTO A BLACK-AND-WHITE MENTALITY

Molding minds is a step-by-step process. Some prospective members will bite off the information and swallow it rapidly. More critical minds will usually have difficulty accepting everything they are told. Concerning the latter, the group may slow down and even back off until these new members accept certain teachings. Then, after the disciples have wrestled with their doubt and rationalized away other negative ideas, they are led to the next bit of misinformation. Exposed to a group using these training dynamics, even the strongest individual can be broken. Yes, even you.

This is why I repeat so often that people don't think they are being unduly influenced because they "came on their own" and received teachings "at their own pace." Nothing appears to have been forced upon them. In the end, though, it doesn't matter if you learned all the redefining of words and all the twisted Scripture in a single sitting, or if it took you a year. The process is insidious. While it is happening, your view of reality is slowly narrowing. Whether in one giant step, or slowly over a longer period of time, they are still molding your thinking to fit their own agenda.

Please don't impute evil motives to everyone who does this. Often leaders in abusive discipleship groups don't see that they are trying to manipulate their followers. There are some sincere teachers who feel they are seeking to follow the truth. Because of this, they believe they have found the one right way of understanding and explaining Scripture. They may honestly believe they understand "God's view" more perfectly than anyone else.

One must not judge the quality of a ministry based solely on intentions. The impact of a ministry on the lives of its members is important, too.

CHECKLIST
Control in Black and White—Chapter 7

Check those that apply to you and/or your group:

❏ I feel grateful because the gray and open areas of my life have been narrowed; I see absolute right and wrong so clearly now

❏ I feel I am free to choose, even though my choices of right and wrong are now narrower than before I joined the group

❏ Even though the gray and open areas of my life have been narrowed, I still feel as though I am using all of my critical thinking skills

❏ God doesn't give me options if I am truly living each moment in His Perfect Will

❏ There is only one way to evangelize

❏ Frequently uses such words as: always, never, must, and only

❏ Believes people are either "all bad" or "all good," totally obedient to God or totally disobedient

❏ Prayer must be and only be specific

NOTE: If you have checked *any* boxes, it may indicate a misuse of Scripture and/or may represent the presence of abuse and excessive control.

Chapter 8

VICIOUS INFORMATION CONTROL

*These disciplers think they are living the Full Gospel when
actually they are living an inferior Christian life because leaders
discredit negative information about their group;
this blinds them to anything bad about leadership.*

In an abusive discipleship environment that controls information, you can be prevented from freely expressing worry, doubt, or fear because you run the risk of being accused of sin. The discipler may say you are not trusting God because of your genuine concerns. They're sneaky though. The disciplers will not label you as being in sin for not trusting God every time you have a worry, just the times they deem necessary—those times when they want to mold your thinking. The discipler doesn't have to directly tell you, the disciples, to suppress your thoughts of sadness or trouble; subtle misdirection is much more effective. The discipler causes you, *of your own volition,* to shun specific thoughts by making you think that your feelings of sorrow or anxiety are from the devil and, therefore, sinful.

STUFF YOUR FEELINGS AND CAUSE YOURSELF TERRIBLE STRUGGLES

One of the most popular verses frequently taken out of context and used to cut off thoughts and feelings is "perfect love casts out fear..." (1 John 4:18). After a period of indoctrination, members are brought to understand that "fear" means almost any anxiety or trouble. If members are bothered by something to the extent that they are anxious or troubled, their group may persuade them that their natural human feelings are sinful while quoting this verse (1 John

4:18). This trick often causes them to "stuff" their valid feelings.

What is the context? Judgment Day! The verse is talking about *standing before God on Judgment Day.* If you have been a loving person all your life, you will not fear standing before God. The love for God as shown throughout our lives will cast out any fear of standing before God.

Some leaders stretch this verse to mean it proves you don't love God if any time you feel afraid. Remember Jesus in the Garden of Gethsemane, sweating blood and asking the Father to let this cup pass from him. Fears are human nature and certainly do not prove whether or not we love God.

Further, Jesus said, "Do not worry about your life, what you will eat or drink, or about your body, what you will wear" (Matthew 6:25). Jesus was talking about food and clothing but this does not mean that we cannot have *any* concern about ourselves or another person. Paul was "perplexed, but not driven to despair..." (2 Cor. 4:8), and he was afflicted in every way with external conflicts and internal fears (2 Cor. 7:5).

Consider the case of "Joanne." She was worried that her family was not being saved. Her discipler constantly reminded her that her faith was weak and that she was not trusting God to convert them. Joanne stuffed her thoughts and misgivings, and she began to lose touch with her feelings. So she would have less anxiety, she began thinking of her family less and less often. If Joanne had not been influenced to discard these feelings, she probably would have prayed more intensely for her family. Instead Joanne said to herself, "Perfect love casts out fear." Joanne eventually became a kind of robot repeating this verse over and over. Over time, this inappropriate use of a Bible verse slowly killed the affection she had felt for her family.

If Joanne had been thinking objectively, she may have disputed her discipler's teaching and said Jesus desires that everyone should be saved; but, because of free will, not everyone will accept salvation. Being concerned for the welfare of her family had nothing to do with a lack of faith, and it was certainly not a sin. Of course, if you *really* speak back to your discipler like this, it is quite possible that you will be accused of being rebellious, unteachable, or full of pride.

Many disciples or members of controlling churches have told me that their families weren't Christians. In fact, the truth was that their families didn't believe in the exact same interpretation of the Bible as they did.

Working with those involved in controlling groups, I have often turned to the parents right in front of the disciples and asked if they had faith in Jesus and if they were baptized Christians. They almost always said they were. It became clear that the reason for the disciples' worry was that family members didn't have a discipler over them. Had they been under the supervision of a discipler, that would have meant they were committed Christians.

The "disciple mentality" finds it impossible to believe that a family can be living a committed Christian life if they do not have "guidance" from a discipler.

JESUS HAD ANXIETY AND GREAT SORROW

Jesus was so troubled and full of anxiety and sorrow in the Garden of Gethsemane that he cried out, "My soul is sorrowful unto death" (Matt. 26:38, Douay). Jesus was genuinely troubled because of those who rejected him and were not saved, and because of the agonizing death he knew he would suffer. Still Jesus had perfect faith.

So you can have faith and be troubled, perplexed, or have fears. We wouldn't say Jesus sinned, yet often disciples who have worry, doubt, or fear can be told they "lack trust in God" and, therefore, they are in sin. Jesus was able to pray more earnestly *because* He fell into a great agony (Luke 22:44). If Jesus had been under a discipler, He might have been told that his sadness and anxiety showed that He lacked trust in God.

Maybe you have been influenced to believe that your sorrowful or troubled heart was sinful when it wasn't. Your discipler may have told you that Jesus wants "the full measure of my joy within them" (John 17:13). The discipler can also remind you that Jesus said He wanted your joy to be full (John 16:24). So, because of the "isolated verse trick," you are expected to dismiss your sadness and replace it with joy.

THE ISOLATED VERSE CON GAME

By careful use of an isolated Bible verse, a clever discipler can label almost any feeling as "sinful" and influence you to suppress it. While there is a real need to be joyful, there are times when we can and should feel sorrow. Listen to Paul: "For out of much affliction and anguish of heart I wrote to you with many tears" (2 Cor. 2:4). He knew it was all right to feel emotion and he certainly didn't consider it sinful. Ask yourself if there have been times when your discipler took unwarranted action by labeling as sinful your emotions, thoughts, or feelings. Perhaps you've noticed this in their work with others. If these practices occur in your group, you may have a serious problem.

God allows us to have trials and suffer for our own good. A discipler can be mistaken if he jumps to conclusions about why sorrow, worry, doubt, or fear is in our life. God doesn't always relieve these burdens, but He does promise not to give us more than we can handle.

Paul prayed three times for our Lord to remove the "thorn in his side." God said, "My grace is sufficient for you, for my power is made perfect in weakness" (2 Cor. 12:9). Here is God speaking to one whom He selected, saying that poor Paul has to just stick it out. God also reminded Paul that His grace would be there with him. Paul understood that this "trial" was to keep him from becoming conceited.

BIBLE ROULETTE

Many disciplers warn against "Bible roulette," the practice of asking a question and then opening the Bible and accepting a random passage as the answer. Even though they may preach against Bible roulette, they often practice it in different forms.

When you have a question, they subtly lead you to accept as the answer whatever Bible verse comes to mind. Your mind, however, has a limited capacity to memorize verses from among the thousands in Scripture. Therefore, you will not always have memorized the proper verse for whatever path God wants you to follow.

Another form of Bible roulette depends on the Bible to solve all of our daily problems. Whatever passage we happen upon is the one the Lord must be using to tell us how to answer our problem for that day. Some disciples become overconfident, believing God is personally leading them in this manner.

We can learn much from the Bible, but it is self-deception to expect to find the answer in such a random manner. Yes, sometimes we can be directed by Scripture. But sometimes we will act inappropriately if we blindly follow a randomly selected Scripture. God wants us to grow in His wisdom by learning all of His Word, and surely He will make good use of the mistakes we make along the way.

THE KIDS ACTED APPROPRIATELY—THE BIBLE PERSON DIDN'T

"Naomi," one of my first controlling-discipleship clients, told me about the time her sister came to the third grade classroom where she was teaching to tell her of their father's death. Naomi looked at her sister, who was profoundly emotional and in tears, and replied, "Praise the Lord!" Naomi thought she was exhibiting peace about the situation, not realizing that she was acting inappropriately.

Naomi then told her class that her father had just died and that a substitute would be taking her place. The little children were saddened and sympathetic (Naomi remembered the sadness on their faces and their asking if there was anything that they could do for her). Naomi, however, was inappropriately emotionally distant from the situation, while these innocent children were responding normally to someone who had just lost a parent.

Naomi always looked for a Bible verse on how to act. She told me she remembered a verse from the Old Testament which read, "Rejoice at death and weep at birth." Perhaps she was thinking of Jeremiah 22:10: "Weep not for him who is dead, mourn not for him!" to account for her reaction; but that is not the meaning of this verse, if taken in context. It would have been better if she had remembered "Rejoice with those who rejoice and weep with those who weep" (Romans 12:15), and responded normally to her sister and the tragic news. Naomi also could have remembered that Jesus also wept at the death of his friend, Lazarus. This story illustrates the danger of expecting random Bible passages to tell us how we should feel. Spontaneity is stifled by this process and, in my opinion, these Christians are hindering the freedom of the Holy Spirit to lead them.

When seeking God's direction, we need time to pray and reflect in a personal relationship with our God. God is able to plant the urge in our hearts concerning which direction we should take (Psalm 20:4). The problem is, so many times we "receive" (really, we remember) a verse that contradicts the desire God has placed in our hearts. So, actually, we are not accepting God's Will but rather some irrelevant Bible verse.

Those who memorize Scripture are to be commended. It is

presumptive, however, to limit God to only those passages you've memorized. Although God can bring to our mind one of the Scriptures that we may have memorized, we serve God more perfectly if we do not expect Him to stick to only the Scriptures we know.

LED BY SCRIPTURE OR HIS OWN BIAS?

I confronted "Mark" about his discipleship. While reading the Bible, he came across the word "factious" and instantly thought of me. He reasoned that the Lord was showing him that I was factious and telling him to avoid me. Instead of reasoning with me and thinking things out with the good mind God gave him, Mark cut me off because of his misapplication of Scripture. He refused to consider my side of the matter because he read "factious" somewhere in Scripture. He even told me that, as he read this passage, he said to God, "Lord, are you trying to tell me that Mary Alice is factious?" Much later, one of his elders would tell him my information was accurate and he eventually began to see I was credible.

LIMITING GOD BY THE SCRIPTURE YOU READ FOR THE DAY

Be very cautious about expecting to get answers for problems from the Scripture verses you happen to read today. We must study the *entire* Bible for a better understanding of God's Will. You might ask, "Doesn't God speak to us by Scriptures?" Yes, but that doesn't mean that if someone challenges me I am to go only to the Bible passage I read that day to solve the problem.

Mark should have allowed me to thoroughly discuss these issues with him. Instead, he avoided me. His problem could have been solved with an open and candid conversation. Of course, I am not saying that studying the Bible isn't helpful. I *am* saying that it is not true that God will always give you His direction for the day and tell you exactly what to do every time you read Scripture. And I am saying that conditioning people to expect God to do this is misleading them.

So how do we know for sure that we are following the desire that God puts in our heart or our own selfish desire?

If the subject is criticism of our discipleship group, as it was when I spoke to Mark, we must be willing to research the matter.

Speak to those who question your group. Be willing to read the comments of former members. Don't be foolishly arrogant and say, "I already know because the Bible and my group give me every answer to life and, therefore, I don't need to look at anything else." Such closed thinking is why some people spend their entire lives in destructive groups—they believe it would be sinful if they read derogatory information about their group. That's exactly what such groups want you to think. If your group has the truth, challenges can hold no fear for you—or for *them.*

Truth will set you free, but only if you are allowed to hear it and only if you don't prejudge the information.

FEAR IS GOOD!

Do controlling groups ever talk about *healthy fear?* Rarely. They will, of course, admit we are allowed to have fear of God, but they usually categorize all other fear as sinful. This is so subtle that we're not aware when some of our healthy fears and doubts start being called sinful. Ironically, these groups rely heavily on fear to keep members in line!

God can guide us by allowing us to feel fear. Suppose that a disciple's family members have a distinct fear that something is wrong with him or her. They begin praying only to find out later that the disciple was really in terrible trouble and needed their prayers. Many families can tell of a fear that motivated them to pray and to seek help, which ended up saving the lives of loved ones. We have to be sensitive to our spirit and carefully evaluate the fear. Otherwise, we may be suppressing doubts inspired by the Holy Spirit.

I certainly have benefited from examining my thoughts to find out if I was unnecessarily fearful. My problems began when I started rejecting too many thoughts that contained traces of worry, doubt, and fear, thinking they were wrong. I started to lose my perspective.

Much later, I was able to understand that I limited my free will because someone had persuaded me that worry, doubt, and fear were causing me unhappiness. When I started suppressing these thoughts, I felt better (temporarily) and presumed they were right.

One day, my mother was very troubled. Instead of being sensitive to her problem, however, I immediately diagnosed her problem as fear. I would pray for her, I said. I thought that was all I could do. *I was wrong.*

Looking back, if I hadn't had a fixed belief that almost all our worries, doubts, and fears were sinful and, thus, were the cause of unhappiness, I would have been able to look objectively at my mother's problem instead of thinking, "The apparent problem isn't the real issue—it's really her fear." I could have helped her solve her problem with a little creative thinking; but I didn't, because my mind was closed. This prevented me from doing anything for her.

RATE YOURSELF

"Monty" isn't greatly inclined to see most criticism as sinful. That's why he doesn't generally get bent out of shape when he hears adverse comments about his pastor.

But what if his friend "Eddie," who goes to a controlling church, should happen to hear the same comment about *his* pastor? Eddie immediately judges the critic as sinful simply because that person had the audacity to voice an opinion. His blood pressure goes up, the volume and intensity of his voice increases, his body becomes rigid, and his facial muscles tighten. Eddie, in effect, has taken on a different personality! Under the influence of his programming, Eddie proceeds to tell the critic that he is terribly grieved because this should have been discussed only in private and only with the pastor.

Scoring these two reactions, Monty gets a 10 and Eddie rates a one (a low score).

Eddie didn't even really listen to anything said about his pastor. These words were only for the pastor's ears, according to Eddie. But what about the possibility that this was something that Eddie should think about? What if the "critic" felt led by the Lord to discuss this with Eddie? It is impossible for Eddie to even think about this because, in his church group, *God does not work this way.* If anything negative is to be discussed, God must use the "right channels of communication."

In these groups, you are likely to be judged as "sinning" if you simply lean over and tell a friend something negative about a leader's teachings. According to them, this is *not* how God would open someone's eyes to a problem. God is squeezed into their one way to do things.

You may say, "I don't usually label those who challenge leadership as factious!" Maybe you don't, but your group may have caused you to have other similar tendencies.

WARNING: Don't discard all you are learning from this book just because this particular point doesn't seem to fit you. If you read some things in this book that don't apply to your group, you might be tempted to deduce that your group doesn't use *any* coercive persuasion techniques. From a single exception, you might leap to the conclusion that yours is not a controlling discipleship. If others have suspicions that your group is using control methods, please keep reading and looking.

PERSECUTION—ARE YOU KIDDING?

Controlling groups really make a big deal out of being persecuted. Perhaps your group does.

This conditioning produces a strong reaction when something negative has been said about your group or its leaders. This emotional reaction usually causes you to discredit those who speak out against the group, its policies, your leaders, or their teachings. "This is persecution," you cry. You don't think about it, you don't analyze it. You conclude it's persecution. This is the language of non-thought.

Once you believe that almost all criticism is a form of persecution, you won't be able to see that you are being manipulated to ignore reality.

If you are struggling to avoid even one negative thought about your group, because that means doubt and doubt is equal to sin in your mind, you will usually overreact to almost all negative information about your group. What if the group labels those who give you that negative information as "the enemy," or tells you that these persons are persecutors? You can be persuaded to project hatred towards these people and to denounce outside influences. Under these conditions, it is nearly impossible for you to objectively evaluate the dissenting comments. You are on a merry-go-round, and you must get off in order to study the information away from the influence of the group.

But how can you realize you should get away? You've rejected all negative thoughts, thus hampering your striving toward independent judgment about the group.

Picture yourself standing in a group of Christians who are about to be thrown to the lions. Present are other Christians who had fingers or arms cut off or eyes gouged out because they refused to renounce their faith in Jesus. (Note: If you want to read more about the suffering endured by early Christians, see Eusebius's *Ecclesiastical History*.)[50]

You don't want to be the only one not suffering, so you mention that your Christian group has also been persecuted. They all hush in respectful silence. In fear and concern for their brothers and sisters and with chills running up their spines, they ask how you and your Christian friends have been persecuted. You cast your eyes downward and whisper that people criticize your leaders.

There is dead silence. You add that, "Parents have hired people to talk to my Christian friends." The audience doesn't seem to be properly horrified. They appear puzzled and begin to question you. They have been horribly tortured and they are preparing to die for their faith. They are obviously having difficulty understanding why you think your group has been persecuted.

"Have your friends been asked to deny Jesus?" they ask you. You don't know of anyone who was asked to do that. "No, no," you cry, "but there are all of these other churches that don't have the correct Biblical beliefs! Some of our disciples have left our Christian group for those dead churches!"

"Do those churches," they ask, "believe that Jesus is God?"

"Well, yes," you reply, "but those other Christian groups are lukewarm because they don't believe in discipling or in rebuking like we do. Our church is on fire and we really care. Those other churches aren't committed to the hilt like ours."

About this time the bedraggled Christians are looking at you a bit oddly. A blind man, clad in rags, gets your attention and asks you, "Do you honestly believe you are being persecuted when no one has tried to force you to deny Jesus Christ?"

Again you mutter that other Christian churches are not as committed and they don't preach the whole truth. They even tell lies about your church.

The blind Christian reminds you that many of his contemporary churches didn't teach the whole truth either. The church of Corinth lived the Gospel poorly and the people there were committing all kinds of sins yet the Apostle still recognized the Corinthians as brothers and sisters in Christ. Paul addresses this troublesome church, which was not following God's commandments, as "the church of God in Corinth, together with all the saints throughout Achaia" (2 Cor. 1:1).

"But," you tell the blind Christian, "these people are *criticizing my leader.*"

The blind man turns his face toward your voice. "They are *verbally* criticizing your leader. Excuse me, but it is incredible to me that you think of that as persecution. Not one person has asked you to deny Christ. No one has tortured you! My brother, no one has cut off your arm, starved you, or gouged out your eyes. Do you really think mere words are persecution?"

His empty eyes look you in the face as he says, "Brother, let me tell you the meaning of Christianity. When people criticize you, love them, be kind to them. You are not to think that they are persecuting you when they criticize your church leaders. Peter and Paul were criticized by my brothers and sisters many times, but our mutual respect and love in Christ was never in question!"

Why do controlling groups and cults have to impress upon their members that criticism of leaders is persecution? To more fully control or influence members.

NO, SON, I WOULDN'T REJECT YOU... BUT *YOU* ARE REJECTING ME

"Adam" was home on a visit and said, "Dad, you may reject my beliefs, but I am prepared to be cut off from you and the rest of the family because of those beliefs."

"Charles" looked at him and said, "Son, I would never cut you off for your beliefs."

Adam quoted Matthew 10:34-36: "Do not think that I have come to bring peace upon the earth. I have come to bring not peace but the sword. For I have come to set a man against his father, a daughter-in-law against her mother-in-law; and one's enemies will be those of his household" (New American Bible).

Adam also quoted Luke 12:51 to his family: "Do you think that I have come to establish peace on the earth? No, I tell you, but rather division" (NAB). The teachers in Adam's church had isolated these verses and ingrained them deeply into the minds of their disciples.

His dad tried to explain that it was the Jews of that time who rejected their children and family members who followed Jesus. These verses were not orders to Christians to reject their parents and all other non-believers. Jesus taught us to love everyone. Non-Christians may slander, revile, and persecute us, but Christians are to return blessings for abuse, and not reject their detractors. We are to "heap burning coals on his head" (Prov. 25:21-22, Rom. 12:20) by returning love for hate.

"Besides," Charles said, "I have faith in Jesus. You can't apply that verse to me. It is not our faith in Jesus that is separating us. It is the faith you have in your group and in their interpretation of the Bible that is in question. This Scripture describes a family rejecting a member for his belief in Jesus. We are only rejecting your thinking about some of your group's practices and beliefs. That is what your mother and I want to discuss."

"Dad," said Adam, "I only believe in the Bible. I don't believe in a group. They just happen to be the only ones fully preaching and believing what is in His Word."

Adam told his family that he was prepared to give them up if he had to choose between faith and family. Adam's mother assured him that he could believe whatever he wanted but that she would never reject him. She assured him that her disagreement with some of his beliefs would not come between them.

However, in the months that followed, Adam's family continued to question his beliefs. As a result, he didn't call or come home much anymore. Adam had cut off his family. Charles tried to make Adam see that he wasn't being Scriptural. "Adam," he said, "even if you perceive me as a non-Christian, the Bible does not talk about cutting off family members because they don't agree with your beliefs."

Charles said the Bible clearly tells us that it isn't the Christian who is to do the rejecting. Adam, however, had made up his mind. He thought he had an obligation to separate from his family because they could not meet his demand to be uncritical of his church.

This is typical of the behavior of persons in a controlling group who have been fed twisted Scriptures.

THE DISCIPLE IS BOSS—GOT THAT, MOM AND DAD?

Typically, programmed disciples—running from challenges and questions—tell their families that they will not listen to any criticism of their group. They take away their families' right of free speech. The families must obey the disciples on this matter. The disciples have become masters of their families.

The disciple dictates to family members and will cut them off if they continue to criticize or question his group. If the disciple's family wants to see him or speak with him, they must accept all kinds of restrictions he places on them. The disciple is boss here— either obey his orders or the disciple may threaten his family that they will never get to see or hear from him again. Despicable, yes— and completely contrary to Christian love as well.

Recognize that it takes courage to sit down with your family members and hear them out. It takes courage to face negative facts and respond logically. What disciplers do not see is that they are teaching cowardice and labeling nearly all opposition as "dero- gatory" and any negative facts as "lies."

Abusive disciplers seldom recommend going home and spend- ing whatever time it takes to answer the worries of family members. They teach disciples to turn their backs on the "opposition."

If you refuse to listen to negative information, it may be because your group has instilled in you the fear that you will hear something negative about your leaders or group. They have you believing that, if you listen to such criticism or questioning, you will fall away by committing the sin of doubting the leaders. They are just trying to scare you into not hearing the truth. If these leaders weren't hiding something, they wouldn't have to do all this controlling of negative information.

Do you realize that by telling your family or friends they cannot speak negatively to you, you may be telling God He cannot give you any negative information about your group through your family or friends? That is what you are doing. Maybe God wants to use your family or friends as His instruments for shedding light on something that may not be right in your group.

Are you going to continue to demand that God jump through your hoops if He wants to enlighten you about something negative in your group? "Hey, God, it has to come from my group's leadership or I won't believe it!"

I pray that you cast off this yoke of bondage.

TRICKS TO KEEP YOU CONTROLLED

➤ Leaders get you to believe that they don't interpret the Bible but just "teach what is in the Bible"—making the Bible synonymous with their interpretation!

➤ Leaders teach you to think that, if you want to be truly committed to Jesus, you must believe every word they teach about the Bible.

➤ Leaders prompt you to think that you are probably committing sins of pride or rebelliousness if you don't believe every word of the Bible as they interpret it for you.

These are some of the ingredients for controlling. The recipe isn't entirely foolproof—some disciples will leave, but many will be caught.

INSTILL FEAR OF NEGATIVE INFORMATION TO GAIN CONTROL

Abusive and controlling groups concentrate on these two essential elements:

➤ Teach the discipled that any negative or critical words are probably sinful

➤ Teach them to fear those "sins" so greatly that they will react forcefully and irrationally toward *anyone* (family, friend, fellow Christian) who dares suggest that their group might be making a mistake in any of its teachings.

If you can cause someone to eliminate nearly all feelings of worry, doubts, and fears, it is likely that you can cause a disassociated state of consciousness in that person. Disassociated describes an altered state. Once this altered state of consciousness has been achieved, the subject will be highly impressionable to all your teachings and may be programmed to trust you and reject all outside influences.

If you consistently denigrate outsiders, labeling them as not committed, demonic, or worldly, you can probably prevent the subject from accepting most information offered by those outsiders. If the information can be prevented from being seen as credible, the subjects will refuse to be informed about the errors you are trying to teach them.

I haven't written much about the tactic of putting down other groups in order to make your group look better, but it works rather well, and it can be the "final touch" to cement a disciple into your group.

Here is how it is done: Teach your disciples to think that no other Christian church is living a committed Christian life and that no other church is so directly led by God. Under this influence, disciples won't want to leave even if many teachings and activities are questionable (members of Jim Jones's cult said that even though things were bizarre, there was no other Christian church that was living the full Gospel). So the idea is to pump up your group as the greatest and demean others.

PERSECUTION COMPLEX = INFORMATION CONTROL

The result of expanding the meaning of "persecution" to include any dissent from your group can produce *information control*. Many Christian churches that twist Biblical ideas to control information in an effort to gain compliance from disciples have been called cults. Some specialists who study cults see that such churches also preach the legitimate Gospel along with their perversions. In order to make a clearer separation between controlling Christian groups and destructive cults, these professionals often apply labels such as "abusive churches," "controlling churches," or "cult-like control." Don't read too much meaning into this technical difference. It simply means that these groups use the tools and controls of destructive cults while also teaching components of basic Christianity.

INFORMATION CONTROL THROUGH FEAR

In Chapter 4, you learned how the Biblical meaning of unity was changed. In some groups, members are conned into believing they are out of unity with "The Body of Christ" when they are in disagreement with whatever the group deems important. As a result, many members will suppress their right to voice their opinions fearing they might be accused of being "out of unity." This is an effective way of suppressing information to make the members highly compliant to the leaders' whims. Also, if you can convince your members that "division" is always wrong, you can ensure maximum cooperation without anyone even noticing the subtle control.

Further, groups often manipulate the meaning of the following verse to control opposing information:

> *I appeal to you, brothers, in the name of our Lord Jesus Christ, that you all agree with one another so that there may be no divisions among you and that you be perfectly united in mind and thought* (1 Cor. 1:10).

Some leaders isolate the words, *"no divisions among you,"* and *"be perfectly united in mind and thought."* By doing this, they can then jump to the conclusion that we are *never* to disagree with the group—to do otherwise always causes divisions.

In context, you will find out that Paul was speaking about a specific problem in a specific church community. What subject was he talking about when he was asking them to have the "same point of view"? Within the church at Corinth, there was bickering and bragging about who was following whom. Some said they followed Paul, others Cephas and Apollo. Some said that they alone followed Christ.

Paul said, "Is Christ divided? Were you baptized in the name of Paul?" He did not want any divisions over this issue of being followers of men, as they were supposed to be united in Jesus. Jesus warned that His mission would bring divisions and dissension (Matt. 10:34-36). Divisions are not always a sign of sin or error; they are the natural result of our human urge to seek the truth and are to be expected.

Certainly there will always be error in our current churches just as there was in Corinth. We will always need brave Christians to stand up and challenge church leaders who are straying. If we habitually see as divisive those who disagree with or challenge leaders' actions, we may miss God's leading. Yes, independent thinkers will often create divisions. Because they may be from God, they are deserving of a reasoned response and careful study.

Another phrase frequently mishandled is "Be of one mind" (e.g.: Rom. 12:16; Philp. 1:27, 2:2, 4:2). Controllers may use this out of context whenever they want to change your opinion to theirs. It is terribly wrong to claim that Paul meant we must always agree with the leaders.

The mere argument that there should be no division tells you that agreement is more important than the truth. When a group stresses "no division" instead of the facts, watch out! They are asking you to be mindless and just accept their view.

If you look at all these ideas (i.e., division, unity, being of one mind, being led of the Spirit, obedience, and submission) in a controlling discipleship, you will see a tendency to reduce all of them to a general meaning of *don't keep your opinion but accept ours.* Thus your freedom to think and act is restricted. Conversely, disciplers of these groups will almost always perceive you as a virtuous person if you consistently give up your opinion for theirs and acquiesce to their requests.

For all of these reasons, "independent" is now a negative word. It means you have different ideas from the leaders and want to keep yours.

"Falling away" is another label commonly used to describe those who don't want to keep the same viewpoints as the leaders. Being accused of "not surrendering" doesn't necessarily have anything to do with not wanting to give up sin, but rather *not wanting to give up your opinions for those of your leaders!*

Are you getting the picture? Everything is starting to mean: *Agree with us, think like us, and speak like us.* To them, that is what's right; whereas, going against leaders is almost always viewed as "wrong."

Remember that I said "almost always" wrong. There will be times that you can actually win when the truth goes against leaders, but the odds are against you. Because you *are* occasionally permitted to win on a few minor points, you will be led to say, "I was able to question this and that and straighten out things." Great! Once in a while you can win; but look at all your friends who had to eat "crow" when they tried to correct leaders even though they were in the right.

"Not committed" can now have the added meaning that a person doesn't want to go along with the group-think. "Rebellious" may mean that you simply don't accept the leaders' errors, even though you may still be committed as ever to Jesus and keeping His commands.

Pretty simple game isn't it? Try to make as many Biblical words as you can come to mean "we must agree with leaders." Adding new meanings to all these words only means more control of information.

DISCREDITING THE SOURCE

Sometimes people refuse to hear important ideas because the person who espouses the information is a poor speaker, makes mistakes in grammar, or has a limited vocabulary. These shallow judgments cause people to miss things that God wants them to understand. In a closed environment (like that of abusive or controlling groups), the habit of rejecting information because of its source is extremely dangerous.

The more reliance listeners place on the background of a speaker before they find their information credible, the less they exercise their ability to reason and make good judgments on their own. If the speaker or writer has a background to their liking, it is easier for them to believe what they are told; if that background is different from theirs, the very same information may be rejected or they may refuse to listen to it.

Manipulative leaders understand that people have this tendency to discredit information if the source is ridiculed. They exploit this weakness by assassinating their opposition's character rather than dealing with facts. This is a ploy which gives manipulators more influence over the thinking of their victims.

Often the leaders do not want their followers to even consider information, attacking the motives and credibility of a critic is an effective way to accomplish this. When members are conditioned by leaders to believe that information is credible only if the source of that information is acceptable, it is unlikely followers will seriously consider anything said by those ridiculed by the leaders. These victims become putty in the hands of these leaders.

I often hear, "Could you send me information on who you are? My friends might discount your views if they do not know your Biblical footing. What is your statement of Faith?" I have no fear of disclosing who I am and what my background is, but it is important to remember that God is not limited. He can use anyone to send understanding or direction. Questions and comments of this sort imply that God does not use unbelievers, Christians whose beliefs differ from ours, or those not in good standing with our church, to teach us anything valid. Questions of this sort also show that people don't want to evaluate information on its own merit. They demand that the source's background be similar to theirs before they will accept it.

If you think about this and find that you want to know the background of the source before you can agree or disagree with the contents, take heed! Intentionally avoid learning the background of information until you have fully formed your own judgments. (Make this a practice to sharpen your ability to critically think for yourself.) Weigh and evaluate new thoughts and data on the basis of what is said, not on the background of the speaker or writer. God used a donkey to speak to Baalum (Num. 22:30). If an ass should speak to you, you should listen and evaluate, and overlook the source.

CHECKLIST
VICIOUS INFORMATION CONTROL—Chapter 8

Check those that apply to you and/or your group:

❏ I am inclined to see criticism of my group or its leaders as sinful

❏ I am inclined to see criticism, slander, or ridicule of my group as Biblical persecution

❏ "Denying Christ" means not giving up all personal wishes, desires, and goals

❏ I find myself suppressing my feelings because they may be sinful or wrong when they are not

❏ Random reading of the Bible can answer every question

❏ God will lead me directly to a Bible verse each time I have a question for Him

❏ My family members feel they can't say anything against my group

❏ I become extremely irritated when someone criticizes my group or leaders

❏ Those who disagree with, or openly challenge, leaders are divisive

❏ If the entire church supports an action or decision of the leaders, I should, too, so I won't be out of unity

❏ "Perfect love casts out fear"—therefore, I should never have fear if I love God

❏ I need to know the background of the person before I give much weight to their information or views

NOTE: If you have checked *any* boxes, it may indicate a misuse of Scripture and/or may represent the presence of abuse and excessive control.

Chapter 9

TRUTH OR CONSEQUENCES

In order to gain maximum influence over people,
coercive disciplers and cult leaders often induce their
victims to accept certain false beliefs that will bring them to
follow a desired path. If the belief isn't followed,
the victims' own minds will generate guilt,
yet they will not feel that they are being manipulated.

Once disciplers have narrowed the disciple's world, there are consequences, some of which appear to be positive. Suddenly the disciple has a strong central purpose in life. Old questions that used to trouble disciples disappear. A new and reassuring certainty about the "truth" emerges.

At the same time, negative consequences abound. Most of these groups point to their rapid growth, dynamic worship, teachings, and strong group commitment as signs that the fruit of their ministry is good. But, to Jesus, the sign of good fruit (Matt. 7:15-18) is not the number of apples on the tree, but whether those apples are healthy or rotten. Abusive discipleship produces some bitter fruit for the committed disciples: unjustified guilt, fear, shame, a loss of normal human emotions, and a highly judgmental mind-set.

Fruit. That's another word frequently misused by many discipleships. If you look up all the places where fruit is mentioned in the Bible, you will find that fruit isn't the number of new disciples you've gathered. Rather, it is the virtue that is growing in your life. When the Bible speaks of fruit, think of the quality of virtuous life. An excellent reference is Galatians 5:22, 23:

> *But the fruit of the Spirit is love, joy, peace, patience, kindness,*
> *goodness, faithfulness, gentleness and self-control.*

"Bad fruit" usually refers to immoral behavior. Many discipleships say that when they are growing in numbers, this "shows their fruit." Look it up in your concordance and you will discover that growth in membership has no connection with fruit.

A GUILT-EDGED SWORD

We all have consciences—that voice of our intellect that warns us when we consider doing something sinful or bad. When we fail to heed that voice of our reason, we feel the emotional response of guilt. We will feel this emotion whether that guilt is genuinely deserved or not, as long as we have accepted and incorporated teachings about moral matters into our intellect. Each of us decides how strongly the voice of conscience speaks—for some of us it is a whisper, for others a shouted warning. "Practice makes perfect," they say, and the same is true of conscience. If you never use your conscience, it will slowly fade away. If, however, you think long and hard and study moral matters, your conscience will be alert and strong.

The key for gaining maximum control over someone's conscience is to influence the person to study and accept certain beliefs. Then, if the person fails to follow those beliefs, a powerful feeling of guilt will be the result.

Guilt is such a powerful motivator—especially in the context of a Christian fellowship—that once the seeds of guilt are planted, leaders need not physically prevent people from certain action because their guilt will do this for them (in other words, turning their guilt against themselves). Many of the teachings and recommended books of controlling groups nurture this result by implanting false beliefs.

To restore your conscience, which has been formed incorrectly by distorted teachings, you need an environment that relieves you of both subtle and overt pressures while you seek the real Biblical imperatives.

INSTILLING FEAR

"Craig's" group had a strange teaching. If they were angry, they weren't supposed to let the sun go down without resolving the issue. They taught this based upon Ephesians 4:26-27: "Do not let the sun go down while you are still angry and do not give the devil a foothold."

Sounds like a good idea, doesn't it? But what actually took place was the discipler and the disciple would sometimes spend half the night in discussion. The disciple soon learned he would be worn down during the night and, when exhausted, would be talked into seeing it the leader's way. Then they all lived happily again. (Apparently no one noticed that the sun had gone down without waiting for them to settle their differences!) The group's members dreaded these all-nighters so much that they would automatically begin to stifle their legitimate anger or criticism. The Bible verse was being used as a weapon to defeat disciples by making them stay awake until all was resolved.

INSTILLED FEAR OF THE OUTSIDE WORLD

"Naomi" left her group and went to a flea market with me. A lady tried to sell us a pair of salt and pepper shakers for $10. We saw them on the next table for $2 which triggered an unusual reaction in Naomi. Suddenly she started spouting doctrine from her leader—he was right, all the world was greedy!

Naomi was gripped with such a terrible fear of the sin in the world that she wanted to get away from all those sinful flea-marketers. Later, after we sat and talked about the incident, she calmed down and realized she had been "switched" back into that "black and white" mind-set.

I told Naomi, "You don't have to feel fear and run away just because your leader is right about the fact that there is greed in the world. You can face sin in the world without fear. You are not alone—Jesus promised He would be with you and He is."

MOLDING BEHAVIOR BY SHAME

When we are excessively sensitive to shame, we may curtail our normal activities.

"Sharon" said that, when she was in discipleship, she would play popular music whenever she went home. However, when she lived with all these committed Christians, she felt that she should be ashamed of her enjoyment of secular music. This was not bad music, it just wasn't religious music. It was neither "black" nor "white." This was not a moral issue at all. It was "gray" music, if you will.

Controlling disciplers mold disciples' behavior in order that anything they say or do might be judged as being sinful. As you can see, this ingrained concern (about being held accountable in every excruciating detail of their lives) forces them to think through each decision to make sure they will not be shamed by their discipler. This results in endless pain, guilt, fear, and sometimes a paralysis of the disciples' normal good sense.

In some other cases:

➤ "Nigel" said she wouldn't let a young man and her daughter ride in a car together because she feared other disciples might be scandalized. While in this group, she began to judge all young couples alone in cars as sinful.

➤ "Doug" mentioned that he wouldn't even play basketball with the guys on campus. He was afraid that, if he sprained his ankle, he would be a bad witness for believers. His group taught that if you ask God to heal you, God would—*if* you have the faith. Doug worried that his faith would not be strong enough for God to heal him. So, to avoid becoming a bad witness, he refused to play his favorite sport.

➤ "Rachel" worked for the leader's commercial business. Two of her female employees quit and Rachel was saddled with all three jobs. She became inefficient because she was continually swapping tasks and deluged with work. Her discipler accused her of laziness for not getting all of her work done! Rachel wanted to sink through the floor as she shared this experience with us.

These are just a small sampling of the stories I've heard through the years—stories filled with the fear of being held accountable and tales of unnecessary shame. Usually disciples don't realize they are even doing these things until they leave their controlling group. Rather, they see their leaders as caring people who are holding them accountable because "that's how discipleship was in Jesus' day."

DON'T RUN FROM THE PEOPLE WHO CHALLENGE YOU

One of the hardest lessons I learned in my life occurred when I was 24 years old. My dad found a book I was reading and wanted to talk to me about it. I huffily refused any discussion. I realized this wasn't like me. I had always enjoyed a good debate. Now I found that I couldn't talk about some subjects. If you find that you, too, are unwilling to have your ideas challenged, then you likely are in trouble. You've closed your mind so it won't be confused by the facts.

Some disciples, when challenged, will sit and listen for a time and then say, "See, I've listened to the information; I *am* able to question my group."

Hold on a minute. You need to respond. You need to engage in conversation. If your friends are still concerned about you and want more questions answered, you are deceiving yourself by thinking you've "got it all because you listened." I've dealt with many who would give a day or so and then say, "That's it!" They may have been in a controlling discipleship for years, but would listen to us only as long as we didn't make them doubt. When they started to feel the first stirrings of doubt, some would get up and walk out.

Can you get to the place where you really question your leaders' practices and teachings, and can you talk with others about this? If you can't, you may tolerate and accept false teachings for the rest of your life. One of my clients said, "But if I have the truth and I know it, I shouldn't read anything that contradicts it!" THAT IS WRONG. In fact, it couldn't be more wrong. I once believed those same things in my closed mental environment. Anyone who has been subjected to such intensive redirection of thinking normally follows this same line of reasoning. It is impossible to pursue the truth honestly and objectively unless you compare your ideas in depth to those who have different viewpoints.

PROPER CHANNELS

"Tammy" asked a discipler, "Mark," for advice about a problem. He immediately replied, "Are you accountable to anyone?" To someone outside the discipleship movement, the question would seem irrelevant—what does it matter if Tammy is accountable to someone? The discipler, however, felt he couldn't answer her question by listening to the problem and analyzing it as you or I would have. No. He had to *go through the proper channels.* Under the rules of this narrowed discipleship mentality, if Tammy were in complete submission to someone, Mark might be overstepping his authority if he gave advice. His obligation would be to send her to the person to whom she was submitted. Normal human interaction is short-circuited by this discipleship mentality.

The Bible admonishes us to seek many counselors (Prov. 11:14, 15:22; Acts 15), and some controlling discipleship groups do have a number of mentors; but these, nonetheless, typically judge you as "not spiritual" if you fail to accept the opinions of your *personal* discipler as your own.

WHAT'S THE PROBLEM?

In one group, disciplers were told, "Rarely is the problem that the disciple presents the actual problem." When I heard this, I thought, "Isn't it great that the first thing these disciplers are programmed to do is to distrust their disciples and assume the presented problem is not the real problem?"

This is "robot thinking." This is not looking creatively for the truth. This automatically catalogues a situation before any effort is made to understand it. These so-called "teachers" are being taught to automatically assume the disciple is probably confused about the issue or lying. You can see their simplistic world view in these statements. You will hear a lot of pat answers to life's problems in these groups.

Genuine feelings and inquiry tend to be suppressed by this labeling process. Not all feelings are lost, just those that do not match those of the group. A person in this situation does not truly evaluate most situations without the bias of the system's faulty viewpoints. The disciple is left to live in only partial reality.

Discipler "Jane" told me I was totally irrational. Jane had been programmed to believe that the problem presented is rarely the issue. Since I said certain techniques of this discipleship appeared to be abusive, Jane instantly assumed that wasn't the real issue. This allowed her to freely select another issue. She promptly decided the issue was me, that I was irrational. Taking no risk of facing what might be a difficult reality, Jane retreated into the partially real world of group-think. She was insensitive to my feelings and opinions.

More likely than not, Jane believed that anyone questioning the discipleship method had to be "totally irrational and highly immoral." She had no need to evaluate my concerns rationally because, in her mind, she already "knew the truth." These beliefs prevented Jane from evaluating the true situation. The result was a complete lack of compassion for others' concerns.

"Doug" is a former disciple who described his own loss of normal response:

For me there was one moment when my compassion was stripped from me. I always had a very compassionate heart. One day my discipler told me, "Doug, you can't allow Satan to take advantage of your compassionate heart." I saw his logic, in that you don't want to be used. You can't always be running around doing things for others. You need to be spending time with the Lord.

My discipler admitted that he used to have the same heart. It seemed kind of odd to me at the time, but I went along with this.

I excitedly told my leader that I went to the home of a lady who was dying of cancer. Twenty years earlier, she had played the guitar, so we talked and prayed together; then I played her a song on my guitar. She began to cry and I felt the spirit of God descend on all of us. It made me happy; I felt that I was really being used by the Lord. When I told my discipler about the experience, he said, "You need to understand that the Lord has brought her to that point. You have to realize that if she was walking with the Lord then she would be healed! Are you sure the Lord told you to go there?"

From that point on, my compassion dwindled little by little. We were taught "if you really love them, you need to show them their sin."

His discipler suggested to Doug that singing for that woman was for his own gratification and pride since it made him feel good. Doug would come to believe this.

ACCOUNTABILITY TO THE EXTREME

Some abusive discipleships teach: "loving is confronting." Perhaps you already see what is wrong with this type of accountability. It is like the parent who tries to make a child perfect by always pointing out the poor kid's mistakes and confronting the child with everything he or she does wrong. You can see that the parent becomes domineering and nagging. This child will probably become insecure, extremely dependent, or may, on the other hand, turn to rebelliousness.

In a disciple/discipler relationship, this kind of treatment leads to many of the same problems. Dependency can stop a previously capable disciple from making the most basic decisions. When accountability, thought to be so wonderful, is taken to these extremes, it actually degenerates normal Christians. Good spiritual directors and disciplers often overlook minor faults, but in abusive discipleships, the disciplers are biased toward aggressive confrontation. Novice disciplers are rarely taught sensitivity. They are taught to confront.

Discipler Jane taught that disciples should judge others as "not really wanting help" if they don't do what they're told. One quote she used was, "They don't really want help if they are not willing to do whatever you say."

A young woman came for help. But, because she didn't want to change immediately and take Jane's advice as an order, she was judged as not ready for help. Later I sat in this discipler's office and asked her to help me understand Scripturally why she was saying that disciples had to instantly accept all of her advice. She dismissed me as "not going to change." Therefore, she had no need to answer my questions. She wanted to enforce blind obedience even on me.

Too often, abusive disciplers cannot see that their mercy has been stripped from them by the demands of the group's way of thinking. They have lost their compassion to feel for those who do not hold their viewpoints, but they think they are helping by leaving them without comfort of any kind.

WHERE'S THE MERCY?

Mercy and compassion in controlling groups are limited to those who conform and are not for the unrepentant sinner. As we show mercy, God will show mercy to us (Matt. 5:7); but it is hard to show mercy when it is constantly reinforced that "confronting means loving."

Think about the number of talks given in your group on the topic of "being merciful." How many prayers have you heard about showing mercy to the sinner? A controlling group will seldom teach much about mercy. If you do find this topic, it is often lip service. In case you are in a controlling group and rarely hear prayers about mercy, here is one I especially love [edited]:

O Lord,
May The Greatest of all Divine attributes,
That of your unfathomable Mercy,
Pass through my heart and soul.

Help me, oh Lord, that my eyes may be merciful,
So that I never judge or suspect from appearances
But look for what is beautiful in my neighbors'
Souls and come to their rescue.

Help me, oh Lord, that my ears may be merciful
So that I may give heed to my neighbors' needs
And not be indifferent to their pains and moaning.

Help me, oh Lord, that my tongue may be merciful...
[and] have a Word of comfort and forgiveness for all.

Help me, oh Lord, that my hands may be merciful
and filled with good deeds,
So that I may only do good to my neighbors...

Help me, oh Lord, that my Heart may be merciful so that I myself
May feel all the sufferings of my neighbor
I will refuse my heart to no one...
May your mercy rest upon me Oh My Jesus
Transform me into yourself for you can do all things.[51]

Notice the part that says, "so that I myself may feel all the sufferings of my neighbor; I will refuse my heart to no one." In abusive discipleship, you generally refuse your heart to everyone who doesn't conform to your standards. That means you don't feel their sufferings to a great degree either. Oh, you may give lip service to having mercy for your parents and outsiders, but this is severely limited. However, if you don't refuse your heart according to the demands of your leader, then what happens? You end up being exploited and abused by the discipler!

If you think this is an odd prayer, I will say that it is typical of prayer throughout the ages. More radical and daring are Mother Teresa's suggestions: "Speak as little as possible of self... mind your own business... accept contradiction... cheerfully... pass over others' mistakes... be kind and gentle (under provocation)... never stand on your dignity."[52]

Spend some time reading old prayers and you will find many of them ask God to protect us from our desire to be extolled, praised, and looked up to, which flies in the face of the practice of many of today's disciplers. Typical prayer through the centuries has asked God for help in minding our own business, not to go around poking our noses into Christians' faces, insisting they be accountable to us for every action that we deem sinful.

Your search of prayer books and hymnals will show you that Christians traditionally accept blame, injury, and insult even when they realize that they are innocent. And Christians are admonished to be gentle even when provoked. But not our abusive disciplers—they always want to get in the last word by confronting those who disagree with them. Abusive disciplers eventually get rid of the tough cases of those who don't obey enough by simply asking them not to come back, thus keeping around them only the more docile and loyal disciples.

SHUNNING

Discipleship groups that are either abusive or controlling practice "shunning," but not necessarily in the way this term is understood by most Christians. Although some discipleships directly dictate whom their disciples may converse with, there are more subtle methods of enforcing a boycott. Disciples are encouraged to feel separated from any who leave their church or discipleship group. This feeling arises from the group's view: "If people were really committed, they too would be discipled as we are."

This is an attitude which implies that those in the group are superior to everyone else.

This kind of environment provides reasons for you to start distancing yourself from former members, but you probably won't see it that way. You may simply have an overpowering feeling that you have nothing in common with them anymore. You may think, "Oh yes, they may still believe in Jesus, but they're not as committed as I am." Your desire to be around these "uncommitted" Christians has died.

Be cautious about accepting limited definitions of essential words like "committed," for there are broader forms of true Christian commitment.

Are there people who have left your discipleship for whom your feeling of closeness has died? They also feel that death. This is why many will tell you they feel shunned. Suddenly their closest friends don't have time for them anymore.

WHERE IS THE COMPASSION?

How often does your group give food or clothing, support orphanages, hospitals, or send medical supplies to the needy who are not in your group and probably never will be? Is such giving in proportion to the budget for your organization? Remember, the Good Samaritan got nothing in return, nor did he expect anything! In controlling churches, one normally sees a lack of charity toward strangers unless recruitment is intended. Yes, they will work to build churches all around the world—but true charity helps all with no strings attached.

Many of these groups find themselves spending most of their time organizing Bible studies for new people and working to recruit more members (who, of course, will in turn get more members) which will produce more money (money which, in many cases, goes to support the luxurious lifestyle of the top leader). Doesn't this begin to sound more like a business and perhaps a crooked one at that?

Twisted discipleships do not love you for yourself. They love you for what they plan to make of you and for what you can do for them.

RECRUITING EQUALS EVANGELIZING—OR DOES IT?

Many controlling groups spend a lot of time recruiting—they call it "evangelization."

Remember, Jesus stresses giving to meet physical needs and spiritual needs. He did good things for anyone, not just those He thought were ready to come to him on his terms. "But," you may say, "our church goes around the world building churches!" Granted, that's a lot of hard work and costs a lot of money, but many cults do the same thing. What about the basic tenet of giving food, clothing, medicine, or shelter to the poor—even those poor who have neither the potential nor the inclination to become members of your group? Does your group stress this as much as it seeks membership numbers, more churches, and evangelization to get more members?

BAD FRUIT—BUT I COULDN'T SEE IT!

A good tree cannot bear bad fruit... (Matt. 7:18).

How much bad fruit are you finding in your group?

If I don't sound very compassionate about such leaders, it is because I understand how group-thinking destroys human compassion. Under the influence of the group I belonged to, I gradually lost interest in my job, in the world, in my hobbies, in friends who were not part of my new group, and in all of the things of my former life. Looking back, I see why I couldn't stay around my family for any extended period of time.

There was a time when my mother invited me home for dinner. I came. I ate. I was not interested in discussing the weather or my day. I thought all this chatter was wasting time because we weren't talking about God's eternal truth. I recall that, as soon as I downed dinner, I had to run. I no longer had anything in common with these strangers.

I looked at my parents through eyes clouded by "group categories." I did not see the people who loved me, who raised me, who instilled faith and values in me. Instead, in bondage to my group's teaching, I only saw people who were "not committed."

My feelings were skewed by my new mind-set. It appeared to me that I was totally separated from my mother—she who had been especially close to me since the loss of my sister and brother several years before. I could no longer remember that we were ever close.

One afternoon, I came home and found my mother crying. She said, "Mary Alice, you're dead, you're already dead." Then she shook me. I just stared at her. I remember labeling her as someone who needed the "truth" I was certain I had. I felt some compassion for her and made a mental note to pray for her. I was at peace. In retrospect, I know this was neither a normal nor appropriate response to the agony of the mother whom I loved.

Looking back I cannot believe how I reacted. I didn't want to spend time with her. Normally, when someone had tears in their eyes, I got tears in mine. In fact, when I was at the airport and saw strangers crying and saying good-bye, I usually ended up crying just from watching. Yet now, here was my own mother crying and there were no tears in my eye. I thought in my heart that I was feeling sorrow and love for her, but it was obviously shallow because I showed no outward signs of love. I was on a different "spiritual level."

That level is where many committed members of abusive discipleship groups dwell. It is the level where God-given emotions are choked off in favor of group labels. This process (the exchanging of one's true feelings for a puppet-like conformity as desired by the discipler) can cause great mental anguish. The pain truly feels like dying, and the disciple may think that this is what the Bible means by putting to death our sinful selves. It is *not*. Rather, it is the death of normal, God-given emotion.

The highly judgmental mind-set produced by these groups is more "bad fruit." These disciples make hasty judgments regarding who is a Christian and who is not. Some Christians have to hear such statements as "God told me to do something" or "I give God the glory for this" before they will believe you have evidence of a Christian walk. Some Christians have to hear the name "Jesus" in every short conversation to come to the conclusion that a person is committed to Jesus Christ. Others think that if you are on the street evangelizing, that is proof. Some Christians think if you didn't "ask Jesus into your heart" with these exact words, then you are not saved. Still others think that, if you don't raise your hands while in prayer, you aren't filled with the Holy Spirit. Many believe you have to be discipled. The list is endless.

Paraphrasing Jesus in Matthew 7:22, many will say, "Lord, Lord... they 'talked the talk' but they did not 'walk the walk.'" Jesus was pointing out that the ones doing works of mercy were going to Heaven, while the others who were saying the right words were going to Hell.

Christians today need to step back and remember what James 2:18 says: "I will show you my faith by what I do." I'd rather see a man give God the glory by his actions than brag all day long about giving God the glory. I see many Christians who reek with self-righteousness. Just because a person always says he is giving God the glory, it isn't proof that in the depth of his heart he really is. Much pride may be involved in these claims.

Sadly, many people are turned off by Christianity today because of the superior attitudes of these Christians whom they rightly find to be judgmental.

THE "WHY" OF INAPPROPRIATE BEHAVIOR—MIND CONTROL

The result of suppressing natural emotional and psychological responses, by imposing upon them so-called Biblical standards of judgment, is inappropriate behavior. Those under the influence of such warped standards typically overreact to disclosures about their group. They may make wildly irrational statements and begin mishandling personal and family relationships. In circumstances where unaffected persons perform well, these individuals frequently make foolish mistakes. In general, their ability to respond with compassion is sharply decreased.

Crises occur with alarming frequency in controlling groups. Does your church always seem to be suffering from some severe problem that requires immediate attention?

I tried to convince an elder that the recurring problems in his church were mostly caused by destructive discipleship doctrines. He saw the problems as isolated events, not at all related to members being under the control of the discipleship group.

If your group suffers from constant crises, look for some of the twisted ideas I've described. If you find them, have the humility and courage to admit your errors and remove them by educating others. Although it may take many months to achieve the goal, your group's problems will decrease, and you will be pleasantly surprised at the difference it will make in your whole church.

If your group refuses to change, your only alternative, for your own sake, is to leave.

CHECKLIST
TRUTH OR CONSEQUENCES—Chapter 9

Check those that apply to you and/or your group:

❑ Equates "fruit" (in the Biblical sense) to large numbers of recruits

❑ I choose not to associate with people who cause me to question my beliefs

❑ I believe myself to be "open" but resist discussing the group's problems or questioning their actions

❑ Members willingly stuff their genuine feelings when they don't match the "correct ones" (i.e., the feelings determined appropriate by the leaders)

❑ Shows little compassion for those outside your group

❑ To a great degree, I am disconnected from Christians outside my group and from those who have left it

❑ I now feel that I was never truly close to my family

❑ I can quickly tell if someone is Christian or not

❑ It's not right if someone receives praise and doesn't claim that only the Lord should receive the glory for their deed

NOTE: If you have checked *any* boxes, it may indicate a misuse of Scripture and/or may represent the presence of abuse and excessive control.

Chapter 10

CONFESSION CONFUSION

*The Bible tells us to confess "one to another"
but it doesn't say confess "one to a group."*

Confession is good for the soul—an old expression that
certainly has Biblical merit. Confession is also something that's
emphasized by most discipleship groups, although they may refer
to it as "sharing." What discipleship groups call "sharing" actually
amounts to confessing your faults and problems, not just your sins.

Most disciplers will suggest that the reason for confession in
their groups is to free disciples from sins and shortcomings that
have been burdening them or keeping them from growth into
Christian maturity.

For many who enter into discipling relationships, such
confession is a new concept and, initially, it can be an emotionally
freeing experience. Many people who have been carrying burdens
around with them are glad to have an opportunity to unload them.
Valid and healing confessions do take place in controlling groups.

However, in coercive or controlling discipleship groups, this practice is often based upon out-of-context application of James 5:14-16:

*Is any one of you sick? He should call the elders of the church to
pray over him and anoint him with oil in the name of the Lord.
And the prayer offered in faith will make the sick person well; the
Lord will raise him up. If he has sinned, he will be forgiven.
Therefore confess your sins to each other and pray for each other
so that you may be healed. The prayer of a righteous man is
powerful and effective.*

Properly understood in context, this Scripture refers to disease
or sickness and a prayer for healing. We are told that if the sickness
is the result of sin, healing may require confessing that sin to "the

elders." This is not a mandate to get together with other ordinary Christians and spell out all of one's shameful deeds.

In many of these groups, unfortunately, confession is driven beyond what is Biblically right and healthy, and it becomes a tool used to manipulate and control group members.

SHARING IN GROUPS IS OPEN CONFESSION

I remember sitting with a group of men and women who were sharing with one another. The man next to me shared that he had raped three women. I was stunned. I found myself inching away from him. This made such an impression on me that, years later, I still remember his confession.

In the same group, a woman shared that she had run a whore-house. Every time I saw her after that, I thought of her sin. I could not help myself. It wasn't until years later that I realized that group confession isn't in the Bible. Based upon these experiences plus interviews I have conducted with many others, I believe I now know why.

A church member told me of a public confession at his church in which a man confessed adultery. As this man attends this church of several thousand members, I wondered how many cannot help recalling his adultery. How many of his fellow-Christians have spread the word of his sin to others like me? This man was sorry; he was forgiven; he didn't need to stand up and confess to the whole church. But abusive leaders encourage this.

I was also embarrassed for the teenage girl who was humiliated when her spiritual director persuaded her to stand before a large group of her peers and publicly admit she had had an abortion. We don't need to know everyone who has had an abortion, but some leaders say that churches must ask such things if they really care for their members. This is simply not a Biblical doctrine. Instead, Scripture requires that we seek the forgiveness of those we have injured and do as much as possible to make things right with them (Matt. 5:23,24).

While non-abusive disciplers and spiritual advisors believe in private confession, most abusive groups persuade Christians to stand before others and confess their sins. There simply is no example in the Bible of people being told to confess to an entire congregation or even a small group. Yet these abusive disciplers profess to be following the Bible more closely than those who accept private confession.

Non-abusive leaders do not pry into their disciples' private lives even when they are confessing in a private setting. Abusive disciplers, to the contrary, expect their disciples to be totally open about all areas of their lives. Worse, they encourage them to expose their failings to their peers.

The group may tell disciples to be "totally open" or "transparent"—encouraging them to hold back nothing of past feelings, problems, and thoughts. In many of these groups, even if a disciple exposes his sins, he may feel as if he is hiding something else, because the group's leaders usually want total exposure of every aspect of the disciple's life, not just sins.

For example, disciples under the influence of an abusive leader will likely feel a compulsion to share that they are buying a new car or looking for another job—actions which have no moral aspect and are not subject to a spiritual advisor's directives. If they fail to discuss such innocent activities, they probably will feel they are not being "totally open." Obviously, the decision to purchase a car is not a matter of spiritual direction and a non-abusive discipler would find it strange if you expected to discuss this.

Many Christians are taught to re-confess (or at least share) past sins. If a sin has been repented, it is forgiven by God, so why do leaders want you to keep sharing something God has allowed you to put behind you? The reason, most likely, is to make disciples more vulnerable to group influence and bind them to their group.

Abusive Groups	Non-Abusive Groups
Encourage open confession	Practice private confession
Want members to expose every area of life, whether sinful or not-sinful	Expect members to confess only sins, not matters which have no moral content

If you feel that you are "not being totally open" because you don't discuss everything with your discipler or director, you are being deceived, manipulated, and possibly abused.

GROUP ACCOUNTABILITY RESULTS IN OPEN CONFESSION

Leaders slyly coerce confession by sugarcoating certain words. Instead of saying, "Now we are all going to confess our sins to one another," leaders may say, "We need more accountability in our lives." This allows them to coax you into a small group meeting where they stress that you need to be transparent to each other and you need to be more open. This is to get you to confess in a group and to cause you to accept the responsibility for holding others "accountable."

The end result is to turn the members of the group into full-time watchdogs for sins.

Abusive leaders phrase it much more politely. They say, "These brothers and sisters will help you be better Christians by holding each other accountable." I receive calls from all around the world describing how this type of "accountability" results in Christian disasters. Accusations of artificial sins, motives judged wrongly, and terrible emotional pain result from this type of accountability. Former members of these groups say they felt extraordinary undue influence on their lives. Some have described it as bondage.

It seems, at the onset, to be a good thing. But, over a period of time, the truth becomes inescapable. The leaders slough off the problems saying there are always a few disgruntled members or immature disciplers in every group.

DISCIPLERS MUST ALSO REACH A HIGH DEGREE OF SPIRITUAL MATURITY

Matthew 7:3-5 tells us to take the plank out of our own eye before trying to help a brother remove a speck from his. This can be paraphrased, "Don't try to hold someone else accountable for their sins until you have successfully removed your own sins." It takes years to reach the spiritual maturity necessary to properly guide others.

Quite honestly, it is dangerous for those of us with average spiritual growth to be put in a position over others on their spiritual walk. We may inaccurately judge the actions of others. Thus, when we think we are holding others accountable, we may be only misunderstanding, or even being inappropriately judgmental.

If a leader asks you to join a group and encourages you to become "transparent" or to "open up," don't fall for it.

This type of "accountability" strays far from Scripture. Mature Christians realize that sometimes it is wise to hold a disciple accountable and sometimes wiser to simply pray for the person and be silent. It takes a deeply virtuous and unusually discerning person to be able to know when to be stern and when to be merciful and patient.

LOVING PARENTS DON'T CONFRONT THE CHILD FOR EVERY WRONGDOING

Even a parent has to find the proper balance between confrontation and loving guidance. Pointing out every error may cause a child to become insecure, lack self-esteem, or begin to hate the parent. At the same time, never disciplining a child is also wrong.

If your pastor or discipler constantly confronts you because he wants you to be the best Christian in town, it may make you a nervous wreck. If all of the people in your group are asked to watch for your personal sins or weaknesses and to keep you accountable, you may be driven to a nervous breakdown. Total accountability to a group is like having the world's worst parent!

Jesus stressed mercy and forgiveness by telling us to overlook the mistakes of others, to forgive insults, injuries, or being slighted by our brothers or our enemies. (See also Prov. 19:11; Col. 3:12 and 14.)

DOUBLE STANDARDS: CONFRONT CHRISTIANS—LOVE UNBELIEVERS

I've observed a number of controlling churches which teach their members to show mercy to non-believers, but, after they are converted, shame them for their past sins and confront them for almost every mistake and weakness.

Laurie Jacobson, a former member of Youth With a Mission (YWAM), wrote an article about her experience with confession in the YWAM Discipleship Training School (DTS) in Hawaii.[53] Her experience illustrates how confession can be abused as a means to control members:

> *After the lecture delineating the steps of Intercession, and a five-minute break, we regrouped in the Lecture Room for our first try at it... I found a seat near the front and sat clutching the blue card they had handed out that listed the magic formula for unlocking the secrets of God. I bowed my head, closed my eyes, and amidst the chorus of "Yes Lord" and "Thank you Jesus," heard Jack, our director, begin to pray. After a few moments, he prayed, "And Lord, we ask that the Holy Spirit would reveal any unconfessed sin." He continued in a soft voice, and I believe that he mentioned various sins, but I can't recall exactly what he said. I had focused my thoughts on God, but in the background I heard Jack encouraging, "Speak it out, speak it out." The next*

thing I knew, someone was sobbing loudly, "Oh Lord, please forgive me!" Again Jack instructed, "Speak it out." Eventually the sobbing girl confessed that she had been sleeping with her boyfriend before she left for Hawaii. She prayed for a few minutes and then several others offered prayer on her behalf. Her confession was soon followed by those of others who felt convicted about sins committed prior to their arrival at DTS. This went on for several hours—people crying out and pleading for forgiveness, and Jack advising them to "Speak it out." We finally broke for lunch at one o'clock.[54]

Laurie describes how confession was initiated and controlled by the leadership. Although, in the midst of the emotional experience of this confession session, it may appear that the Holy Spirit is acting, Laurie discovered otherwise:

Given the diversity of the students attending, it seemed plausible that the confessions had been spontaneous and necessary. Later, I learned that YWAM has labeled these sessions "Openness and Brokenness," and that they always begin a discipleship training session. This made me suspect that the staff had more to do with engineering the confession time than has the Holy Spirit.

I might not have wondered so much if we had stopped after the first few days. By the third day, we did move on to the second step of Intercession, but that did not signal the end of Openness and Brokenness. Throughout the first three months, many hours were specifically set aside for confession and self-exposure, including an eight-hour ordeal focusing on masturbation, lust, and homosexuality. On that particular occasion, we were instructed to place our chairs in a large circle in the lecture room and then had to sit quietly and wait for someone to feel "led by God" and confess.[55]

FORMING INTENSE FRIENDSHIPS WITH THOSE WE COUNSEL—A MAJOR BLUNDER

The discipler blurs his position by presuming ministerial authority and acting as a spiritual director and hearing confessions, all while remaining a layperson and an intimate friend of the disciple.

Many disciplers have admitted that, to some degree, they did confess to the disciples they directed. Whenever two people open themselves so completely to each other, an intense feeling of intimacy inevitably develops. This creates a tight bond and makes the disciple more willing to follow the suggestions of his discipler, causes dependency, and pressures the disciple to stay in the relationship—even when he or she doesn't feel that it's right. This abnormal dependency is fertile ground in which to grow a perverse influence.

Professional therapists and counselors understand that intimate friendships must not be formed with clients. But, in the discipleship relationship, this is completely ignored. Instead of the caution with which professional counselors approach patients, the novice discipler usually seeks to become quite close with those he guides.

OPENNESS AND BROKENNESS

Remember that YWAM labeled confessions as "openness and brokenness." That gives one the feeling that if you aren't confessing, this group will accuse you of "failing to be open or broken to God." Most members look at people as "lacking spiritual virtue" if they are not led to confess in a group.

Some disciples tell me, "I don't have to confess." If you feel that way, ask yourself if there are any negative repercussions if you don't confess or if you feel guilty for not opening up. If you don't freely feel like opening up, you have to consider that perhaps the Holy Spirit is giving you this feeling in order to guard you.

Here is another true account of coercive confession:

We were just sitting there when three people approached Judy at different times and said to her that the Lord told them that Judy had something to confess and that she had better not deny the work that the Holy Spirit is trying to do in her life. Judy kept refusing. Helen put her hands on Judy's shoulders and began massaging her and said that there was something that Judy had to release. Then she came to me and began the same therapy and also spoke in tongues over me. I freaked! Judy was crying so hard I couldn't take it. I ran outside.

"I felt like people silently pressured me to confess sins," one student remembered. A lecturer insisted, "You are secretive if you are up to something bad." Therefore, if a student went too long without confession, people assumed she was trying to hide something; that she was not being honest.[56]

In abusive discipleships, leaders presume they have the right of ownership to the disciple's thoughts. Making the confession is also important in their opinion because it acknowledges there are no secrets, no thoughts hidden from the leaders.

Several groups I've studied said that being secretive was a sin. You will not find this taught in the Bible. If one hides from their spiritual director a sinful habit or intentionally conceals a serious moral wrong like murder or adultery, this type of secretiveness is wrong. Discretion, however, is often a wise position to take. Reserve can prevent hurt feelings and may even be an act of charity. To teach that all secretiveness is wrong is just another manipulative trick.

"Sharon," a former client, said that when she really didn't have any problems to discuss, her discipler would say, "Come on Sharon, everyone has problems." Following this pressure tactic, Sharon would always come up with something to confess. Disciples who do not frequently share all ideas or emotions are often told that they have a bad attitude, are not humble, not broken, are full of pride, or something else derogatory. With all these ideas planted in the disciple's mind, there is tremendous pressure to confess.

Another misuse of confession involves artificial sins. Laurie Jacobson gives an example of this in her account of YWAM:

> The following two mornings were so filled with hours of crying and confessing that I was emotionally drained. We all commented that we felt as if we had spent the morning engaged in grueling physical exercise. I remember feeling confused and frightened during these sessions, and guilty for not confessing everything. I shared my feelings with one of the staff members and was advised to confess my fear as sin. I did.[57]

If I told you I was afraid of crossing a busy intersection because of heavy traffic, would you call me a sinner? Would a responsible leader tell me that I should confess my fear of traffic? I seriously doubt it. There are often good and healthy reasons for fear. But notice how the leader simply equated fear with sin. What a simple equation it is, especially when the motive is to get the confession.

When we do things because we have been convinced by twisted Scriptures that God has asked us to do it—even though it might painfully go against us—this is oppression.

NON-BIBLICAL DELIVERANCE

"Deliverance ministries" are frequently non-Biblical and full of controlling techniques. These groups emphasize what is, in reality, a type of confession which is emotionally harmful. I have intentionally resisted talking about the groups that place great emphasis on the devil and are highly focused on casting out demons, for fear that some of my readers might say, "But my group never did that weird stuff" and ignore all the other manipulations that may apply to their groups. Many of you may find this next section controversial, but please read the entire section before you put this chapter aside.

Adrian J. Reimers, Ph.D., wrote an article describing the manipulation during prayer which he experienced as a member of "People of Praise." Reimers said:

> *I never knew I was a sexual pervert; not until the leader of our covenant community and his wife prayed with me for deliverance. During this prayer in our living room, the leader discerned that for most of my life I had been unknowingly oppressed by an evil spirit, a spirit of sexual perversion. I had never acted perversely. But our leader identified this demon, which was crippling my life in the Holy Spirit and interfering with my ability to live and to love. When he cast the demon out, then its hitherto undetected, baneful influence was gone from my life...* [58]

Reimers just passively participated in allowing someone to pray for him, but he got a lot more than he expected. I call this a "coercively demeaning prayer." The victim is subtly pressured to accept a suggestion. The victim can't easily respond that it isn't true, because it is understood that these leaders are "spiritually advanced" and able to "discern" whatever so-called demon is possessing the victim.

The implication was that this leader was able to spiritually see others more clearly than they could see themselves. It is difficult to question such disciplers under the conditions which Reimers describes.

In most controlling discipleships, the error is in thinking that leaders can discern your sins better than you can. However, they don't tend to blame it on the devil nearly as often as do "deliverance ministries." If you have never been accused of sins and told what your problem is by a "spiritual leader," you may think that this is a weird con game that no one would fall for. But being told your sins (instead of freely confessing your sins) is an abuse that persists in some controlling groups.

Many "deliverance ministries" present you with an authority who can tell you your sins or the reasons for your problems (these ministries blame demons for nearly everything that is wrong). Orthodox theologians agree that there are demons, but in many of the deliverance groups, the demons are only in the minister's mind.

If you believe in your discipler's ability to know your sins better than you do, you may allow his or her perceptions to overpower your better judgment. The same can happen if you believe those who claim that they can see your devils. In this way, you can unwittingly become putty in the hands of the manipulative leader.

BRUTAL CONFESSIONS

Many "sharings" are downright brutal, as in this true story of "Tom" and "Paul":

In one such incident during a meeting, Tom told Paul, "Brother, I have been thinking about the way you've been coming across in meetings. I talked to some people and we've decided you would be a better example if you showed more physical affection for your wife during the services. You know, hug her or hold her hand." Paul laughed and agreed that he always struggled with being a "Mr. Spock." He said that he would pray about it, and expressed his feelings, "Don't you think that something like showing affection should be from the heart? You don't want me to pretend or put on a show, do you?"

Tom responded, "There are many things we do as Christians that we don't want to do at first, but feel right about later." Paul argued that he didn't want to force himself in a public assembly to hold her hand. Then Tom, leaning forward and pointing, said, "That's the trouble with you, Paul. You are stubborn and prideful. You can't do this simple thing. Your marriage must be a mess, but you won't ask for help. I am sick of trying to hold you accountable. I think you are using your job for an excuse. What is an obstetrician anyway, but a glorified plumber?"[59]

Obviously, it is not sinful to hold hands or not to hold hands in public. Yet this incident is typical of the hundreds of ways that disciplers decide what is right and what is wrong for their disciples to do. They want to mold them into the perfect character *they* think they should be.

There are other sins that are "created" in abusive discipleships to be confessed by their members. Things that were not sinful during the first 2,000 years of Christianity, now become sinful. It can be a sin to buy a car, if your discipler doesn't agree with the idea. It could be a sin to go to college, not go to college; to buy a house, not to buy a house; to decorate your house; to decide to go to a family reunion; or, as in Laurie's case, not to confess! The list is endless. Anytime you don't acquiesce to the wishes of your discipler, that discipler can choose to call it sin. You may feel guilty and confess it as a sin; but it is an *artificial* sin.

Confessions are full of artificial sins. Countless hours are wasted kicking yourself for not wanting to obey advice you have been conned into believing is Biblical.

Public confession is contrary to Christian tradition and is not taught in the Bible. So why do these groups demand it? They insist upon this type of confession because it makes members vulnerable and easy to manipulate.

When confession is engineered and coerced, it becomes a great emotional burden on the disciple. The disciple becomes more and more introspective: "What am I doing wrong now? Is this sin? Should I confess this?" Too much time spent on confession or sharing leads many to a lack of confidence and an over-dependency on their discipler. True, we don't want to be blind to our faults, but constantly digging up our past sins, looking for new sins, and rooting out artificial sin can be harmful.

Take the sin of immoral sexual thoughts and desires. The more you focus on this sin, the more you think of sexual thoughts and desires, which defeats the purpose. What if I told you that, no matter what, you are not to think of a pink elephant. Well, you'd probably etch an image of a pink elephant into your mind right away!

After dwelling on past negatives or sins, you will start to see your past in a distorted way. After I became involved with a controlling group, my own past began to look dark and dingy. When I left the group, I could again see events in my past as I had before joining. I once again understood that there was a lot more good in my life than I saw when I was focusing on all the sin in my life.

I personally believe in confession, but I have much wiser counsel now. My present advisors don't ever press me to confess. I am not even pressured to meet regularly with them. They don't call me, wondering why I "missed" a session, because I am not expected to be on a time schedule now.

CHECKLIST
CONFESSION CONFUSION—Chapter 10

Check those that apply to you and/or your group:

❑ I have confessed (in front of a group) sins or problems that were unrelated to the persons present

❑ My group doesn't call it "confessions"—but we are pressured to expose our inner selves and our past

❑ I frequently feel I am not being open when I don't confess or share

❑ Most human problems or weaknesses are "evil spirits" or "demons" which need to be searched for and cast out

❑ Often I feel emotionally drained after sharing

❑ I would feel uncomfortable allowing a new person in our small group

❑ I would feel uncomfortable if a family member heard our intimate group discussions

NOTE: If you have checked *any* boxes, it may indicate a misuse of Scripture and/or may represent the presence of abuse and excessive control.

Chapter 11

WALLING OFF THE WORLD

*Some Christians have embraced the idea of
developing a closed personal and professional network that
functions like a "Christian Yellow Pages." This tends to isolate
Christians from the rest of the world.*

At times even non-abusive churches isolate Scriptural verses that separate Christians. A common example is the verse, "Do not call anyone on earth 'father'" (Matt. 23:9). Members of the church then point accusingly at other churches that use the title "father," while they ignore the rest of the Scripture: "Nor are you to be called 'teacher'…" (Matt. 23:10). Was Jesus making the point that we should never use these words again? Not according to the Apostle Paul, who still referred to Abraham as the father of us all (Rom. 4:16), and used this word many other times referring to earthly fathers. (Note: For honorable uses of the word "father" in the Bible, you might refer to these verses: 1 Tim. 5:1; 1 Thess. 2:11; Eph. 6:2; 1 Cor. 4:15; Rom. 4:11; Matt. 19:19.)

So what's the Biblical point about calling someone "father" on earth? The point is, "For whoever exalts himself will be humbled" (Matt. 23:12). The Pharisees who sat in Moses' seat were setting bad examples. They wanted to look good and be honored, all while they laid heavy burdens on others, and Jesus was warning against this. He didn't want his Apostles to be similarly arrogant. It's this pride that Jesus was warning against—that's the point of the whole passage. Christians may think they are learning the Bible when they are really missing the principles that the Scripture is trying to teach.

WE CAN BUILD OUR OWN WALLS

Even without being subjected to the manipulation of "special" words or Biblical ideas, sometimes our minds randomly "wall off" the world.

"Joan" told me she was thinking of suicide when she prayed to God for help. Suddenly there was a knock at the door. Two Jehovah's Witnesses stood there smiling. Joan's mind jumped to the conclusion that God wanted her in this group because they had rescued her. It's possible God used them to help her in her need—but should she jump to the conclusion that she must believe everything this group teaches because they saved her life?

I often hear such phrases as, "This is where I met the Lord." Then no matter how bad things become, these disciples won't even think about leaving. Some tell me of a healing that took place, which led them to stay in the group even though they were having problems there. Even members of dangerous groups tell me that they stay in their group because of healings and conversions. Finding the Lord in a particular group or receiving a healing does not prove that this is where God wants you to stay. The good that you found is wonderful, but you need to realize that evil can also exist in a place where good things happen (Eccl. 3:16 NASB).

If you see your group has become darker, it may be that God is showing that you need to discuss those problems with others in your church. Then, if that doesn't resolve the problems, look into other churches. If you have allowed your leaders and your teachers to convince you to think all other churches are "dead," then you will have a hard time even thinking about leaving.

BUT JESUS SAID, "WHO ARE MY MOTHER AND BROTHERS?"

Mark 3:31-34 is often used to persuade disciples to wall off their families and friends outside the group:

Then Jesus' mother and brothers arrived. Standing outside, they sent someone in to call him. A crowd was sitting around him, and they told him, "Your mother and brothers are outside looking for you."

"Who are my mother and my brothers?" he asked. Then he looked at those seated in a circle around him and said, "Here are my mother and my brothers! Whoever does God's will is my brother and sister and mother."

By using this verse, our group was powerfully driven to feel isolated from all outsiders we believed weren't committed as we were. Those of us within the group truly felt as though we were brothers and sisters. I emotionally distanced myself from my blood relatives. They didn't count as much.

After I left the group and stopped thinking in this twisted mode, I heard another explanation of this verse: Jesus wasn't saying that He didn't feel close to His family. As we know from other Scriptures, Jesus wanted to be as close to everyone as to His mother. He is telling us that to be close to Him (to be His family), we just need to do the will of God.

The love He had for his mother was well known. At a wedding, Jesus lovingly fulfilled His mother's request even though He wasn't ready to begin His ministry (John 2:1-11). When Mary and Joseph found Him in the temple at 12 years old, Jesus said He needed to be in His Father's house (Luke 2:41-51); yet, in obedience, He went with His earthly parents, showing us that it is pleasing to God when we respect our family.

What happens when your family or friends ask you to join them in analyzing your discipleship? Do you regard this as persecution? Do you think that they don't have renewed minds so they can't understand? Did you refuse to discuss your involvement in your discipleship until your family or friends persisted? The disciple usually makes the excuse that "since people on the outside can't understand, I don't need to waste a couple of days to go over all their concerns." Most disciples in controlling groups show a lack of love by refusing to spend whatever time it takes to help their families understand. Why is this? Often these groups make their members paranoid by admonishing them not to allow their own families to challenge the groups' teachings, and they warn disciples to absolutely avoid persons who work with victims of such groups.

Sometimes members are told that they will lose their faith if they listen to professional counselors. Hogwash! Not true, my friends. I may be a professional worker in this field, but I am also a Christian.

Why do I find it so hard to get disciples to listen? Because they are conditioned to believe their group already has the highest truth available, and it would be literally a waste of time to talk with me. Well, I've been there, too! I used to feel this way when I was part of that elitist mentality. You don't feel elitist, you just believe you have the whole truth.

When you have truth in its fullness, you won't mind being put to the test. When you have the whole truth, you will enjoy probing this truth because it will stand any challenge. If you fear shining a light into all the practices and beliefs of your group, then you don't have the truth. When you have the truth, you can question things without the presence or permission of your leaders.

After several months of studying with my group, I got to the point where I wouldn't even read critical information about my group. I didn't want to hear it. If I did hear it, I knew it wasn't true, so I wouldn't believe it. Later, after leaving the group, I told my family that if I ever reach that point again, they have my permission to keep me as long as they like until they have satisfied every question they have. I grew up during that period. I now realize that when I cannot discuss information that questions my group, I am refusing to be objective. Now I have no fear of any information about a group of which I am part. I can discuss anything now—*try me!*

If you are a member of a controlled environment, you usually will not allow yourself to discuss thoroughly criticism about your group. You may not be willing to validate factual information. You may try to discredit negative information so as not to have even one critical thought in your mind about your group because you think you might be "doubting God." What makes me think I know how your mind works? I've been there.

It is normal for you to have a few complaints about situations in your church or group. When you don't voice one critical thought about your group, big red flags should go up!

I had been trying to persuade "Teddy" to sit down with me and discuss some issues concerning his discipleship group. He avoided me for quite a while, but finally said he would meet with me in a couple of months. Two months passed, and he still tried to say no. Finally, after three months and against his discipler's advice, Teddy did meet with me.

He would never admit that anything negative happened in his discipleship. Oh, he confirmed that my material was accurate; other discipleships had these problems. However, he would not mention anything critical concerning his own group.

When I confronted him on some false ideas, Teddy pushed me away saying "we differed theologically" and that he wouldn't listen anymore. Later he would say to me, "See, I was willing to talk with you." Actually, I did all the talking and he just listened, but he thought this was a dialogue. With what depth did we have a two-way conversation? He never admitted that any of the group's teachings were wrong. He just became vague and cut me off whenever I got too close for comfort. Teddy had walled himself off from me by refusing to freely discuss the problems in his group.

Are you walling off people from your life? Maybe you don't see it that way from your perspective, so be brave and ask your old friends and your family if they feel distant from you. Ask them if they now feel there is an invisible wall or barrier between you. Can you talk critically about your group with them? This is the big question. If they need answers, then you have a responsibility to go home and spend some time with them, even as Jesus did with His parents (Luke 2:51) and just as Paul and Barnabas agreed to meet with those who had concerns (Acts 15:1-6). After you have satisfied their questions and thoroughly discussed these issues, then you can say you have evaluated your situation and that you are at peace concerning your continued involvement with your group. Simply saying, "My spirit doesn't bear witness to your ideas," when you don't want to face confrontation is just a method of walling off others' ideas. It is a cop-out to claim you "have peace" when your family and old friends are greatly troubled about your life.

When I was locked into my elitist mind-set, I felt so emotionally close to the people in my group that I wanted to be around them continuously. I wanted to talk with them and spend all my spare time with them. I lost all interest in outsiders unless they were potential recruits to my group. I felt closer to the group than to my own family. Today I hear this echoed by people in many abusive discipleships and controlling groups. If you can identify with this feeling, you may be experiencing some form of elitism. Or you may not be able to believe the label fits. However if your family is hurting because they are isolated from you, you have a serious need to step back and do some deep soul-searching.

From my personal experience and from my work with many disciples in such groups, I can tell you that many of us stepped back to evaluate and regained the intimacy with our families that we had lost. True spiritual growth should not diminish your feelings of closeness with your family. True spiritual growth should cause you to love your family as you do your new Christian friends.

THE DIFFERENCE IN CHRISTIANITY

Christians should be different. Those who have faith in Jesus Christ should act and think differently than those who do not. Over the centuries, the church has wrestled with this issue. The meaning of "being different" has changed as cultures changed. Some aspects of being different in Jesus' and Paul's day (e.g., ceremonial washing or eating meat sacrificed to idols) are not necessarily relevant to our time. A related issue is whether these differences should lead to separation of the faithful from the world. Different groups in the church have also given different answers to this question. Some have thought the church should blend in with the surrounding culture and serve as "salt" or "leaven." Others have concluded that the church is to withdraw from the surrounding culture in order to act as a "light."

Some controlling-discipleship churches make a big deal of "being different." Disciples are taught to differentiate themselves even from Christians in other non-discipling churches. The separation from the world, if there is any, is also extended to most of the churches outside the discipleship. A subtle feeling of superiority and condemnation filters into the thinking of disciples in abusive groups. This separation becomes another means of exerting undue influence over disciples.

THE UNEQUAL YOKE TRICK

Elitist Christian groups frequently use 2 Corinthians 6:14 (KJV)—"Do not be unequally yoked together with unbelievers"—to foster separation from outsiders. This verse is employed as a tool to cut off these discipling Christians from non-believers and even from some other Christians.

Many groups overextend the meaning of "unbelievers" or sometimes label anyone who is not in their group as an "unbeliever." There are many cases of leaders even persuading members to divorce just because spouses left the group. This type of thinking is absolutely wrong! (Malachi 2:14-16; Matt. 5:32)

Similarly, groups sometimes persuade single members that they should marry only within the group, not someone from one of those other "less committed" churches. A well-known discipleship writer states, "A formal (legal) bond with an unbeliever, be it... business partnership or whatever, is unacceptable to the Christian."[60]

It is hard to understand how this writer arrives at an interpretation that contains the word "formal" or "legal." There are practical aspects to this. I don't think we will convert our business partners to Christianity by telling them we are breaking up our business because they don't share our faith. Ousting good business partners will only create havoc and hatred for Christianity, but this author thinks he is teaching Christian principles. Walling off the world this way is brutal and uncharitable behavior. Can you imagine Peter the fisherman refusing to fish with his partner because he didn't have faith in Jesus?

If you believe this teaching, then you must think that:

➤ your secretary can be a non-believer but not your business partner

➤ your boss can be an unbeliever as long as you have no "formal agreement" with him, but as soon as you sign a contract you must find another job

➤ if a non-believer buys one-third the stock in your company, you have to get out or buy him or her out because it would be sinful to continue this business relationship

➤ if your Christian business partner turns agnostic, you will have to dissolve your business.

Jesus did not refuse to be intimate with unbelievers and sinners (Mark 2:15-17; Luke 19:1-10). What was the problem that Paul was addressing? Read the entire passage in context. Paul seems to be addressing a specific problem in the church at Corinth where Christians may have been going to pagan festivities worshipping false gods. Paul would certainly have warned them this was forbidden. If they were going there to witness for Christ, then Paul would have congratulated them and encouraged them to do more.

The Pharisees complained because Jesus was hanging around sinners and eating with them (Mark 2:16). Jesus replied that He did not come for the righteous (Mark 2:17). Paul knew this well, and would never have admonished the Corinthian Christians for being friendly or working with the unrighteous whether formally or informally. No, it seems obvious that he was warning them about being yoked to unbelievers by participating in their disbelief or evil. Charles B. Williams translated this verse (2 Cor 6:14), "Stop forming intimate and inconsistent relations with unbelievers."[61]

Paul clarifies, a few verses later, the type of unbeliever with whom we are not to be yoked. Read all of chapter six of his second letter to the Corinthians and you will learn that Paul is talking about not being yoked with those who worship idols or with those who practice lawlessness or wickedness.

Jesus gave us His example by dealing gently with prostitutes, so obviously we can spend time with unbelievers. There is a great deal of difference between trying to save a sinner and joining that sinner's evil activities.

CHECKLIST
WALLING OFF THE WORLD—Chapter 11

Check those that apply to you and/or your group:

❑ Business relationships with non-Christians are discouraged

❑ I do not wish to include non-believers in my social life

❑ Other churches simply "do it wrong"

❑ I agree that we should not call anyone on earth our father

❑ I am not interested in discussing critical ideas about my group with my family or friends

❑ It's important to stay in the group where I first found my personal relationship with the Lord

❑ It is difficult for those whose spouses leave the group to remain married

❑ I view most Christians not in a discipling relationship as less committed than those in our group

❑ Since my involvement with this group, I perceive most Christians outside our group are not really believers

❑ I do believe the leaders when they say one of our members has "fallen away"

NOTE: If you have checked *any* boxes, it indicates a misuse of Scripture and may represent the presence of abuse and excessive control.

Chapter 12

WHAT GOD
AND THE DISCIPLER
HAVE JOINED TOGETHER

*Discipleship control is worse than having a domineering
mother who tells you whom to marry! You usually will be
viewed as "going against God" if you act in opposition to the
advice of your discipler, but seen only as a headstrong child
if you go against the wishes of your mother.*

I met "Sally" in 1993. Sally was unmarried and had been in a
Catholic community that used a form of discipleship called
"shepherding." When she met someone she liked, she would seek
approval from her pastor before dating. When her relationship
began to be serious (but the pastor didn't want them to marry), he
would ask them to pray because "he was not at peace" with the idea.
All her pastor had to say to end the relationship was that the man in
whom she was interested was not as spiritual as she was.

One day her pastor suggested that Sally should pray about
marrying a man named "Joe" who was also in her group. Joe
prayed, too. They had peace about it and were married. Only after
she left this discipleship did she realize that her marriage was made
under the undue influence of another person. *She* did not choose her
husband. Sally had been conditioned to trust and obey her pastor in
all areas of life—not just moral issues. So, when he advised her to
marry Joe, Sally was highly inclined to obey without question.

This control over marriages is a controversial issue, and not one
which many groups or disciples are comfortable discussing. Most disciples balk at the thought that someone else is picking out their marriage partner for them. They may say something such as, "I made the
choice and my discipler merely confirmed it as God's Will."

183

Some discipleships lead their disciples to feel that marrying a person who isn't being discipled by their method is being "unequally yoked." You may want to date a person not being discipled or who's in another church, but your discipler may persuade you to go against your inclination which may indeed have been God's Will for you. One of the results of this constant influence is that many couples' engagements and weddings are subtly controlled. Many don't date people because their discipler is giving negative signals such as "pray about it a little longer." Of course, one should pray for guidance in selecting a spouse; but, in these groups, being told to "pray more" is simply manipulation.

THE MARRIAGE MATCH GAME

Let's say that there is a young man who wants to get married, and there are 20 women who are possible partners. Each time the disciple mentions the name of a woman he would like to date, the discipler may freely let him choose to date without any restrictions.

If the relationship begins to look serious and the woman does not meet the discipler's requirements, then the discipler may start working on the disciple. The discipler may indicate that it might not be God's Will for them to be together. It can be just a tone of voice or just a lack of response whenever the woman's name is mentioned. The discipler may just not seem happy when the love-struck young man talks about his beloved. Or he may avoid saying anything positive about her, and this may be enough to suppress our young man's interest. If the discipler really wants the relationship to break up, he may say he "doesn't feel that she is right" or "she isn't spiritually advanced."

On the other hand, the discipler may show obvious happy excitement when speaking about the person "selected" for you. It is very difficult to fight this influence and freely pick your partner when you have been taught that the discipler is God's appointed authority over you.

Do you see how this works? You decide who to date but your discipler will discourage you each time he wants you to change. Instead of your discipler telling you that "Judy" would be a good match, he may approve of your dating "Ashley"—but if you start to get a little serious, he will become negative about her. Finally you ask "Judy" out, and suddenly he is positive and reinforces your decision to see her. He doesn't make your choice directly, but rather by a process of elimination. He just withholds approval and positive feedback until you make the choice he thinks is better suited for you.

You might say, "But my discipler tells me to pray about it myself and really just double-checks my decision of wanting to marry this person." This is a common way disciplers give negative feedback. It would be unusual for a discipler to come right out and say, "You can't do this." Then you could see that you were being controlled. Although some discipleships can be this blunt, they are normally a lot smoother. They just keep asking you to pray about it until the relationship dies for lack of progress.

You might also say, "Sometimes the discipler does agree with me and finally gives consent." This is not graciousness. Disciplers should not normally meddle in these matters in the first place. If it comes down to it, a discipler who definitely wants you to follow a certain path will not give in and may call you in sin for not obeying. Whereas, a wise spiritual leader would not accuse you of sin for merely failing to take his advice.

THE PENCIL DEMONSTRATION

Here is a demonstration of subtle influence I use in classes: I ask for a volunteer to walk to my desk and open my drawer, take out three pencils and put them on my desk. Then I choose another student and ask them to select the best pencil. I then ask the class if they made a free choice. Inevitably some will say, "Yes." I then ask, "Who told you to walk to my desk? Who told you to open my drawer and take out three pencils? Who eliminated all the other pencils in the other desks? Who decided it was going to be pencils that you chose?"

By now, the class can see who is in charge. I did allow a selection of three but that doesn't mean it was a choice that you would have made had you been given more alternatives. I am still the boss. If you chose a particular pencil without my manipulation, then you may have thought you weren't being controlled. It is when you really want something else and I narrow your options that you start "struggling" in the program.

Struggling in an abusive discipleship doesn't mean that you want to commit a sin. It means that your discipler has narrowed your options until they do not include one that you would have picked on your own.

The disciple can be made to think he is choosing freely when it has already been decided which of the three he will choose. See what happens if I give an opinion about each of the three choices. For example, I could say one pencil probably will break since the lead is so soft and that another pencil is terribly short. He will probably pick the pencil I really wanted him to have. If he does not, I will tell him how wonderful the third pencil is. If they have been taught to trust you, it is possible to control people's lives almost completely by continuously giving your opinion about nearly everything they do.

You can hardly resist believing what your discipler says in most cases. It is very hard for anyone, no matter how well prepared, to see this mind game when already in it.

THE (FORCED) WEDDING MARCH

A manipulative device frequently used to maneuver disciples toward marriage is the "programmed doctrine" (i.e., that when a decision has been made to marry, one must never back down). Here is what an author popular with controlling disciplers has to say:

> *After the decision [to marry] has been made, it is important to protect yourself (and your potential mate) from backing down on your commitment, so verbalize your commitment!*[62]

One discipler told me he often reminds those who have doubts about a marriage that "they have made a commitment." This reinforcement of the term "commitment" can subtly force disciples into the marriage.

Speaking to those who decide not to marry after having dated, this same author writes, "...*it is essential that you make a clean break.*"[63] If the disciple does not want to marry a person after dating for a while, then the advice from the programmed discipler is simply not to date this person anymore. They must make a *clean break*.

This puts enormous psychological pressure on a couple. They enjoy each other's company, but their disciplers think they have been dating too long and need to decide one way or the other. They are both hesitating to marry, but they feel pressure from their disciplers to marry or break up completely. This can be a terrible predicament. If one has been dating too long (according to their disciplers' clock!), an irrevocable decision must be made, or *one isn't following God's Will*.

I have witnessed couples, who enjoyed each other's company (but did not feel ready to marry), go ahead and marry anyway because they didn't want to break up completely. Were the couple allowed the freedom to become better acquainted (by dating for the period of time that they need), many of these weddings would never take place. Sadly, some people avoid marriage for years because of this constant manipulation. If the discipler is always advising against the people the disciple wants to date, the disciple may think that he or she is sinning by failing to feel just as the discipler says.

Most disciplers are not intentionally making their students and followers dependent on them, but in reality the program is set up to do exactly that—to make disciples dependent on disciplers. These programs make disciplers into little gods. They can interfere in disciples' everyday decisions without compunction because they are made to believe that this is "total accountability." But, as you have seen from our study of Biblical references, Christian leaders have no Scriptural mandate to dominate all areas of our life.

Disciplers from abusive programs deny they are forming dependent disciples. They say they want their disciples to be dependent on God. I believe they truly feel this way. But "feelings" are often wrong. These disciplers must study the results of their actions. When they condition disciples to trust and obey them for fear of probably disobeying God, they create an unhealthy and unspiritual dependency.

Abusive discipleships take you back to infantile dependency. The discipler wants you to check with him for most of your decisions as though you were a child. The discipler can question your motives just as your parents did when you were young. There is a major difference, however. You are now an adult. Why do you need to refer all of your decisions to another person? Some discipleships will try to convince you this is the way Jesus treated his disciples. There isn't anything in the Bible that tells of Jesus spending hours reviewing all their decisions. What does the Bible record? Guidelines! What do you get in abusive discipleships? Control!

But coercive discipleship control is even worse than having a domineering parent. Often you are seen as having some sinful fault or tendency if you go against, or don't trust, the advice of your discipler. This technique is a subtle form of coercion to accept the advice of your discipler regardless of your personal convictions.

Many disciplers feel the discipleship program gives them ecclesiastical authority. This is absolutely untrue. The final responsibility for these decisions is still yours and yours alone. By merely joining a discipling program, you should not have given the discipler authority over every area of your life.

CHECKLIST
WHAT GOD AND THE DISCIPLER HAVE JOINED TOGETHER—Chapter 12

Check those that apply to your discipler:

❑ Exerts control that's as bad or worse than that of a domineering parent

❑ Belittles the person I'm dating

❑ Delayed my wedding because he or she never "felt peace" about the marriage

❑ Helped me—either subtly or overtly—select a certain person as my spouse

❑ Talks about being "unequally yoked" when discussing potential mates not in our group

NOTE: If you have checked *any* boxes, it may indicate a misuse of Scripture and/or may represent the presence of abuse and excessive control.

Chapter 13

THIS CAN'T BE MIND CONTROL, CAN IT?

When committed Christians regularly see other members'
salvation questioned when they leave their church,
it is very difficult for them to consider leaving—
God, salvation, and the group seem to be synonymous.

The phrase "mind control" conjures up images of people locked in prisons, deprived of sleep and food, and subjected to the kind of verbal assault and mental torture that causes them to break down and parrot the ideas and phrases of their captors. We may suspect that certain oppressive governments and possibly some very extreme political and religious groups practice mind control, but never a Christian group—and certainly not *our* group.

You might be surprised to learn that none of these extreme measures is required for mind control. All that's needed is an environment where the information can be controlled, and more importantly, the way people perceive that information. To be fair, this definition may seem to apply to parenting, school, even political campaigns. But children eventually grow up and strike out on their own; students can read a variety of books at the local library, and, in every political campaign, there is counter propaganda from "the other side." However groups that practice mind control often suppress the desire to seek outside sources or accept what these sources reveal.

"Jeanie," a former disciple, said she was not being unduly influenced, but also told me she didn't even want to read anything "against her church." If she did, she would not have believed it anyway. If something made her doubt that the group was totally right, Jeanie figured that the doubt was from the devil or that she might be lacking spiritually. Jeanie thought she was keeping her mind free of evil influences. Actually, Jeanie's mind was trapped inside a closed box. Check carefully and honestly to see if you have fallen into similar thoughts or feelings.

Before joining this particular discipleship, Jeanie never thought this way. During her training, those "older in the Lord" helped her understand the "truth." If something causes doubt about the group, it must be wrong.

As a disciple in this group, she believed that it was the devil, her carnal mind, or bad influences from other people that made her doubt the group. Later, free of the abusive group, Jeanie realized that she had reached a point where *she herself* was suppressing her critical faculties.

When you can allow yourself without fear or guilt to discuss and read material critical of or contrary to your group's teachings, you have a chance to be objective. The reason I say "chance" is because I have witnessed disciples so emotionally tied to their group that they would read material for a short time (to get mom and dad off their backs) but wouldn't face the facts with an open mind. Their minds couldn't validate the information even though it was true. They hurried back to their destructive groups as fast as they could.

If you feel that you must get back to your group and don't want to thoroughly discuss issues with friends or family, you should recognize your fear and uneasiness as "red flags."

I know you will rationalize this behavior as wanting to be with your Christian friends. You may think, "People on the outside just can't understand!" Well *you* are never going to understand *them* if you don't give outsiders the time that they desire to speak and discuss the issues with you. If they want to spend a week with you discussing this subject, then, for your own mental and spiritual health, you should require it of yourself. What's a little time to reach a decision that may affect the rest of your life?

COULD IT BE CONTROL IF YOU ARE TOLD TO CHECK IT OUT FOR YOURSELF?

Ethical Bible teachers sometimes will say, "Don't believe me; check it out for yourself." Disciplers in extremely controlling groups tell their members the same thing. That sounds as though they surely couldn't be controlling. But please don't forget to check out the *environment* as well. Look at the difference in the pressures that exist in one group versus another. Disciples in the abusive and controlling groups are in a closed environment with their closest friends. They know if they disagree it probably will be looked upon as a lack of spiritual development. And they've heard about disagreeable and painful things that happened to disciples who left the group.

Do you think these disciples' minds can truly be objective? Not likely! Not unless they enjoy being looked down upon, being rebuked for "having a hard heart," and possibly losing the respect of friends.

THERE'S THE DOOR—WE'RE NOT CONTROLLING YOU

One of my favorite comments from controlling leaders is: "There's the door; no one is forcing you to stay; no one is controlling you." This statement is supposed to lead followers to believe that they are not being controlled, because the preacher said they can leave. But in nearly every instance, disciples have been frightened with misleading stories of terrible tragedies that befell members who left. What if some of your closest friends left and it was said of them that they are now living in grave sin since leaving? If you believe this, could your mind really be objective under this pressure? I've spoken to many former members who say the fear of what might happen to them if they left was so great that, when they had questions or doubts, they would try to ignore them.

It is very difficult for such discipled Christians to leave after hearing someone's salvation called into question when they leave their church. The former members of these types of controlling groups will tell you that they were trapped psychologically. They couldn't leave because, in their minds, it would be the same as spiritual suicide.

REINFORCE THE NEGATIVE—IGNORE THE POSITIVE

"Deidra" loved her job but, once in a while, she would mention something that annoyed her boyfriend, "Mike." Mike never complimented her about the good work she did in her tough job. When she made one of those rare negative comments, however, he would seize the opportunity to reinforce her negativism. Deidra found that when her opinion was the same as Mike's, things were fine. When she opposed his viewpoint, however, he became irritated and occasionally irate.

Mike sometimes said her opinions weren't rational. Sometimes he condemned Deidra for opposing his ideas. As a result, Deidra began to withhold her opinions because she liked being around him. She could no longer be herself. Deidra had been an extremely confident person with high self-esteem. Over a short period of time, her self-image and self-assuredness lay in ruins.

Eventually, though, she identified the problem. When she did, Deidra stood her ground and became herself once again. When Mike found that he could no longer control her, he left her.

Healthy friends allow room for differences. There are people, however, who are insecure and have a need to control. Their hidden agenda is to change us to fit their mold. They are often so subtle that a professional may be needed to point out their manipulations.

Disciples have told me that accepting their disciplers' advice usually did not bother them. I pointed out to them that, when we are already conditioned to accept the leaders' advice and understand the group's demands, of course there will be little, if any, conflict. What you must do is examine what happens when you don't agree. Is there often a negative response from the discipler, or some other form of negative feedback?

QUICK! I'VE GOT TO FIND A COUNSELOR— THE BIBLE TELLS ME SO

I recently sat through a disciple program. After one of the sessions, I felt as though I should run out and find a counselor as fast as possible. The man who led the session made sure he expressed in at least a 100 ways how desperately everyone needed counsel. By using out-of-context Scripture to support his perspective, this discipler was molding within us a deep desire to receive counseling.

Although I've spent years studying these motivational psychology tricks, it still had an effect on me! Even though I recognized he was isolating verses from other texts, I felt compelled to find a counselor after this class though I didn't have a real need at the time. That is how subtle yet powerful these control techniques are.

Of course, everyone uses some of these techniques on occasion. Every good speaker tries to put the facts together in a persuasive way that is most supportive to his or her case. Each of us has the capacity to influence our friends in some way. Destructive groups, however, consistently use the controlling techniques I've described.

I've been asked, "But doesn't the military use mind control?"

The military does use some behavior modification techniques to assure that, under battle conditions, soldiers will respond instantly to a command. The difference is that the army's conditioning interferes with only limited areas of the soldier's life. There is no attempt to disguise the purpose of the training. The military does not have the hidden agendas we find in all abusive groups. Military recruits know in advance what is expected.

On the other hand, controlling groups systematically and without warning try to change your feelings or views about your family, friends, your church, and/or the values and morals with which you were raised. They conceal their true goals from members, disciples, and the public in general. Misdirection, deception, and secrecy are pervasive. To the contrary, we seldom hear complaints from parents, relatives, and friends that the military changed someone's religious/political views or relationships.

Fear that their group might be guilty of excessively controlling members' lives actually causes some disciples to deny the possibility of mind control. Many Christians in and out of discipleship groups find it hard to believe that any group which preaches the Gospel, evangelizes, and baptizes people for Christ could use a sophisticated program to control members. Denial, unfortunately, does not change the facts. Mind control techniques can exist in *any* group or organization.

Mind control is a combination of techniques that change personalities and suppress many normal responses. One can be conditioned to control one's thoughts in a narrowed range, depending on how domineering the group leader is.

Dr. Robert Lifton did a study on "brainwashing" or "thought reform" in China. As a result of his studies, he proposed a model consisting of eight "psychological themes" which reveals if a group is using "thought reform" techniques.[64] Lifton found these psychological themes in Chinese universities as well as prison camps. The characteristics that Lifton discovered are also found in abusive or controlling discipleships. The themes he outlined are proven effective in keeping members motivated, indoctrinated, and under leaders' control. As few as six of Lifton's steps are enough to control the lives of group members.

This is a summary of Lifton's Thought Reform Model (Note: Dr.

Lifton's technical language has been paraphrased, and I have added some explanatory comments):

1 - Milieu Control

The group influences not only what we should hear and see, read and write, but also our judgment of that material. For example, we prejudge negative criticism of the group as invalid. Negative material is usually viewed as divisive, factious, or non-Biblical even before the facts are weighed. Almost anything that goes against the group is to be viewed as illogical, irrational, or non-Biblical. You don't give it much thought. You feel confident that you are seeing objectively.

Judgment of right versus wrong is not necessarily based on the content of the information, but by the fact that it goes against the group or its teachers. If new information, independent judgment, and self-expression do not conform to your disciplers' viewpoint, you are subtly pressured to change it to the "truth" as the disciplers see it.

Milieu control also influences how we view people outside of our group, good or bad, saved or not saved. These divisions are much sharper than they are in non-abusive churches.

By not allowing members to voice publicly the smallest negative thought about the leaders (and equating criticism with disloyalty to Jesus), these leaders place themselves on a level with God. Lifton found this same kind of control in communist China: "...any thought or action which questions the higher purpose is considered to be stimulated by a lower purpose, to be backward, selfish, and petty in the face of the great, overriding mission."[65] This deprives the individual "...of the opportunity to exercise his capacities for self-expression and independent action."[66]

2 - Mystical Manipulation

The group's leaders contrive events (which then appear to occur spontaneously) within the group; this impresses members and thus makes them more easily manipulated. As a result, members are made to feel they have a higher purpose than any other group on the face of the earth. They come to think that God is leading them more closely than most any other group. Their leaders subtly lead them to think that they have more understanding of Biblical truth than anyone else.

The more convinced you are that this is the most flawless group of all Christian groups, the more likely you are to be "deprived of the opportunity to exercise [your] capacities for self-expression and independent action."[67] With this comes the feeling that it is necessary to submit to the leaders' manipulations and even painful abuse in order to fulfill the group's mission.

3 - The Demand for Purity

Based on the group leader's twisted definition, everything "impure" must be purged. "Reality is sharply divided into the pure and the impure, into the absolutely good and the absolutely evil."[68] Extreme accountability is used as a way to purge everyone of their "taints and poisons" and members are encouraged to watch one another. This purging of impurity is the source of much rebuking in these groups. Although leaders cannot see our hearts or motives, they constantly judge them; their views on even non-moral matters are generally held to be correct.

4 - The Cult of Confession

This is founded upon a pressure to continuously reveal "artificial sins." In abusive discipleship, this concentration on the self brings about self-degradation and distortion of one's past. Evading emotions or ideas to prevent the need of exposing them to our discipler causes us to feel still more guilt. We come to feel we are more sinful for not exposing all of our feelings, sinful or not.

Compared to the Biblical understanding, the effects of this type of confession are quite the reverse of healing confession. People are made to feel sinful in some way if they aren't "totally open" or for keeping personal secrets even if these are not sinful. Total exposure intensifies personal secrecy and erects walls of conflict between group members.

It is interesting to observe these close-knit disciples at large meetings. They tend to flock together because they feel an intense intimacy, having totally exposed themselves to each other. The shallow nature of this relationship becomes evident, however, when a disciple decides to leave the group. At this point, the remaining members regard the one who left as having very little in common with them anymore, and often they presume the former member has fallen away from God.

5 - The Sacred Science

Abusive groups often forbid any challenge to their methods. If you ask these disciplers to prove their practices are Biblical, they often become angry and defensive. Their reaction is to judge anyone who dares to criticize as immoral, irrational, irreverent, or lacking faith. In their opinion, their doctrinal methods are straight from the Bible. They generally will not tolerate discussion and insist they are doing what anyone who wants to totally serve God should be doing.

There is one group bold enough to put it in black and white. This is from the manual of a nationally-known discipleship: *A critical attitude of fellow staff, of the ------ ------- ministry or of other individuals or groups shall be considered as evidence of disloyalty to Christ, and shall be accepted as an act of resignation.*[69]

Lifton again hits the nail on the head when he talks about an environment of thought control: *This sacredness is evident in the prohibition (whether or not explicit) against the questioning of basic assumptions, and in the reverence which is demanded for the originators of the Word, the present bearers of the Word, and the Word itself. Thus the ultimate moral vision becomes an ultimate science; and the man who dares to criticize it, or to harbor even unspoken alternative ideas, becomes not only immoral and irreverent, but also [illogical or totally irrational.]*[70]

6 - Loading the Language

Many words are changed to mean "Godly terms" or "evil terms." The loaded language pressures members "...to censor, edit, and slow down spontaneous bursts of criticism [or restricts criticism altogether] or oppositional ideas and actions."[71]

7 - Doctrine Over Persons

"Doctrine over persons" means that the group leadership remolds personalities without regard for the individual's talents and spiritual gifts. Spurious and repetitious cataloguing of feelings as sinful, right, or wrong becomes more real than truth.

Disciplers have told me the problem presented is rarely the problem. In other words, "The complaint you make is not what you really are concerned about. You have some other problem which you are hiding beneath this complaint. Let's dig that other problem out and examine it, instead of answering your questions." This clearly demonstrates that these leaders are much more concerned about maintaining the belief system of the group than about the people they are supposed to guide. Those who dare contradict, argue, or criticize are labeled by leaders as negative or even sinful—further evidence of doctrine over persons.

8 - The Dispensing of Existence

Most of the time those challenging abusive leadership have no rights. They will recognize the challenging members' existence and speak with them usually on the condition that they might eventually agree.

These groups, who feel they are "the only ones doing it God's way," have an elitist view. They feel that you were spiritually "dead" before you joined them and that you are worthless if you leave (and are even, perhaps, their enemy). Such an environment fosters paranoia, causing members to distrust anyone outside the group. In other words, they dispense with the existence of anyone outside their group.

PICTURES CAN TELL A THOUSAND WORDS

The photograph on the left was taken before my involvement with an abusive group. I was outgoing, had a positive attitude toward life, and possessed a great sense of humor—and I believe those qualities are evident in this picture. The photograph on the right was taken while I was under mind control. I think I appear lifeless in this picture. To me, my eyes look dull and I appear tense and worried (in fact, at this time I felt euphoric and was convinced that I'd never been happier in my life).

In retrospect, I now realize I had little tolerance for people who did not agree with me. At home, I participated in family conversation and games—pastimes I'd previously enjoyed greatly—only to avoid being rude.

Not everyone trapped in mind control groups will show such a dramatic change. I include these only as a personal example. You must also remember that the depth of a victim's involvement can vary widely from day to day. The group's program and the intensity of the discipler's efforts also have a profound effect.

Fortunately my family cared enough about me to do something about my condition. During the second day of my family intervention, I experienced an abrupt change of feelings during which much of my former personality returned, although I did not fully recover my normal reactions and emotions for months.

MONASTERIES

People frequently ask, "What about monasteries and convents—don't they demand unwavering obedience? They have lots of rules; so aren't they using mind control?"

Rules cause outward conformity and do not necessarily mean mind control is being used. What I've been describing is the coercive control that changes your thinking without your consent. It is true that, in most destructive groups, a symptom of control techniques can be too many rules or excessive "do's and don'ts." But mind control doesn't need a lot of obvious rules.

There are distinct differences between monasteries (that allow plenty of room for free will) and high-demand discipleships (that erode a person's freedom). Similar to the military, religious orders let recruits know exactly what they will face, do not mislead members, and have no ulterior motives. Further, neither religious orders nor the military expect "quick commitment."

Unlike abusive discipleships, monastic orders are not excessively introspective, unwilling to answer challenges, nor overly concerned about controlling negative information about themselves.

In my study of monastic orders, I've not found excessive "loading of the language" as there is in control groups using the mind control model. Neither have I found shunning of former members. (Note: Sister Oresta, a nun who ran the Vatican Library for years, told me that her community went to the weddings of former members of her order and attended their baby showers.)

Monastic groups did not give me icy silence when presented with hard-hitting questions. Rather, they willingly answered all my inquiries. This is markedly different from the reaction I found in groups I suspected of using control techniques. On the contrary, legitimate religious orders seem to be spontaneous and willing to admit their faults. Most members of religious orders don't hesitate to comment on teachings that they don't like, and they often tell me what they don't like about their specific group or order. Of course, there are some monastic orders that are deceptive, cover up things, and are defensive. In these rare cases, however, I usually also find excessive control.

Here are some ways in which religious orders are different from mind control groups: Religious orders...

- ➤ typically don't feel their group has a higher purpose than other convents, monasteries, or other churches

- ➤ don't think God is leading them more closely than any other Christians

- ➤ don't typically feel they have a deeper Biblical truth than lay persons

- ➤ are not usually made to feel they will lose their salvation if they leave the monastery or convent

- ➤ confession, as practiced in formal orders, is not exploitative and sins are not repeated to others, as often occurs in abusive discipleships

- ➤ do not relentlessly judge others' motives or hearts as part of the order's program

- ➤ don't generally bash other religions or groups

- ➤ criticism of leadership is usually freely accepted

- ➤ reveal up front what is expected of members

- ➤ do all that is possible to care for elderly or sick members; whereas, I have often heard about abusive discipleships that neglect caring for members who were incapable of participating in the group's activities.

CHECKLIST
THIS CAN'T BE MIND CONTROL,
CAN IT?—Chapter 13

Check those that apply to you and/or your group:

❑ I avoid reading books that might challenge my beliefs

❑ I've been told examples of bad things that happened to people who've left

❑ I have heard a leader say: "There's the door; you're free to leave"

❑ I sense that God and my group are truly one

❑ I've been told to "check it out for yourself" but still the group uses isolated Scriptures to reinforce conformity

❑ I believe my group is not controlling because it is not as intense as other groups I've heard about

❑ I sense my leaders relax their control temporarily, perhaps to establish "credibility"

NOTE: If you have checked *any* boxes, it may indicate a misuse of Scripture and/or may represent the presence of abuse and excessive control.

Chapter 14

COLLISION WITH LEADERSHIP

God said He would spew out the lukewarm but He never
commanded us to reject the lukewarm; that is why this
discipleship method is nothing more than a "hate program."

It is not "discipling" that I am against, it is the abuse of disciples by their trusted teachers, group leaders, and pastors. If these leaders are unwilling to listen to reason and bring their teachings back into conformity with the Bible, then it is up to you, the disciple, to confront them. Please know it is not just non-denominations that pervert the Gospel in order to control members. So don't think it only happens in other churches—look carefully at your own.

But be prepared! These personal experiences will demonstrate what you might expect when you collide with your group's leadership.

In March 1994, I was delightfully surprised to be allowed to sit in a special discipling program being brought from a large, prominent Baptist Church in Atlanta, Georgia, to a local church near my home in Chattanooga, Tennessee. I was looking for balanced discipleship. What I found was appalling.

I wrote "Jane," one of the group's leaders, challenging the non-Scriptural basis of some of the organization's ideas. The following is part of my letter (edited and expanded to include some clarification):

Dear Jane:

This letter is about the "uncommitted" that you spoke about in the second session. You talked about a woman who came in for counseling; you said she was living in an adulterous relationship and that she wanted prayer for the wrong reason. The woman didn't want to change immediately so you said that she wasn't really wanting help. The lady was asked to come back when she could say, "Whatever you want me to do, I'll do it!"

I was greatly disturbed. If I took this attitude, I would be making slaves of whomever I counseled.

Then yesterday you mentioned in the discipling counsel class that you gave another woman an ultimatum: she had to pick only one counselor. Such an ultimatum is simply a restrictive control trip, putting the client in a box. Professional counselors only need to know if the client is working with another professional so that they can cooperate in the treatment. I have seen times when two counselors were asking for the Holy Spirit's guidance, and had two different directives. Both were backed by Scripture. To exclude [my clients] from other counseling may be doing them a great disservice.

I have asked many times: If we don't allow the lukewarm and the cold to sit in our churches, be in our discipleships, and receive counseling, how will they ever have a chance of catching fire? God said that on Judgment Day He would spew out the lukewarm. God never commanded us to do that. I feel that it is God's place alone to judge who is not ready.

You said that, "There will come that point when a person is obviously choosing to waste your time." It was said that a person should be given every opportunity before we turn them away. The theme, "don't waste your time with those you judge as not ready," was more prominent in the second session. You determine who is wasting your time based on their obedience to you.

One discipler told me, "You don't want to just pour yourself into someone who doesn't really want to learn." A red flag went up in my mind after she told me this. When I questioned her further, she continued, "One doesn't want to spend an entire year on someone and then they leave and don't go on further with the Lord." Although stunned, I thanked her for sharing such telling information. I reminded her of the Scripture of "leaving the 99 (saved) and going after the lost sheep." The idea of not putting up with the weak or lost runs counter to this Scripture and also to 1 Thessalonians 5:14.

Another problem is that the burden on other Christian counselors is even greater since another brother in Christ deemed these weak ones as "not ready." These Christians aren't willing to carry this burden because they only want the easier cases; those willing to be putty in their hands and do what they say. What an easier life I could have if I could, in good conscience, drop all the people who didn't quickly respond to my directives.

I cannot imagine facing God on Judgment Day telling Him that I left a drunk lying in the ditch because "he wasn't ready to change." Jesus made the point that the good Samaritan didn't judge before he was willing to help. That is a prime example of unconditional love. It takes a lot of Christ's unconditional love working through us to give us the strength to handle these cases. (Also think of Jesus reaching out to tax collectors and sinners [Matt. 9:10-13, Mark 2:15-17, and Luke 5:29-32.])

It takes even more effort to convince the uncommitted, who have been abandoned by other Christians, that we truly care. I feel the damage produced by deserting may sometimes cause more damage then the original problem.

I have colleagues and Christian friends who have worked with people who didn't want to change their life for weeks, months, or years before conversion took place. As Christians, we don't give up when people aren't ready to change. We leave the 99 and go for the lost one, pour ourselves out to them as Jesus and the Apostles did for the unbelievers as well as the believers. I have seen the greatest miracles that anyone could possibly imagine as a result of this philosophy.

If I had the luxury of judging by your standards and deeming people as "not ready," I would have turned many cases away. Because I was willing to stick by them when they didn't seem ready to change, their conversion was possible.

Jesus gave Judas, the lost soul, every opportunity to accept love and care. This is our best example of how counselors should be directed. Jesus knew that Judas was a thief and would sell Him for money, yet Jesus chose him to be one of the 12. Jesus poured himself out to the very end for Judas. Jesus never abandoned Judas because he was not "ready to come to God."

Another statement made during your talk was: "Sometimes we should leave people hungry!" This rubs me the wrong way. It seems to imply that we could set ourselves up as judge and decide who to feed and who should go hungry. I am having trouble finding any Scriptural basis for this authority to decide who we should help and who we can allow to starve.

Another comment I heard was: "If I become a cushion, give them relief, or give them comfort in some way that is in direct opposition of what God is doing, I just interfered with what God is doing." I am having difficulty in finding verses in my Bible that tell me that I am not to comfort certain people who need help. Where do you find the Scriptural references for turning people away who are judged as not being ready or wasting our time?

Your rationalization was that we may be going against God's Will if we try to help these people who don't want to change immediately to our way of thinking. But I am using Jesus' treatment of Judas, His acceptance of sinners like the tax collectors, and His story of the good Samaritan as the Scriptural basis for my conclusions. I am also standing on the promise "Whatever you do to the least of these..., you do unto me" (Matt. 25:40). I know whatever effort I make to comfort, Jesus promised that I am doing it to him. How, then, can we be going against God's will if we try to help?

I feel that the practice of rejection is harmful not only for those turned away but also to the believer who is taught to judge instead of help. Rejection is much easier but Jesus didn't turn away Judas, who would never change. Is this a cross that we need not bear? Jesus bore it with Judas.

We need to go after the lost sheep, stay with them, and pour ourselves into them with the compassion and love that Jesus gives us for these "uncommitted."

After sending this letter to "Jane," I met with her about it. I thought that she might quote Scriptures to me because of my challenges. Instead, her first question to me was, "What makes you tick?" Jane was looking for my weak points. She was looking for something that would allow her to dispense with my existence. If she could discredit me, Jane wouldn't have to deal with anything I said.

Jane told me that she would not respond to this letter, saying I was "totally irrational." Without realizing it, Jane was keeping herself from thinking objectively by categorizing me and thus dispensing with all I said. From her viewpoint, I had no rights. I did not deserve to be given an explanation because I was a non-person. My questions couldn't possibly be valid because I didn't accept her beliefs.

If you find yourself categorizing people this way, know that you are keeping yourself from getting outside, possibly valid, information. You cannot be objective if you are not willing to be open.

You will have a healthier balance and be more objective if you allow yourself the freedom to talk with people whose views conflict with your own. The Bible says, "Seek and you will find" (Matt. 7:7). Controlling discipleships stifle you from examining negative ideas about the program, so you cannot find the truth. Don't be afraid of negative information. This fear is what most controlling groups want. Fear of negative information can keep you in their group.

Jane said she would not respond to my questions because I wouldn't change. The cliché that I "wasn't going to change" was also a thought-stopping technique which meant Jane would not think any further. She could not be objective because she refused to admit the possibility that anyone who disagreed with her might possibly be right.

THE PROGRAM OF HATE

In many dictatorships, there is a very real threat of extinction if one does not obey the law. The threat of death is a powerful means of coercion, to say the least. For Christians, the threat of losing eternal salvation is even more serious. Such a threat can cause extreme emotional damage to those who "fail to measure up" and are rejected by their church.

Expulsion is a very real threat in the discipleship methodology. Whereas, in most mainstream Christian churches, you can be lukewarm or even "deadwood," and not be asked to leave. Abusive discipleship, however, doesn't always put up with such members.

I know a medical doctor who was discipled by one of the largest discipling groups in America. At the time, the doctor began her internship and was therefore unable to meet all of the obligations of this particular discipleship. This group refused to continue to disciple her. The leaders of this discipleship program apparently felt superior to Christ's church and thought that they could decide she did not belong because she was not "committed" enough.

This discipleship's attitude is this:

We don't have to pour ourselves out for those outcasts who aren't ready to change. We don't have to spend time counseling them. We are God's elite so we don't have to accept those who aren't ready to obey almost all that we request of them. Truly loving consists of helping to "hit bottom" those who don't want to change. If we comfort them, we are going against God's will. We can help them "hit bottom" by withholding our help until they are hurting so badly that they will do whatever we say. We can help force them into God's will for their life by giving an ultimatum: It is either our way or they don't get help and can't be part of our program. (Note: Biblical calls for treatment are invariably meant to be love; see Acts 20:31-35; Rom. 15:7; 1 Cor. 4:14; 1 Thess. 5:11, and 14; 2 Thess. 3:15.)

What about "tough love"? Tough love refers to giving an ultimatum to those who are stubborn in outright sin or self-destructive behavior in order to pressure them into changing or seeking help (Matt. 18:15-17; 1 Cor. 5; 2 Cor. 12:20,21; 13:1-2,10; 1 Tim. 5:19-20; Titus 1:10-13: all of Jonah). Would it be wrong to comfort them? Perhaps, because—although comfort isn't wrong— it is often misinterpreted by addicts, and may have to be withheld for their own good. But, just because this sometimes works, would you also withhold food from a drunk or drug addict? Of course not, because you know that psychological comfort is not the same as material aid.

"Tough love" usually applies to deep psychological sicknesses like drug and alcohol addiction. Most importantly, remember that disciplers are not usually trained professionals with the knowledge and authority to use powerful spiritual (or mental) medicines and procedures on disciples who may have nothing worse than the spiritual equivalent of a head cold.

A lack of charity is also produced by twisting Jesus' words in Matthew 25:40: *"whatever you did for one of the least of these brothers of mine, you did for me."* Abusive groups often teach that Jesus meant that you only receive rewards for doing good for brothers in Christ (believers). This is one interpretation that self-centered groups might use (and many destructive cults) to find excuses of why they do not to have to spend their money on the needy who are not in their group.

If you have this belief, study Matthew 5:46-47 where Jesus says, "If you love those who love you, what reward will you get? Are not even the tax collectors doing that? And if you greet only your brothers, what are you doing more than others? Do not even pagans do that?" If you do good mainly for those in your group or those that you can win to your group, what reward will you get? Are not even cult members doing that?

Jesus reinforces the idea that we will be repaid for doing good for strangers: "When you give a luncheon or dinner, do not invite your friends, your brothers, or relatives... *if you do... [as I say]...* you will be repaid." (Luke 14:12) Yet what I hear from former members are examples like this: "When my neighbor died, I didn't even buy a sympathy card because I was so busy with church." How many of your neighbors (not in your group) have needs but because you are so busy, you do not have time to find out? Your capacity for truly loving the way the Bible speaks is greatly reduced under these leaders who demand so much of your time.

Many of you realize that your church requires so much of your time that you don't have the proper time to do good deeds for strangers unless you are trying to interest them into coming to your church or Bible group. If you plan on voicing your concerns to your leaders, or if you are in an abusive group, please take note:

➤ It is not likely you will "win" in a confrontation with your group's leaders—as a matter of fact, there is very little chance that you will change even one leader's mind.

➤ Knowing this, you must understand that the longer you try to reason with them, the greater will be your chance of suffering an emotional beating. Think hard about the risk to your own emotional health before you decide to meet with these leaders, and remember that you are under no obligation to take any abuse from them.

➤ Once the pattern of mishandling disciples becomes obvious to you, your first responsibility is to protect your own spiritual and mental welfare. Only after you are certain you are safe should you consider meeting with your group's leaders.

COLLISION WITH LEADERSHIP—Chapter 14
A short review:

Comparing Discipleships

Abusive	Non-Abusive
Refuse to pour themselves out to the uncommitted who do not fully accept and follow the leader's orders or advice	Serve others whether they are committed or not
Typically reject dealing with those they judge as "lukewarm"	Offer the lukewarm love and a chance to learn
Distance themselves from any member who leaves their group	Treat kindly those who leave them, as Jesus did Judas
Judge who they should "feed" (counsel) and who they should let go hungry, based on obedience	"Feed" (counsel) anyone in need, regardless of how well they obey
Love, and meet the needs of, only those who are committed	Know that Jesus commands us to love the uncommitted as well as the committed
Judge that those who don't fully obey them or "are not ready" are "wasting their time"	Are willing to invest time and love in working with disobedient or difficult disciples
In practice, change the Biblical: "Whatever you do to the least of these, you do unto me" to "Whatever you do to the least of these (unless you decide that they are wasting your time) you do unto me"	Teach that we are to love the weak and the obstinate by being willing to counsel and disciple them too
Usually refuse to admit any error in their teaching; and try to discredit the critic rather than listen to the complaint	Usually give a careful hearing to complaints about their teaching and presume the critic is sincere

Chapter 15

THE NEW INQUISITION

The downfall of this "accountability" is that it establishes human beings, and not God, as the ultimate judges.

The Spanish Inquisition in the Christian Church during the 13th century was intended to search out and convict non-believers and heretics. The original inquisitors believed they were doing God's Will. Today, we have new inquisitors (i.e., abusive, controlling disciplers and church leaders) who claim to search out and eliminate what they consider to be every taint and poison in their disciples' lives. They believe that they are doing this better than any other Christian church on earth, and they feel justified when using coercive and controlling means to accomplish their goals. As with the original inquisitors, they often destroy those they purport to help.

These new inquisitors wield a weapon that they call "accountability." You may think it is not possible to have too much accountability. Perhaps you think that "more is better."

You may recall I said abusive discipleship groups don't necessarily call themselves "discipleships" but go under different names. I grouped many of these controlling discipleships under the category of "More Accountability," because "accountability" is their key word which they load with new meaning.

Regardless of what they call themselves, these discipleships promote a form of accountability which is misleading and damaging. The distortion of meaning is subtle, and many Christians fall for it because it sounds like a good idea and the spiritual thing to do. These discipleships teach that every Christian ought to be accountable to someone or some group. In some of these groups, it goes as far as reporting nearly every detail of the past week and being totally open to a person or to a small group in order to "make sure you're not in sin." Again, the Bible does not support this high level of scrutiny as a justifiable practice nor does it teach this kind of "watchdog" operation.

"Accountability" simply means "responsibility." We are responsible (to God, our employer, our customers, our parents, our children, our spouse) for fulfilling our duties and meeting our obligations. Also, pastors, and disciplers are—or at least should be—accountable to those under their care; to nurture and respect them and not dominate them (1 Pet. 5:1-3; Ezek. 34:1-4).

Beyond that, we are accountable to each other in the sense that we have a responsibility not to sin against one another.

It is important to note the difference between an abusive group that has a particular, strong, tightly controlling authoritarian leader and one that does not. You might think the latter is not as damaging, but it can be. Take a look at the following examples.

GETTING PERMISSION TO SING HIS SONGS

I recently went to a Christian concert. "Mat" commented, "Every song I write, I submit it to my church." Mat belongs to a Presbyterian church. I mention this only to show that this problem exists in a variety of churches.

Mat went on to mention that we all needed to be accountable. I slumped a little in my seat and an eerily familiar feeling swept over me—extreme accountability had just popped up in my favorite Christian singer. I had gone to the concert to enjoy myself, to take a break from work. But, because this false teaching is so pervasive, I was brought right back to this subject.

Later I mentioned Mat's comments to a staunch advocate of accountability. This person defended the practice saying that the singer probably just wanted to make sure his songs are theologically correct. I thought to myself, "Rarely is there any theological depth to his songs. Yet he submits every song he writes and not just the ones that he might have questions about." This is a dead giveaway. Somehow Mat had been taught it was wrong for him to make these decisions himself. Others had to verify his work. In short, he was accountable to others for everything he wrote.

Accountability is extremely me-focused and time-consuming. When you are in it, however, you usually will not see this extraordinary self-focus as a flaw. If every Christian submitted in this way, we would spend a lot less time caring for the poor, preaching the Gospel, etc. It is difficult to believe that the leaders of Mat's church have enough time to meet all of the needs of their whole church when so much time has to be spent deciding if Mat can sing the songs he wrote. It is impossible for them to avoid becoming mired in needless time-consuming decisions.

The time demands of abusive accountability can become extreme. Members of these groups often carry appointment books filled to capacity. What are they doing with all of that time? They are usually confirming to other adults that what they want to do is okay with them, while believing it's actually helping them grow spiritually. Put this way, it appears rather silly, doesn't it? Yet this is exactly what is happening in many Christian discipling groups and churches today.

THE GROUP COMES FIRST, THEN YOUR FAMILY

Recently "Rheta" spoke to me about her husband, "Gene." Gene had gone to a huge men's rally where they praised the Lord. It seemed wonderful. The organizers said there would be no follow-up, that they weren't asking anyone to do anything but develop a deeper relationship with the Lord. A few days later, however, there was a follow-up. Gene brushed off this deception and joined a small group of these men for prayer and more accountability in his life.

The leader orchestrated certain agreements for the men. One of those commitments was to come every Tuesday night to their meeting. This didn't sound so bad at first. All groups have rules, Gene reasoned. But when Gene and Rheta's daughter's birthday party landed on meeting night, he felt his agreement with the group took priority. In these high-demand groups, they think the pursuit of their goal *"supercede[s] all consideration of decency or of immediate human welfare."*[72]

One would have thought Gene had taken a vow of obedience to this group. He felt pressure not to miss the meetings just as he felt a need to keep his promise of being totally open with these guys.

One day, Gene started to reveal to Rheta some of the group dynamics he had begun to question. He mentioned that "Spencer" had complained that something he had done really bothered him and Spencer wanted to hold him accountable. Several others jumped in and said Gene's action also bothered them. Gene felt he was being interrogated for an insignificant incident and was being unfairly judged. Gene felt frustrated because they saw him as having a fault when he knew their complaint had no substance.

These disciples were all too eager to call each other into accountability. There was little room for mistakes anymore. They were nitpicking at each other, thinking they were helping their companions rid themselves of every little sin—accountability gone haywire.

THE TYRANNY OF TIME DEMANDS

"Ted" reported that, during a discipler's meeting, he discussed a potential convert. He gave an account of this friend, saying how many activities he regularly attended—except for Sunday worship. "Stan," the leader, scolded him for his poor assessment of his friend's openness. He said conversion was hopeless unless disciplers got their candidates to Sunday morning service.

Ted really felt that his friend could be reached despite his lack of church attendance and wanted to explain why he thought this person might make a spiritual commitment soon. Stan became angry when it was obvious Ted didn't immediately accept his view of the situation.

Ted began to question, "Am I not supposed to think for myself?" But he quickly suppressed his questioning, succumbing to the mind control that caused him to stay in the group for many more years.

Ted said, "To think that the leadership was wrong was similar to blasphemy against God. There was a pressure to avoid mentioning wrongdoing on the part of the leadership." But, even with these thoughts, Ted was so shaken in good conscience about the leaderships' mishandling of people that he wrote a letter with each charge and then asked for a meeting for some explanations.

Instead of explanations, Stan began the meeting by saying:

Ted, we all love you here and want you to resolve this problem you are having. I think the real problem here is your heart. You are prideful and independent.

Your marriage is a mess, as well as your family. You haven't done anything spiritually since you left Dallas in '78. You were away too long from the Movement and were influenced in Boulder, Colorado in a negative way. Once you recognize the sin present in your life, these things (pointing to a copy of the letter from Ted where he complained of systematic abuses of leadership) will clear up. All of us here can see it, Ted. You are totally blind in your pride and sin.

I know of hundreds of similar instances in which discipleship leaders have attacked their disciples whenever they had a legitimate complaint. But Ted had thought this through and was ready for the attack on his character. He presented Stan with a letter containing his objections. Ted recounts what happened next:

I told him, "Let's talk about the topics I presented in my letter. Even if I am completely evil, I came to have an explanation of these matters. My conscience is at stake here, not whether I am a good disciple."

Stan and I went back and forth. He wanted me to confess that it was personal sin that led me to bring up these issues. I was unmoving, saying conscience was the key question at this meeting. I argued that an individual's conscience is important and that questions can arise in a person who is trying to do what is right. I said asking such questions does not imply personal evil. He would reply by saying my life was without "fruit."

He implied I was useless as a Christian and seemed to want me to defend myself by listing accomplishments I had done. I kept a level tone of voice, which seemed to make Stan even more loud and angry. Throughout this discussion, Pat and Joe watched speechless. Joe told me later, "I thought you were done for the way you and Stan went back and forth."

After about an hour of Stan refusing to discuss the topics in my letter, I was exhausted trying to maintain my contention that a good conscience can have questions about church leadership.[73]

This is typical of the way in which these discipleships handle people.

I discussed these examples with a man who had been a spiritual director in a monastery for over 40 years. He found them ghastly. He felt it was outrageous to tell someone, "You are prideful" or "You are totally blind in your pride" or "Your marriage is a mess." He didn't feel that, even though he was charged with leading the spiritual development of a group of dedicated Christian monks, he had the right to make the kind of final judgment these disciplers made routinely.

COMMONLY DISTORTED BIBLE VERSES

What twisted Scripture verse can you think of which would give you the right to say that a person's different ideas, concerns, and expressions of doubt could mean that you should throw them out of your group?

Many controlling groups like to quote Romans 16:17-18:

I urge you, brothers, to watch out for those who cause divisions and put obstacles in your way that are contrary to the teaching you have learned. Keep away from them. For such people are not serving our Lord Christ.

Abusive groups will ignore the rest of the passage and fail to see that it's really talking about those who use smooth talk and flattery to deceive. The people labeled as "divisive" or "factious" are simply raising legitimate questions and concerns.

Another favorite weapon in some controlling groups is 2 Thessalonians 3:14-15:

If anyone does not obey our instruction in this letter, take special note of him. Do not associate with him, in order that he may feel ashamed. Yet do not regard him as an enemy, but warn him as a brother.

Taken out of context, this verse is interpreted as giving permission to shun people if they fail to obey instruction from leaders. Paul qualified his injunctions: Anyone who was "acting disorderly" referred specifically to those who were in opposition to the teachings of Christ and were disorderly. Paul was trying to restore order in the church community at Thessalonica. Some of these people were apparently refusing to work, being busybodies, and not living the teachings of Jesus. Paul ordered these unruly members to be temporarily shunned. Paul said nothing here about kicking them out of the community or out of the Church.

Another passage frequently misused is 1 Thessalonians 5:22:

Avoid every kind of evil.

Some controlling disciplers define evil to mean "uncommitted believers" (e.g., parents who still celebrate such "worldly holidays" as Christmas, a cousin who drinks wine, and all other Christians who aren't being discipled). This isolates the disciple from nearly everyone he or she has ever known, loved, and trusted. Of course, this also effectively prevents the disciple from discussing any questions about the discipleship group with outsiders.

The disciple does not feel that his thinking is controlled, because he changed his view on his own without a discipler or teacher telling him directly how he should perceive his parents (and all of those other good people). Brought gradually to this point, he doesn't realize that a year ago, he never would have considered his parents as uncommitted believers. With the new ideas placed in his mind, he perceives most Christians outside his discipleship as "not committed."

Now, if the disciple wants to visit mom and dad during the Christmas holidays, the controlling pastor need only repeat, "Avoid every kind of evil." Because of his new but twisted understanding of this verse, the disciple makes the "choice" not to go home for the holidays.

There are numerous Scriptures that can be used by controlling the application or by redefining a word. You must keep your eyes open and give careful thought to any move by your group to redefine the meaning of any verses from Scripture.

In most controlling groups, the definition of "living a Christian life" is changed. Since selected verses (e.g., those on receiving counsel, submission, obedience, and evangelism) are stressed, the disciple begins to perceive those who do these things as more genuine Christians and those who do not as evil or uncommitted.

Suppose we emphasize caring for orphans and widows (James 1:27), or feeding the poor, visiting the sick or those in prisons (Matt. 25:35-46)? Or how about stressing the importance of the many verses that direct us to do physical works of mercy? Few in our group would then be led to evangelize, because that isn't what is being taught. The one thing Paul was told by the great Apostles James, Peter, and John was to "remember the poor." We read: "All they asked was that we should continue to remember the poor, the very thing I was eager to do" (Gal. 2:10).

Eventually, if I continually pounded this home, I could cause you to distort your definition of Christian. You might begin to see people as not committed if you didn't see them physically caring for the poor. In fact, you might start to think of them as not Christian at all.

Nothing is inherently wrong with stressing these verses. The problem comes when groups teach that living a more committed Christian life can *only* be done in terms of these few verses.

Remember:

The body is a unit, though it is made up of many parts; and though all its parts are many, they form one body. So it is with Christ. For we were all baptized by one Spirit into one body— whether Jews or Greeks, slave or free—and we were all given the one Spirit to drink. Now the body is not made up of one part but of many. If the foot should say, "Because I am not a hand, I do not belong to the body," it would not for that reason cease to be part of the body. And if the ear should say, "Because I am not an eye, I do not belong to the body," it would not for that reason cease to be part of the body. If the whole body were an eye, where would the sense of hearing be? If the whole body were an ear, where would the sense of smell be? But in fact God has arranged the parts in the body, every one of them, just as he wanted them to be. If they were all one part, where would the body be? As it is, there are many parts, but one body. The eye cannot say to the hand, "I don't need you!" And the head cannot say to the feet, "I don't need you!" On the contrary, those parts of the body that seem to be weaker are indispensable, and the parts that we think are less honourable we treat with special honour. And the parts that are unpresentable are treated with special modesty, while our presentable parts need no special treatment. But God has combined the members of the body and has given greater honour to the parts that lacked it, so that there should be no division in the body, but that its parts should have equal concern for each other. If one part suffers, every part suffers with it; if one part is honoured, every part rejoices with it. Now you are the body of Christ, and each one of you is a part of it (1 Cor. 12:12-27).

Does everyone understand that? None of us has anything over the others. We are all important. Don't feel superior because you think your church is more spiritual because emphasis is placed on evangelizing or accountability. God sees the church that is taking care of the poor as honorable, and also loves a church that intercedes for others in prayer. If you are taking care of orphans, don't think that you are doing more than others. Messing around with the meanings of ideas may cause superior feelings to arise in your group, but it doesn't change God's love of those outside your group.

DO YOU HEAR BRAGGING IN YOUR GROUP?

Recently I was in my favorite restaurant and overheard a conversation. One couple was bragging to a pastor that their church was so exciting and "brought down the roof" every Sunday. The preacher had been to their church and said that, if he weren't so busy preaching at his church, he would be at their church, too.

I can relate. I used to make statements just like these. I judged whether the pastor was deeply spiritual by the enthusiasm in his voice and by how much I was moved by his sermons. I judged whether members had the spirit of God by how vibrant their greeting was, by how enthusiastic they seemed, and how well they could express themselves in song and spontaneous prayer.

I now realize those who preach the simple Gospel without a lot of commotion may love God as much as the "fire and brimstone" preachers. I have learned that the quiet people in the church, outwardly unenthusiastic, may have virtues beyond those attending the more demonstrative churches. People simply have different personalities. Each day I realize more and more just how dim was my vision.

Are you attracted by the popular high-powered preachers? Do you rave about your spirit-led church? Do you view the more formal worship services in other churches as less spiritual than yours? When Christians develop their prayer life to a greater depth, their relationship with Christ becomes much closer and they have more peace within themselves. With this closer personal relationship with Christ, it could very well be they often find little need to worship with great noise and physical activity.

THE MOST FAMOUS MISUSED VERSE

Luke 14:26:

If anyone comes to me and does not hate his father and mother, his wife and children, his brothers and sisters—yes, even his own life—he cannot be my disciple.

What member of a controlling group doesn't know this verse? Stressing this verse in the wrong way can drive psychological wedges between church members and their families. It can even lead members to feel disgust for those who love them. Now, compare this to the next verses:

1 John 4:20, 21:

If anyone says, "I love God," yet hates his brother, he is a liar. For anyone who does not love his brother, whom he has seen, cannot love God, whom he has not seen. And he has given us this command: Whoever loves God must also love his brother.

Controlling groups often selectively focus on verses that can be used to support the leaders' agendas. Most disciples who have been subjected to stressing of Luke 14:26 did not receive equal instruction on these words of John. I find this interesting and enlightening.

Luke (14:26) is not saying we are to hate anyone. It is a term used for contrast. Jesus would contradict the commandment to "Honor thy Father and thy Mother" if He really meant for us to hate them. In using this idiom of contrast, Jesus was making the point that we must love God far more than we do any mortals. In fact, we are all familiar with Jesus' love for His own human parents, but He loved them less than God. We must make God foremost in everything we think, say, and do. The "inquisitors" appear to have lost Jesus' message but picked up His admonition as a whip to make members shun their families.

Controlling groups have another favorite verse that they misuse: that of the man who wanted to go bury his father before he followed Jesus. Jesus told him to "let the dead bury the dead" (Luke 9:60 and Matt. 8:22). One must look at the cultural context to "bury his father." This meant "wait until my family responsibilities are over." Jesus was not suggesting that this man's father should not be loved and honored. Rather, He was addressing a different problem: Jesus is warning those who delay following him for "perfectly good reasons." You've known people who have said, "When the kids are out of college, I'll start going to church, but right now I've got too much to do!" We don't know the whole story of this man. But Jesus knew, and we can be sure that Jesus had a good reason for gently chastising him.

2 John 9 and 10 is another that is regularly misused:

Anyone who... does not continue in the teaching of Christ does not have God... If anyone comes to you and does not bring this teaching, do not take him into your house or welcome him.

I witnessed a man trying to speak with his sister from whom, because of her church's twisting of this verse, he had been separated by 31 years of silence. Because her brother had left that church, she believed he was not even to be greeted. This poor, misguided woman did not even go to her mother's funeral because of this verse. It is wrong to isolate verses to make them say whatever you want!

The words of John, "do not give him a greeting" (2 John :10 NASB) or "do not... welcome him" (NIV), are better understood if you look at the Greek word *chairo*. Used here, it literally means "rejoice" or "be glad."[74] This text literally says "do not say to him 'rejoice.'" This was much more than a "hi" or "hello" as we understand it today. This is a particular type of greeting between close friends and those of the same religion, not used for greeting strangers except in rare cases. Therefore, John's instruction does not tell us to treat non-Christians and strangers with total silence.[75]

John also says, "If anyone comes to you and does not bring this teaching, do not take him into your house..." Here, John is speaking about traveling preachers or teachers who had become fairly common figures in his time.[76] To give these preachers a place to stay and teach would encourage false teachings.

In Chapter 4, I showed how leaders misuse Matthew 18:15-17 to squelch criticism about themselves. However, Matthew 18:15-17 is often subjected to another atrocious misapplication:

> *If your brother sins against you, go and show him his fault, just between the two of you. If he listens to you, you have won your brother over. But if he will not listen, take one or two others along, so that "every matter may be established by the testimony of two or three witnesses." If he refuses to listen to them, tell it to the church; and if he refuses to listen even to the church, treat him as you would a pagan or a tax collector.*

Abusive leaders insist that Matthew is commanding us to follow this process every time we see our brothers or sisters doing wrong. Confronting sin, say these groups, is the correct loving action.

These "inquisitors" think they always have the right to confront everything they view as personal sin. But here, Matthew writes about a grave, Biblical wrong that threatens to affect the whole church. Personal weaknesses, imperfections, and immaturities are not Biblical issues that affect the faith or morality of the whole church. Therefore, there is no reason to trumpet them to the entire church.

Abusive discipleships believe they have a mandate to interrogate members anytime the disciplers or leaders deem an action as sinful. These verses are used as an excuse to rough up members with the ultimatum that they will be taken before the whole church if they won't quit "sinning."

CAN YOU BECOME AN "INQUISITOR"?

I've witnessed another tragic phenomenon. It seems that most abusive disciplers keep their spouses accountable just as they do their disciples. This process causes mental problems similar to those experienced by battered women. The patterns that emerge are similar to those Dr. Susan Forward describes in *Men Who Hate Women and The Women Who Love Them*. Dr. Forward labels these men as misogynists (i.e., woman haters).

Many of the controlling patterns that Dr. Forward describes also appear in abusive discipleship programs. In these programs, members are taught that they are helping people by confronting them for anything these members view as wrong. Members of these groups are encouraged to accept this confrontation, and to actively encourage others to point out their faults. This leads these members to become abusive themselves.

"Sandy" is married to a discipler, and was being psychologically and emotionally abused. As I began to analyze her situation, there emerged a pattern I've found in many other wives of disciplers. These women are granted very little margin for error without their spouses pointing out faults or otherwise confronting them.

Early in her marriage, Sandy was delighted that her husband, "Ray," a knowledgeable man well-trained in the Bible, was going to help her grow into a woman of God. He would keep her accountable by pointing out when she had pride or any other sin in her life. At first, this did not appear to be damaging; but the cumulative effect over a longer time was emotionally devastating. Naïvely, Sandy thought that this continual confrontation was what a good Christian husband was supposed to do.

For example, if Sandy expressed any criticism of someone, her husband would remind her that she was "in the flesh." That's a nice way of telling someone they are sinning and better change their attitude or behavior. Sandy usually thought Ray must be right again because he knew so much about the Bible. Sandy was being limited in her innocent expression of feelings and thoughts, regardless of whether her comments were justified or not.

Ray would also tell her that she was "going ahead of the Holy

Spirit." These manipulations were covered by a religious veil, but the bottom line was that Ray was molding Sandy's behavior to conform to his ideas of how she should act and think. He thought he was showing her what was Biblically right. But, since he was only human, his fallible judgments were causing Sandy serious emotional turmoil.

Any display of behavior unacceptable to Ray was viewed as sinful and he would hold her accountable. No matter how hard Sandy tried to do what, in Ray's opinion, was right, he always pointed out more of what he said was sin. This psychological abuse is insidious because it is disguised as a way of helping her to be a better woman of God.

Perhaps Sandy was in sin and perhaps she wasn't. Regardless, she had no options. If she had said, "You are wrong," Ray would have judged her as not obedient, unteachable, or proud. His judgment was final and she just needed to recognize it as the truth and change her ways.

There was another problem. Ray often became angry at trivialities. Once, when Sandy had spoken to a disciple of Ray's without telling him, he accused her of going behind his back. His overreaction to a normal occurrence was a sign of the unhealthiness in their relationship. Ray's behavior was aggravated by his discipleship training that called for members to be totally open about everything they do.

Not all disciplers behave this extremely, but the tendency exists when the discipleship program methods are brought into the home. It has been my observation that these tendencies are often related to discipleship. Family and friends of many disciples note that this unusually demanding behavior and fault-finding began only after the person became involved in the discipleship program.

Sandy was to face another subtle but common form of mistreatment. She soon found that her husband belonged first and foremost to the group. Only after the group's obligations were first satisfied was there any time left for the two of them to be together. This became especially apparent once Ray took up a leadership role.

He was tied up nearly every night, often past midnight. If Ray wasn't acting in his leadership role, he and Sandy were expected at some church function. Sandy was also expected to go to many activities for the women of the church. Being the wife of a staff person, she always felt pressure to show up although she increasingly tried to find legitimate excuses so she could gracefully miss activities without being viewed as unspiritual. Even when Sandy and Ray went to church activities together, these functions often separated the men and women. This created a loneliness in the first year of her marriage. In time, Sandy began to feel rejected by the man she had married.

Although Ray often told her he loved her, Sandy came to understand that his words were not matched by his actions. She lived her whole day looking forward to these crumbs of affection, hoping things would get better. The harsh reality was that they were enmeshed in a controlling group. Ray's first priority would always be the group unless they could escape.

Some of you might blame Ray for not being able to say "no." Some of you will already have figured out that the bombardment of teachings (emphasizing obedience and submission to your leaders in every area of your life) creates great pressure to do whatever is asked. In addition to this pressure, these groups also place great value on "serving."

SERVE, SERVE, SERVE

Because of the warped teaching about serving, Sandy couldn't figure out that she was being mistreated. Sandy believed what her leaders taught: "It is a lost opportunity to serve when you say no." With this teaching deeply ingrained, Sandy wanted Ray to do for others, but often felt guilty for wanting Ray to be at home. This conflict caused another emotional beating that Sandy accepted.

Destructive cults often teach their members to serve their parents when they go home for a visit. They want to look good to the mothers and fathers who might have been suspicious of their demanding group. I remember the parent of one Moonie who began to think that maybe the group wasn't so bad after all because their child came home and did the dishes and offered to do all this work around the house—something that had never happened before.

Cindy, a member of an extremely abusive group, was similarly taught that she must serve her parents whenever she went home. Cindy related, "I would go home and jump out of bed early Saturday morning and ask mother if I could wash her car or clean the house." This was abnormal for her, to say the least. In the back of Cindy's mind was the thought that she could report to her discipler that she had "served her mother."

Be aware if your leaders regularly remind you to serve your parents when you go home to visit. If you are in a nurturing Christian environment, the desire to help will happen automatically without having to be admonished as if you were still a child.

One wife of a discipler said, "I just love it when Vince goes to these conferences and they pump the men up to serve their wives. He comes home and tries so hard to serve me! But it wears off after a couple of days."

Your first reaction might be that teaching the flock to be serving is good. But even this teaching must be balanced.

One booklet tries another sleight-of-hand trick when it says, "Another right we must forfeit is in the area of Christian liberty."[77] Actually, the Bible teaches that our Christian liberty is constrained when we refrain from indulging our sinful ways, and it is not necessarily constrained in other areas (Gal. 5:13). After making this statement, the pamphlet gives an example of how Christians should allow themselves to be abused:

> We had 400 people there for a one-day conference in the dead of winter. After each meeting, we would have to take up all the chairs and then reset them for the next event on the program. We worked till past 11:00 p.m. Friday night just preparing for all those people.
>
> Early the next morning at 5:30, my friend woke me up with, "It's 20 below zero, and you need to light the fire in the meeting room." So I went and worked at the fireplace getting the fire going. Then I worked on the traffic crew for three hours, and it wasn't getting any warmer. Then more chairs had to be moved. Finally the conference was over, but we had to clean the whole place before the next morning, for a wedding was to be held there.
>
> We didn't have carpets in those days, just hardwood floors that had to be swept, mopped, waxed, and buffed. I was washing the floor at 11:30 p.m. when in my tiredness I knocked over the whole bucket of soapy water. It was well past midnight before I was done mopping up, and I knew I had to start again early in the morning.

But during a rest period that day I had read this: "Do you not know that your body is a temple of the Holy Spirit, who is in you, whom you have received from God? You are not your own; you were bought at a price" (1 Cor. 6:19, 20). With God speaking to me from His Word in that way, the whole issue was settled. I realized that if I was not my own, then it was not my right to say what I wanted to do or not do. But it was the prerogative of the One who owned me to assign my work to me.[78]

Many of us would have read this Scripture and thought God might be telling us to avoid self-indulgence and fleshly pleasures. Because of this man's warped understanding of serving, he read the group's slanted teaching into this passage. Teachings like these act to form behavior which accepts excessive intrusion by others into your life.

It is interesting to note that, even when abusive disciplers acknowledge their errors (a rare occurrence in itself), they seldom apologize. Sandy also noted this trait in Ray. He rarely acknowledged or apologized for judging her wrongly, even when she got him to see it her way. For example, when Sandy had explained why she had not mentioned her conversation with the disciple, Ray went immediately from rage to charm, but although he now realized that he misjudged Sandy, he did ...*not show any remorse for his tantrums.*[79]

Be wary of accountability advocates who feel no remorse for misjudging you and are often "on your case." Once you tolerate this kind of behavior, ...*you are setting yourself up for an even more painful phase.*[80]

As battered women often do, Sandy began to doubt her own perceptions and began to accept Ray's accusations. Applying this type of accountability to a spouse erodes self-esteem. Even though this type of abuse can be extremely subtle, it *can effectively erode your ability to think and evaluate clearly.*[81]

Your sanity is at stake here. If you accept this kind of abuse, you cannot expect to stay mentally and emotionally healthy. If you find yourself in this situation, I strongly urge that you seek professional guidance at once.

INQUISITORS RARELY OVERLOOK A BROTHER'S SIN

Take this wisdom from Proverbs 19:11 and study several versions:

...And it is his [man's] glory to pass over a fault (Pro. 19:11 ABPS)

...and it is his [man's] glory to pass over a transgression (Pro. 19:11 RV)

...it is his [man's] glory to overlook an offense (Pro. 19:11 BER)

If you want to truly help others, here's some good advice: "As for the faults of others, the best you can do is give a good example, [sometimes] offer a bit of advice where it will help, and say a sincere prayer for the persons involved."[82]

CHECKLIST
THE NEW INQUISITION—Chapter 15

Check those that apply to you and/or your group:

❏ Believes the Bible calls for men and women to hold each other accountable for almost every imperfection

❏ I have missed important personal commitments in order to attend group meetings or church activities

❏ Members in my group are free to tell me what my sin is

❏ Displays little patience with sinners because imperfection should be confronted

❏ Accuses me of disloyalty to Christ if I have any criticism of our group

❏ My definition of "evil" is much broader than before I joined the group

❏ Since my involvement I feel my family members are uncommitted believers

❏ My spouse regularly brings my attention to the way I should act

❏ Since my involvement, I have little time for family

NOTE: If you have checked *any* boxes, it may indicate a misuse of Scripture and/or may represent the presence of abuse and excessive control.

Chapter 16
BOXES WITHIN BOXES

*This controlling church was sheltering
a controlling discipleship!*

I was studying a discipleship group in a prominent Southern Baptist church for its control methods. At the same time, I was trying to help "Edward," a discipler there, understand that he was wrong in threatening to ask me to leave if I continued questioning a leader's actions.

I was surprised when Edward was willing to go to his elder with me so I could prove that his discipleship was abusive. I was shocked when this elder only mildly admonished Edward. Some of Edward's comments to me had been extremely abusive, but the elder acted as if Edward's only problem was a little overreaction.

As I studied this church more thoroughly, I discovered that the church leadership itself was using many control techniques. It was no wonder the elder didn't see Edward's actions as highly inappropriate, and it was no wonder Edward couldn't see his errors—his church leaders were teaching him by example that his actions were acceptable.

Edward continued to deny that his group was abusive because his leaders didn't confirm my critical analysis. That was a double whammy. I had difficulty helping Edward overcome mind control because he was in a controlling discipleship *within a controlling church*. This is not always the case. Many controlling discipleships operate in churches that do not endorse control techniques.

While analyzing the conduct of Edward's church leaders, I continued to work with him, pointing out their errors and inconsistencies. If Edward had not been subjected to all these mind games, assisting him to recover would have been less difficult. I would have presented the facts and Edward could have objectively weighed and evaluated them. But Edward was conditioned to always be "humble and broken" before leaders in every area of his life. In this group, that meant trusting leaders' teachings. This effectively blocked Edward's ability to think objectively about his situation.

As a result of this programming, Edward sometimes lacked spontaneity and failed to respond normally. It was difficult for him to see his leaders as wrong, even when I found typical patterns of destructive cults in what his leaders were saying and doing. I continued to hope that Edward would snap out of it. Sometimes coming out of an altered state of mind is like a light turning on—suddenly one can see.

I showed Edward that, although his church had beautiful and moving services, destructive control methods were entwined in this wonderful Gospel. Listed below are some similarities between Edward's controlling church and destructive cults:

➤ Leadership avoids answering challenging questions by attacking the questioner

➤ Leaders assume the authority to encourage members to leave

➤ Any reason may suffice for public rebuking

➤ Members can be asked not to participate in their small groups if they miss a meeting

➤ Leaders coerce subordinate leaders to change their opinions

➤ A false idea of Christian unity is taught: "Agreeing with leaders is essential"

➤ A false definition of slander or scandal is taught: "Saying anything negative about the leaders"

➤ Members can be rebuked for expressing an opinion different from that of leaders

➤ Leaders often make negative judgments about people's hearts and/or motives

➤ Leaders express hate for their enemies

➤ Leaders put "gag orders" on members by telling them they cannot speak about certain subjects lest they be barred from attending church

➤ Contributions of time and money are so intensely requested that members often find it difficult to meet the ordinary obligations of life

➤ Failure to meet financial giving goals is considered an indication that a member's spiritual life is unhealthy

➤ Open confession is practiced either in small group meetings or before the entire congregation

➤ Members are encouraged to confront minor mistakes or inconsequential differences, as well as actual sin

➤ Leaders are judgmental about such non-Scriptural issues as failure to mention Jesus in the course of a conversation.

The fact that I found all of these characteristics in Edward's church led me to conclude that it was a controlling church. I dug deeper to show him where his leaders were departing from Scripture and wielding unethical control.

The previous list are things I discussed with Edward, hoping they would finally bring him out of denial. Please know that I have no bias against Edward's church—or any other church, for that matter. My only goal is to help church leaders and members recognize an illness that may afflict their church life; and, by facing that illness, cure it.

REDEFINING CONCEPTS—SIMPLE TRICKS

I sat in a mainline church's training class of 40 people working to become discipleship counselors. One of the first things the instructor, "Jane," did was to redefine the words "organism" and "organization."

Jane said, "True ministry that is of the Lord is an organism, not an organization. Organism has life and it flows. *Organization has order, but it's just keeping rules for the sake of keeping rules.* It always will not succeed but often they [organizations] will hinder the work of the Lord."[83]

Jane continued to tear down the concept of organization by attacking the word "organized," saying that churches that were organized were not true ministries of God.

At the end of the lecture, I might have had a real disgust for church organization had I not recognized this as a subtle technique designed to influence my thinking. After such a lecture, listeners normally will have a highly negative response to the word "organization" whereas, before the class, they wouldn't have thought either positively or negatively about it.

Jane's conditioning will have the effect of causing the group to perceive other churches as organizations, now a highly negative term. With this new definition, other churches are not "true ministries" of God. A church might be carrying out the will of God very well, but a person with this distorted view of organization would not likely perceive it that way.

If, after learning this new definition, one of the students speaks with a friend and comments, "Oh, the church you are going to is an organization," the friend won't hear anything negative in the remark. If the friend understood this new meaning of organization, he or she would probably be insulted. However, since these students' friends and families do not know that certain words now have different and special meanings, they are no longer communicating on the same level. This leads to a psychological isolation that grows insidiously because *neither* party realizes what's happening.

I am an Exit Counselor. This means I help victims of cults and controlling groups to critically analyze the control techniques that have influenced them, in an effort to obtain the victim's cooperation in freely choosing to stay or leave such groups.

I look for loaded terms such as these and explain them to the victim. Defining key words correctly is often an important step in releasing victims from bondage.

Jane says her church isn't an organization but an organism, which she defines as having God-like characteristics. This makes her group think of their church as better than others, creating an elitist attitude. Taught enough of these new definitions, their world view will change, which in turn leads them to change their actions. The manipulation of words becomes manipulation of persons.

Jane says that organizations "always will not succeed." This is an absolute statement. I've cautioned you to watch out for the words "always," "never," etc., because there are usually exceptions to any rule. Perhaps Jane feels that if she only waits long enough, they will eventually fail and prove she was right.

Even though you will find that Christians follow rules in order to do God's will, no one in this class questioned her extreme statements. Apparently they all felt that, if Jane said it, it didn't contradict the Bible and so they just believed it. In reality, Jane's church probably has as many rules as any other. The members don't perceive themselves as "keeping rules for the sake of keeping rules"—only *other* churches keep rules for the sake of keeping rules.

Here's a slight twist to the example above that comes from a different group. This other group claims it is not an organized religion yet it publishes newsletters that connect it with "house churches" (i.e., those who meet only in the houses of members and who often feel, by doing so, that they are more closely following the Bible than those who congregate in churches) all over the world.

Members meet at conventions, but boast that theirs is not an organized religion. On the contrary, groups such as this are very well organized, maybe more so than some mainline churches. By redefining "organized," they can deceive themselves in an attempt to set themselves above other churches.

Groups that redefine churches and religion frequently redefine Christianity as well. One man vehemently told me that his church "wasn't a religion, but Christianity." Based upon his understanding of the new definitions of these words, he felt that only churches that claimed they weren't religions were the ones truly practicing Christianity.

This business of defining a church as "not-a-religion" is simply a way in which leaders influence members to feel that their church is better than others. But, if you examine these "non-religions" closely, you will see they are doing things much as the groups they profess to abhor.

Each leader may say it a little differently, but their objective is to guide you to see other churches as "dead" and your church as "alive." Once they convince you of this, even if you see faults and injustices in your own church, you will have a hard time leaving. Former members of these controlling churches often say that, when they left their group, they thought that they were turning their back on God because they believed that there wasn't any other church living and preaching the Gospel.

HOW DO YOU BREAK OUT OF THESE BOXES?

Warning! When you challenge church leaders about these manipulations, they will likely try to deflect your challenge by questioning you: "What gives *you* the right to question our leaders? What right do *you* have to question God's authority?"

Anyone (Christians included!) has the right to question authority. If you don't have as many college degrees as some of these leaders, so what? Leaders should honor others by answering questions, because those who are genuinely God's anointed don't feel threatened by questions, nor do they mind fielding difficult inquiries.

I remind you again that in controlling churches you can see (but only if you will look) evidence of manipulation in your personal experiences, in sermons, in recommended readings, or in teachings. You can often determine if there is a problem by reviewing members' notes from lessons or interviewing former members.

CHECKLIST
BOXES WITHIN BOXES—Chapter 16

Check those that apply to your group's leaders:

❑ Change the meaning of "organization," "religion," or other words thereby leading their members to feel superior to other churches

❑ Apply negative words to other churches

❑ Cause me to be psychologically isolated from others who don't know my new definitions of common English words

❑ Avoid some of my questions

❑ Accuse me or others of having a bad heart

❑ Encourage certain members to leave

❑ Publicly rebuke or discipline members for matters that are not necessary to expose to the whole church

❑ Ask members to no longer participate if they miss meetings

❑ Ask members to not speak to other members about certain subjects

❑ Repeatedly and emphatically request money (and stress that a lack of financial giving is an indication of an unhealthy spiritual life)

❑ Must personally ask members to attend certain groups or studies before they are allowed to participate

NOTE: If you have checked *any* boxes, it may indicate a misuse of Scripture and/or may represent the presence of abuse and excessive control.

Chapter 17

THE WAY TO FREEDOM

*Mind blocks cause you to stop your own thoughts
whenever you begin to be critical of others.*

You may still be rationalizing that yours is not an abusive discipleship, even though you admit to seeing at least some parallels to the groups we have been discussing. "Yes," you say, "I've seen abusive discipleship and I agree with much of what this book says, but there is so much good in our fellowship." Or you may be thinking, "I haven't personally had a bad experience." Or, perhaps, "There is still a lot of good in my discipleship." Then there are those who say, "I know mine is not abusive. I am not being controlled. I make all my own decisions."

Denial of the facts may mean you are using "mind blocks"— those patterns of thinking that allow you to dismiss a source of doubt or worry without even thinking about it. When you hear something negative about your group, the mind block works this way: *If you criticize, you are bad; if you are bad, your information is wrong; if your information is wrong, I don't have to listen.*[84]

What does it mean if you admit there are parallels between your group and abusive discipleships, but turn around and say, "Our discipleship is not abusive." It means *denial*. Unfortunately mind blocks imposed subtly over a long period of time are nearly invisible to the victim.

Let's check this out: All of us use mind blocks at various times when we want to cling to a bias but reality keeps hitting us in the face with contrary facts. In abusive groups, mind blocks are systematically instilled and are especially insidious because they are made to sound as though they are Biblical principles. Take a look at this teaching of the leader of a well-known abusive Christian group:

233

When you criticize us, you criticize him, God.
When you criticize us, you criticize him, God.
When you criticize us, you criticize him, God.[85]

This leader equates his group with God! Any criticism of the group becomes criticism of God, thus creating a typical mind block. Although it may be said in various ways, the bottom line is that abusive leaders want you to feel guilt when you criticize the group. This is absolutely not a Biblical principle. If we follow the Bible, we must not be overly critical; but, if something is wrong, it is our responsibility to seek justice.

There are other mind blocks you may have been taught that effectively cause you to avoid holding leaders accountable:

Leaders are responsible only to God

They'll have to stand before God—therefore, it is not my role to judge

I cannot be responsible for their actions.

GOD IS IN CONTROL

"God is in control." I was frustrated by a discipler who would parrot those words whenever I tried to get him to think critically about something that might be wrong. Later it dawned on me that instead of being in control, God is *sovereign!* A sovereign king doesn't control the individual decisions of all those in his realm. If God didn't allow free will, then we could say that God is in control. Saying that God is in control denies the existence of free will.

As I observed this discipler more closely, I saw that there were several issues here: (1) a false concept had been implanted; (2) parroting "God is in control" gave him permission to remain passive even when he was shown an error in his church; (3) when this discipler, himself, made a mistake, saying "God is in control" gave him a nice excuse; (4) this helped shut down his critical reasoning skills because, once this was said, the conversation was over.

When you point out a legitimate problem about someone's cult or church group and you hear, "God is in control," you are really being told, "I can't do anything about it." That is wrong. God gave us free will to do something about wrongs. Yes, we can do something about errors and problems in our church or group.

So the next time a disciple hit me with "God is in control," I merely asked, "Does that mean God is responsible for your sin? If God isn't responsible for evil, then you can't say God is in control, you are." God in his sovereignty allows evil as a consequence of free will, so don't say he is in control unless you honestly believe that you don't have free will.

Another common mind block is the concept that "doubt is sin." This concept may be taught directly or by implication. Over time, one gets the sense that those who doubt are weak. Actually, it is just the opposite—those who are willing to admit some doubts are generally those who have the stronger self-identity and are more able to think critically.

Remember the times when you had doubts in the group or. struggled with a situation? Perhaps the Lord was talking to you; or, perhaps, your conscience was speaking to you. You may have gone to your discipler who washed away all your anxiety by giving you answers that "sounded good." Looking back now, you may see that what you were "hearing from the Lord" was actually right. You may see that the leader talked you out of your valid feelings by saying that the doubt was a sin or the devil or weak faith.

These are only a few examples of denial patterns, but they may help you be aware of what you're doing to shut off your ability to evaluate objectively. There are hundreds of ways to keep you from doubting your group.

Now is the time! Make a list of all the doubts that you rationalized away, or that your discipler talked you out of. You should also talk to some of those who have left your group. Maybe God will use those former members to open your eyes so you can see what is wrong in your discipleship, group, or church.

Members who survived David Koresh's group told stories about his rude behavior, foul language, his obsession with guns, and his physical abuse of members. Koresh had answers for everything. His followers should have asked, "Are they really the right answers?" Those who stayed with Koresh used rationalizations that probably sound the same as your own: "We have a lot of fun fellowship here. Leaders really care about our members and are willing to confront them and discipline them. God is perfect but He uses imperfect instruments. No other church is living Christianity to the hilt the way we are, so why leave even if there are a few problems?"

Those inside controlled environments can't see objectively

although they think they are seeing everything normally. Most of you reading this book probably think that, if you heard David Koresh's bizarre teachings, you would have reacted differently than did most in his group. Under the same conditions, however, most of you would have reacted the same! If you insist that you would have acted differently, then you fail to appreciate just how powerful the mechanisms of control are.

This book has, I pray, helped you to more objectively evaluate the teachings of your group and the actions of your leaders. Still, you may vacillate. If you acknowledge that the characteristics of control exist in your group but you can't bring yourself to classify your group as abusive, you are caught in a web of control the same as were Koresh's members.

You might still ask, "But how do I know if it is a Biblical idea or if it is just my pastor's opinion? Or if it is a teaching which just sounds Biblical but actually is not?" It can be tough to tell, because the opinion of controlling leaders can sound Biblical, especially in the closed environment of the group. This is why you must be willing to obtain counsel from leaders outside your group, possibly even from other denominations. If you hesitate because you think other Christians are not being led by God as perfectly as your group, it is probably because your group has given you this perception or because you have not been exposed to sound wisdom that often exists in other churches. The Bible admonishes us to seek many counselors (Prov. 11:14, 13:10; Acts 15:1-32). A variety of answers is needed to make healthy decisions.

WHAT TO EXPECT WHEN YOU LEAVE THE GROUP

Many of you have succeeded in making it past all these stages of denial and are now taking steps toward breaking free from control. Coming to the realization that control is being used in your church can be pretty startling. That is why you may have trouble sleeping or even experience nightmares. You may feel nausea, physical discomfort, sadness, irritability, loss of appetite, depression, a loss of concentration, or any number of other problems.

A desire to return to the group may be the result of fear and the paranoia resulting from the group's indoctrination. The fear of thinking that leaving the group is going against God may cause you to ignore the group's control and abuse. Ask yourself: Is my eternal salvation based on this group, or is it based on Christ's redemptive work? Do I have to belong to this group to keep the commandments of God? Is my salvation the result of my own hard work, or is it the result of God's grace?

Another element that holds members in controlling groups is peer pressure and the false teaching that you should never break a commitment. Herod was pressured to behead John the Baptist (Mark 6:17-19). If kings have difficulty because of peer pressure, imagine how much more difficult it is for us ordinary persons. Keeping commitments is not always the right thing to do.

It is difficult, if not impossible, to gracefully leave a controlling group. They commonly question your commitment to Christ and make you doubt your salvation. Often your reputation is smeared. Remind yourself that your commitment is not to the group but to God. This was probably your commitment before you met this group, and it must remain your commitment now. Even if you became a Christian because of this group, that does not mean that you must stay in the group to be saved. Jesus, not the group, is your Savior.

When you stop attending these groups, people you thought were your closest friends will drop you instantly. You may agonize over this loss and the loss of what you perceived to be the most perfect church. Then you will realize that your group is in more serious trouble than the other churches upon which you used to look down. Perhaps you may feel there is no longer any purpose in life.

Study this recovery book and others. Take sufficient time to reflect; speak with former members of similar groups and read about abusive churches. Of greatest importance, speak spontaneously from your heart with God throughout the day.

There is one practical and powerful practice that will help you reestablish your personal strength based on your trust and love for Jesus. This bit of advice has been practiced by Christians throughout history. The Little Way is what Theresa of Lisieux called it; Brother Lawrence calls it Practicing His Presence; Andrew Murray names it Abiding in Christ:

The Lord is your constant partner, so when you clean your room, you are working with him beside you. Start your car in the morning and think of Jesus sitting beside you, sharing every part of your day. You will eventually find the fulfillment that you previously gained from group activities. Making yourself conscious of Jesus' presence is especially healing during the transition from abusive control and readjustment to independence from the group.

During your recovery, Bible readings may trigger turmoil because of the added meaning which your group's leaders taught you to read into the text. Devotional books offer you an alternative to reading nothing but the Bible. Later, when you return to reading the Bible, buy a different translation because you may still feel that certain phrases have meanings which are not true to the original Biblical intent.

Still, after you leave a controlling group, Bible verses will come into your mind and cause you to feel guilty because these verses were twisted by your leaders. Find someone who can help you understand these verses in the context of the passages; this will free you from this false burden of guilt. Ignoring this problem will only make the pain linger. I, too, tried to steer clear of some verses at first. But once I learned how these verses had been misused, I was freed from the wrong interpretations and I stopped trying to overlook these scriptures.

It may be months, or even years, before you can discern the truth from the distortions or additions to the Bible which your group taught. Be patient with yourself; God knows what you have been through and He will not push you to hurry.

Learn from your experiences and persevere in prayer. It may take you a long time to recover from a controlling group's abuse, but you can return to normalcy. It will take you a while to mellow out after you leave this kind of influence, but it can be overcome with God's help.

There may be buzzwords or certain situations that will set you off. Be alert for them. Analyze your behavior. Try to see what you are telling yourself. Keeping a journal may help you to reflect on events like this.

You will also begin to see some of the legalistic ways you picked up from your group. "Brenda" told me that she had thrown away a silver charm bracelet because her group had convinced her the little symbols on the bracelet were superstitious and evil. She now regrets the loss. The bracelet had merely been intended to remind her of happy family events. You, too, may have some regrettable losses, but learn from your experiences and persevere in prayer and seeking the Lord. Recovery is a process. It may take you a long time to recover; but, believe me, you can return to normalcy.

When I returned to my non-controlling church, I felt as if my fellow parishioners were dead because they didn't sing with the same enthusiasm as my controlling group. The preacher didn't seem to have much zeal when he spoke. Later I realized these people were singing voluntarily with no pressure. Slowly I began to understand that I had no right to judge the commitment of my fellow Christians by the volume of their voices. And they didn't have to pray or preach in a certain way to hold my interest.

PUT SCRIPTURE BACK IN PROPER CONTEXT— STUDY DIFFERENT VIEWS

Abused disciples often tell me they feel guilty because of manipulation of the "rich young ruler" story (Matt. 19). Leaders of controlling groups imply that this young man was going to Hell because he was not following Jesus' disciples during their day-by-day activities. For example, an immensely popular Christian book teaches: "The young ruler... missed out on eternal life."[86]

Twisting the meaning of this story can cause you to believe that you will miss out on the Kingdom of God if you aren't with your specific group of disciples. The rich young ruler was already keeping the commandments, as Jesus said he must, in order to gain Heaven. He asked Jesus what more he must do to be perfect. Jesus answered: "If you want to be perfect, go sell your possessions and give to the poor, and you will have treasure in heaven. Then come, follow me" (Matt. 19:21). Jesus first gave the rich young ruler a mandate to get to heaven, and then later, a choice if he (and you and I) wished to strive for perfection.

FINDING YOUR WAY BACK

Controlling environments usually cause you to distort your past life to some degree. Take every opportunity to spend time with old friends and family reminiscing about old times. This will help you regain the perspective of your former life that you may have lost.

Many of you were encouraged strongly to live together with other group members, as controlling discipleships often promote the idea that you need to live with other Christians. After baptizing the eunuch, Philip didn't try to prevent him from going back to a non-Christian country (Acts 8:27-39). But controlling and abusive groups often tell Christians that they aren't strong enough to live by themselves, much less go to a foreign country.

You may have had the idea planted in your mind that non-Christians will pull you down. This leads members to move in with other members, and gives controlling leaders much more influence. If you are committed to God and living His commandments, you can be a great witness regardless of where you live.

You may feel guilty about enjoying privacy now. You don't have to feel you are being selfish because you want your own room or apartment. Being a Christian, you must deny yourself sin, not privacy.

Disciples leaving controlling and abusive groups often have financial problems. Sometimes this is partially due to pressure placed on members to support the group, often far above a tithe. Most of these groups also strongly endorse going abroad to evangelize. This can be very expensive and often puts members in a financial bind. Many group members never had financial trouble before joining the group, but now find themselves in debt. If credit counselling is needed, go get help. Worry about such worldly problems will aggravate the difficulties you face in recovering your independence. Don't let temporary difficulties stop you from regaining your strength and distract you from rebuilding your Christian foundations.

THERAPY AND THERAPISTS CAN HELP—OR HINDER—RECOVERY

Such post-traumatic symptoms as emotional or physiological problems often result from exiting a thought-reform environment or a controlled group.

> *It is difficult to find trained counselors who know how to effectively deal with former members exiting abusive groups. In patient treatment, therapists often have little knowledge of coercive persuasion. They address childhood, but do not thoroughly educate the victim on the methods of control that were used on them and how that normally affects human thinking, behavior and decisions. Ex-members are often told to put the past behind them and get on with life. Professionals tend to blame the victim, thinking the individual must have had some problem in order to be seduced in an abusive group.*[87]

Often victims of abusive churches aren't fortunate enough to reach professional help with experience handling their type of case. Be open and honest with your therapist; ask if he or she is willing to learn. Try to find an experienced counselor in this field who can advise your therapist. Check Appendix 1 for ideas on where to call for information.

I find that therapists who do not specialize in cult or abusive-group recovery seldom understand that the history of individual members of abusive groups has been deeply distorted by the group's influence. Some therapists may try to heal family relations based on the indoctrinated victim's opinions. Many therapists make the mistake of catering to the victim's new identity and values formed by the controlled environment, but since these views were imposed on them by the group, this retards recovery.

Unless victims had a negative view of their families prior to joining the controlling group, it is most effective to bring the victim's siblings, relatives, or friends into sessions to describe their view of parents and family and to show the contrast with the victims' distorted viewpoints. Usually the victims' view will not match that of the others, and the victims will find they only developed this conviction after being influenced by the group. Victims often claim they always felt this way, because they cannot remember ever thinking differently. Generally, after being away from the controlling environment, their prior feelings surface.

You may want to seek therapists who have dealt with "False Memory Syndrome." Victims of memory-recovery therapy seem to have been abused in a way similar to that used by controlling churches. Therapists working with those who have had false memories provoked understand how your history can be distorted by group involvement.

At the time of this writing, there is only one residential operation, *Wellspring* (see Appendix 1), that specializes in helping former members of abusive Bible groups. The founder, Dr. Paul Martin, was a victim of a controlling Bible group for eight years. He and his staff of professionals are exceptional in their approach and understanding of the special needs of these victims. If you cannot afford counseling, ask local churches or synagogues if they are willing to help you pay for a short stay at Wellspring. Don't give up just because you don't have money. Keep asking.

Another source of help for those with limited funds can be counselors who work with battered spouses. They may be listed in your phone book under *domestic violence, family violence, sexual assaults, abused* or *battered spouses*. These counselors usually understand destructive environments, psychological control, and the issues involved when leaving a controlling environment. Still, you may need to discuss your own particular experience with these counselors. You might qualify as "battered" since you have experienced similar psychological abuse from your discipler, leader, or programmed spouse. Don't let financial restrictions keep you from seeking the help you need and deserve. The fees of many such agencies are based on the ability to pay.

Remembering and recognizing the abuse is extremely important because there may be days when you think you've made a mistake by leaving your group. Sometimes this can cause *floating, spacing out,* or *disassociation.* (These words all describe an altered state of consciousness.) This can happen especially when you are depressed or lonely. Bringing yourself out of this lapse and back into objective and critical thinking is partly the goal of the exercise in Appendix 3. Whenever you find yourself in this situation, please review this exercise.

The areas of recovery listed below were taken from Dr. Paul Martin's lecture.[88] These areas should be given adequate attention to speed recovery: (1) the purposes of rehabilitation; (2) the recovery process; and (3) the imposed pathology of the totalist (totalist describes a group that narrows reality in mostly a black or white— good or evil) group. This is only an overview. Books that thoroughly discuss recovery issues are listed in Appendix 1.

REHABILITATION

After you leave your controlling group environment, you must prepare yourself to face a number of new challenges; some of these are very easy to work out, but others may be very difficult for you to handle. If you seek professional help, it will be helpful to talk about the following items with your therapist:

1. *Living in freedom and what that means*
2. *Learning how to handle feelings, emotions, disillusionment, disappointment, grief, and time wasted in the group*
3. *Regaining physical health*
4. *Resolving dependency*
5. *Relearning decision making and independent thought*
6. *Adjusting to society; overcoming social awkwardness*

7. *Accepting yourself*
8. *Reestablishing family and social relationships*
9. *Sharing experiences with other former members*
10. *Reevaluating personal and career goals*
11. *Nourishing healthy theological inquiry*
12. *Nourishing healthy supernatural and discriminating philosophical inquiry*
13. *Resolving sexual problems*
14. *Educating yourself regarding mind control, methods of manipulation, and totalist movements*
15. *Preparing for encounters with current members of abusive groups*
16. *Educating yourself on the recovery process*
17. *Resolving emotional issues created by the group's teachings (e.g., fear, anger, paranoia)*
18. *Resolving "floating" (the feeling of being disassociated or disconnected from society, your peers, and fellow Christians, which causes you to want to rejoin the group rather than maintain independence)*
19. *Reevaluation of why you joined, with a new understanding of how uninformed you were about the group's requirements then*

HELPFUL IDEAS FOR RECOVERY

1. *Seek medical attention if you feel physically ill*
2. *Recognize your need for validation and compassion*
3. *Restore your personal dignity*
   a. *Self-esteem*
   b. *Identity*
   c. *Spirituality*
4. *Tell your story*
5. *Understand and accept your need for privacy*
6. *Strengthen family communications*
7. *Prayer*
8. *Understand that you were a victim, that you are normal, that you are okay*
9. *Have faith in God and never lose hope*
10. *Commit time for counseling*
11. *Get a standard psychological interview and assessment*
12. *Be willing to talk about both the positive and the negative aspects of your group*
13. *Work through the shame process*
14. *Seek validation for yourself*

15. *Resolve your sense of loss, disillusionment, depression, and guilt*
16. *Arrange your time so that you have a daily structure that allows for concrete directions and problem-solving tasks*
17. *Allow your significant others to offer love and care*
18. *Seek solid, conservative information on philosophy and metaphysics*
19. *Recognize that you were subject to the stress of being in a totalist movement, leaving, and now you're facing the stress of starting your life all over again*
20. *Give yourself permission to be kind and caring to yourself*
21. *Understand sexuality and your sex role within the context of Christianity*
22. *Seek career counseling if needed*
23. *Seek financial counseling if needed*
24. *Explore how teachings of the group differed from mainline Christianity and determine if they were really Biblical teachings*
25. *Make time for leisure activities*
26. *Seek out empathetic and loving Christians to form an ongoing support network*
27. *For a while, avoid reading the Bible, watching religious television programs, or participating in any intense or emotional church activities*
28. *Avoid occult literature*
29. *Maintain a personal log or journal*
30. *Get plenty of intellectual stimulation*
31. *Open yourself to previously squelched feelings*
32. *Seek out every possible support resource in (another) church, community and social agencies, family and friends*
33. *Face the future with hope[89]*

WATCH OUT FOR SYMPTOMS

The following is an overview of emotional and mental health problems that may be expected after being subjected to manipulation and deception. The following list is from Dr. Paul Martin's lecture. Some of the terms are technical terms from the Diagnostic and Statistical Manual of Mental Disorders, 4th Ed. (DSM-IV), which is the standard used by the American Psychiatric Association. Although this list is primarily intended as a reference for professionals, DSM-IV is available at most public libraries for those non-professional readers who want to make a deeper study of these problems:

1. *Alienation or despair, feelings of hopelessness, not belonging*

2. *Experience of culture shock when reentering society*
3. *Religious abuse*
    a. *Realization of victimization*
    b. *Bitterness and rage*
4. *Personality doubling (There is the former personality and a newly molded personality that emerged as a result of group indoctrination and group influences. At times the old spontaneous self will emerge and at other times the fabricated identity will surface.)*
5. *Feelings of psychological and intellectual rape*
6. *Induced psychosis with no prior history of psychosis is experienced by some ex-members for one month to two years*
7. *Atypical dissociative disorders*
8. *Anxiety combined with memory problems*
9. *Stress reactions*
10. *Continuing enforced dependency*
11. *Fear of the specific psychological, physical, or spiritual threats and procedures made by the group if one leaves*
12. *Formal methods of dissociation (i.e., systematic means employed to produce dissociative states)*
13. *Feeling screwed or squeezed*
14. *Distorted view of the world*
15. *Paranoia*
16. *Inability to find a job*
17. *Loneliness*
18. *Disillusionment*
19. *An urge to do deliberate harm to self and/or others:*
    a. *Self-mutilation*
    b. *Suicide*
    c. *Homicide*
    d. *Abuse of drugs or alcohol*
20. *Reactive psychosis*
21. *Post-traumatic stress syndrome*
22. *Chronic shock syndrome*
23. *Multiple personality disorders*
24. *Hyperventilation: changes the blood chemistry and alters mood*
25. *Cognitive inefficiencies, memory impairment*
26. *Atypical anxiety*
27. *Relaxation-induced anxiety*
28. *Altered state, or trance state through induced or taught techniques*[90]

Many former members are diagnosed with "Dissociative Disorders Not Otherwise Specified." For more information on this, you should study DSM-IV section 300.15.

CLOSING THOUGHTS ON A PERSONAL LEVEL

If you still find it difficult to break your emotional attachment to your group, it might be helpful to spend time away on a long vacation pondering all that you have learned.

I'll admit it. The break was tough for me, too. I studied for months trying to understand. One night, as I lay on my bed at one of my lowest of lows, a question popped into my mind: *Does God really exist?* I knew how sincerely I had prayed for truth when I first became involved with the group. The only possible conclusion was that there was no God, because I had prayed for truth and instead was deceived. I felt that I would be doing myself an injustice if I tried to make myself believe in God.

I was hanging on by a tiny thread of faith, not wanting to give up my belief in God, yet thinking that I was not being logical. I felt in my heart all of the pain from problems of years past, especially the deaths of my sister and brother, and how my friends had rejected me. I had thought all these pains were cured by my group but now they resurfaced. Although there seemed to be no God, I resisted—I wanted to hang on to hope.

"Help!" I cried soundlessly from the very core of my being. Instantly a presence came into my heart and removed all my pain—pain which has never since returned. I knew I would never again question the existence of my loving God. I now realize God heals hearts as easily as He makes grass grow. I pray that God will send this same healing to everyone who is suffering through the experience of leaving an abusive group.

Epilogue

Leader of Heaven's Gate Undermined Free Will

Had Marshall Applewhite changed his mind the
night before the suicides, the members of Heaven's Gate
also would have changed their minds...

During the last week of March 1997, 39 seemingly sane men and women living in a palatial home near San Diego, California committed an unthinkable act. Led by a strange, wild-eyed man named Marshall Applewhite (aka, "Bo" as in "Bo-Peep") and working in teams, they assisted one another in ritualized mass suicide. The news media treated this horrific act with astonishment and shock. They did so not merely because it was the largest mass suicide in U.S. history, but primarily because the members of the Heaven's Gate cult had appeared to be so reasonable and ordinary.[1]

I am amazed that so many in the media persisted in saying the victims of Heaven's Gate freely chose suicide simply because these cult members videotaped themselves making such remarks as, "We are all choosing of our own free will to go the next level."[2]

To fully understand, one must examine the pressures that exist in such environments before believing commonly circulated reports. It is important to know about the backgrounds and the personalities of the persons speaking on these videotapes. Many reporters and commentators simply did not recognize the classic patterns of control that existed within this group. Marshall Applewhite employed many of the same basic tools of control that are used by cults and abusive churches everywhere.

One victim's parents commented about the suicide video made by their daughter. Their child said she wanted to commit suicide and that she was so happy about the idea. The grieving parents said that in the past their daughter would always look you in the eye when she spoke to you. They observed, however, that during the farewell video she appeared to be looking around nervously while uttering what seemed to be peaceful words. Which would you believe, the words or the eyes? The parents are revealing to us something very significant in these insights. Throughout this book, I have described the patterns of control and you can now understand why we should believe the body language instead of mere words.

Below are some of the steps that Applewhite used to undermine free will. Over time these methods, when systematically used, bring individuals into an altered state of mind. This causes the subjects to be extremely vulnerable to the leader's suggestions and domination. These are the same basic tools commonly employed by destructive cults and manipulative groups.

FREE WILL WAS UNDERMINED

➤ Personalities were destroyed

➤ Human characteristics were generally viewed as negative

➤ Commonly used words were given new definitions

➤ Members were led to believe there was no reason to exist outside the group

➤ They were isolated from family members and friends

➤ Obedience was demanded even when it conflicted with conscience

➤ He created a sense of urgency for there to be total commitment

➤ Fear, guilt, and shame were instilled in the members

➤ Personal affairs were closely monitored

➤ Applewhite had the group excessively confess non-moral issues

➤ Within the group, he fostered a highly developed sense of elitism

➤ True thinkers were systematically weeded out

➤ Criticism of the leaders was not tolerated

DESTRUCTION OF PERSONALITY

Heaven's Gate members were told to overcome "all that was human about them" [3] to "have no likes or dislikes." [4]

In destructive cults and abusive discipleships, members are falsely taught to believe that they need to die completely to all of their goals, desires, or wishes. Members who accept this belief become putty in the hands of their leaders. More properly led churches teach their followers to give up only evil goals, desires, and wishes.

In Applewhite's group, "Picking or choosing certain tasks"[5] was considered an offense.

In controlling groups, members are persuaded to "be flexible and obey" whatever they are told to do. If a leader picks a task for them, for example, they are to do it. This is the definition of humility in these groups.

Family members described changes in the personalities of their loved ones who were in Heaven's Gate. They related how they changed from being kind, loving, and considerate individuals to being cold, evasive, and robot-like.

These observations are strikingly similar to what other parents and siblings have said in describing the children, sisters, and brothers they have lost to similarly abusive groups. "This was not the person I knew" is a common refrain. Others comment, "They suddenly lost interest in their lifelong goals. Their personalities changed dramatically. Their spontaneity diminished. They lost their sense of humor. They didn't look the same." When people die to all their desires, wishes, and goals, they lose precious aspects of the personalities God gave them at birth.

In Heaven's Gate, members were commanded to "relinquish" their thoughts.

In abusive church groups, you are told to "be of one mind" or "have no divisions" if you want to get to the Kingdom of God. The bottom line is: "Your thoughts are wrong and ours are right. You'd better let go of your ideas if you don't want to miss out on heaven."

Heaven's Gate taught that "Trusting my own judgment—or using my own mind"[6] was wrong.

Destructive cults and other abusive groups often employ an identical form of "anti-intellect teaching" to undermine and destroy critical thinking skills. These groups usually impress upon members that it is a sin to trust their own judgment. By contrast, it is viewed as Godly to relinquish one's opinions and replace them with those of the leaders.

These are simple tricks to gain control. If classroom instructors were to teach that it is honorable to give up personal opinions and to always accept their teachings as right, students would be quickly encouraged not to think for themselves. This same type of instruction leads members to relinquish their own perceptions and to gradually lose faith in their own abilities to judge.

Leaders of these groups might also say:

> Your mind (i.e., your intellect) is evil and knowledge will cause pride

> Your old self is keeping you from fully experiencing the new truth

> Your old concepts are dragging you down

> Looking at the circumstances from a human perspective is self-centered

These are simply more tricks to keep you from using your mind and to accept the group's will. Once you believe that you can't trust your own thoughts and feelings, you are under enormous psychological pressure to accept the group's views. Generally, most people under these conditions will comply with the group's wishes, goals, and desires.

HUMAN CHARACTERISTICS ARE ALWAYS VIEWED AS NEGATIVE

Heaven's Gate taught that "desiring attention or approval—wanting to be seen as good"... "putting myself first, wanting my own way, rebelliousness-selfishness" [7] was offensive.

It is true that it would be selfish if we always put ourselves first. Depending upon our motivation and the circumstances, though, it may not be selfish to do so. We must be free to examine these factors ourselves. If, however, we have been conditioned to accept the idea that wanting our own way is wrong, we will no longer make the choice ourselves but will always acquiesce to others.

This is a tricky way in which to control minds because members will vehemently deny that they are being manipulated. Further, since the members firmly believe that relinquishing their way is the right thing to do, they will police themselves to ensure that everyone does what the group wants. At times, members may endure painful struggles while forcing themselves to give up their own way. Eventually, those who succeed will delude themselves into believing that doing so is a great victory.

Some controlling church leaders claim that virtually all personality traits are self-centered. For example, self-confidence, focusing on self, putting personal needs before others, and any dependence on one's own abilities[8] are often viewed as self-centeredness. The leaders of these groups can assert that members are "putting personal needs before those of the group" whenever they do not want them to continue certain actions. It's an easy gimmick with which to gain mindless compliance from almost anyone.

When you read certain phrases and words used by members and leaders of abusive groups, you must understand that the words don't necessarily have the same meaning for you as they do for them. For example, "rebelliousness" to them means "doing something different than what they were advised to do." Of course, it may not be true rebelliousness in the sense that it is morally wrong. Leaders often view as rebellious those who simply do not agree with their opinions. For example, if you want to scramble your breakfast eggs when the leaders tell you to poach them, you can be considered rebellious (it's important to note that this example is not an exaggeration). When any procedure is not followed, one can be accused of rebelliousness. In more properly run churches, rebelliousness is normally described as disobedience when it pertains to moral issues.

Being "self-centered" or "selfish" within a Heaven's Gate or other destructive cult may be nothing more than taking care of a physical need. A little rest for a tired body may be seen as "selfish" when the group wants you to work on a project right away.

There are many ways to silence members without making them aware that they are being manipulated. One way is teaching that "wanting attention" is always wrong. Jesus wanted attention when he spoke and there was nothing wrong with that. Once members are accused of wanting attention and then convinced that it is sinful, they will silence themselves. It's important for you to grasp the distinction: the leader doesn't say "You cannot talk" but rather causes you, the follower, to perceive talking as wrong. This will cause you to voluntarily refrain from speaking.

REDEFINING WORDS

In the preceding paragraphs, you learned how the negative perception of human traits can cause people to change their actions. The redefining of words is also used to manipulate people into changing their behavior. Chapter Five explains how the meanings of concepts and words are commonly altered in controlling churches

(for examples, refer to the listing on pages 94 and 95.)

Heaven's Gate also used this technique of deception and control. Here are a few examples of terms they redefined for their own purposes:

➤ "Leaving the planet" meant ending one's own life

➤ Suicide was reversed to mean "saving your life"

➤ Bodies were dehumanized by calling them "containers" or "vehicles"

➤ Heaven's Gate's home was called a "space ship" or referred to as a "temple"

➤ "Relinquish" meant that members had to give up all of their own thoughts and desires as this was the only way they were going to enter the "Kingdom of God" or advance to the "next level"

NO PURPOSE OR NO REASON TO EXIST OUTSIDE THE GROUP

A Heaven's Gate female member said in her farewell video, "Maybe they're crazy for all I know, but I don't have any choice but to go for it because I've been on this planet for 31 years and there's nothing here for me." [9]

Members of abusive Bible groups are led to believe that they have no other place to go if they truly want to follow God's will. This creates within them the feeling that no reason or purpose exists outside the confines of their group. The next step is for controlling groups to cause members to believe that leaving the group is turning their backs on God's will and, conversely, staying with the group is God's will. The result is that members eventually believe their group is virtually the only hope they have of entering the Kingdom of God.

Most members who do walk away from these groups describe feeling a sense of profound failure by the mere act of leaving. They feel they were not strong enough to persevere to the end. They feel that they could "not handle it" although the truth is that it is they who are the strong ones by not relinquishing their human perspective. This important remnant of self is exactly what helped them escape the clutches of the cult.

Guilt, failure, and sadness were expressed by one Heaven's Gate member who did leave. He was sad because he felt he was not strong enough to go on to the next level. Most cult members who walk away from their groups echo the same sentiment. Eventually—if these cult members can be shown the contradictions, lies, and methods of control used on them—this sadness eventually fades.

ISOLATION FROM FAMILY MEMBERS OR FRIENDS

One of Applewhite's members told his mother that "having contact with his family would hinder the group's goals" and "tug at their vibrational level."[10]

Heaven's Gate member John Craig was visited by his daughter but was not allowed to sit with her or spend much time alone with her. Craig's daughter commented in television interviews that her father couldn't even walk her to the car when she was leaving. She described her father as one who would have never acquiesced to this type of control in his previous life.

When groups teach that contacts with family will hinder the goal of reaching salvation, one should anticipate the severing of contacts. If a group teaches that the vibrational level of those not "on the path" will bring them down, it is normal to see members cutting off relationships with their families.

Many former members of destructive church groups say that their relationships were severely restricted, although many still talked to family members. The frequency of contacts, however, decreased greatly and conversations were not as spontaneous because of the subtle and sometimes overt teachings about their blood families. The groups also tied up so much of their time that when they do go home, visits had to be short.

Members usually feel that they can't wait to get back with the group when they are with family or outsiders because they view most everyone outside as doomed, dammed, unsaved, uncommitted, or perhaps not Christian at all. This puts an incredible psychological wedge between members and their families.

When members do consider visiting their families, there is often a discussion regarding whether they should even go. "What will they accomplish by going home?" they are asked. "Will there be any purpose?" These questions are designed to make members feel as though they would be wasting their time by being with family or old friends. Many members feel there is no purpose in going home unless they plan to bring acquaintances into the group. Members who do visit home may be doing so just in order to fulfill the command to "honor thy mother and father" and to avoid having the appearance of being a cult.

OBEDIENCE IS DEMANDED IN AREAS NOT DEALING WITH MORAL ISSUES

Hohertz, a member of Heaven's Gate said, "For preparation, they'd follow the recipe exactly, no deviation."[11] Breaking any instruction or procedure knowingly"[12] was considered a major offense in Heaven's Gate.

In destructive cults or abusive groups, not following the leader's advice or opinions is commonly considered sinful. Obedience is often demanded even when it conflicts with one's conscience (I am speaking here about areas of opinion and not Biblical mandates, of course). Not taking advice often results in the members being told that they are "hard-hearted," "disobedient," and/or "rebellious."

URGENCY—TOTAL AND IMMEDIATE COMMITMENT

"...You can follow us but you can't stay here and follow us. You would have to follow quickly by also leaving this world..."[13]

Most cults create a sense of urgency when explaining why they need such a quick commitment. This urgency helps to separate recruits from their friends and family. There is the threat that commitment must be right now or members will risk missing enlightenment or even heaven. Urgency combined with the insistence upon total commitment is a powerful motivating factor that helps create instant decisions for members to join and participate fully in the group's activities.

INSTILLING FEAR, GUILT, AND SHAME

Heavens' Gate members were deeply impressed with the idea that if they left, it would prove that the members didn't "have the strength to remain"[14] to continue to the highest thing that they could do to help mankind.

This idea repeated in the group was a guilt trap designed to keep members in the group. It helped assure that if members did walk away that they would feel tremendous guilt, shame, and sadness. Much of the guilt came from believing they had turned their backs on God by leaving.

There were other rigorous rules in Heaven's Gate (e.g., sleeping only four hours at a time and overcoming within themselves "all that was human"[15]). The standards were impossible to accomplish, making it so difficult to follow the rules that the members were certain to fail. Thus, members were kept in a constant state of guilt and shame and were much easier to manipulate.

MONITORING OF PERSONAL AFFAIRS

In Applewhite's group, "taking any action without using... [your] check partner"[16] was an offense. "It was like school. If you were observed doing something that was not procedure, somebody would let you know that doing it this way is not procedure."[17]

Members of cults and abusive groups watch each other closely— an act they describe as "accountability." Members are encouraged to hold everyone "accountable" in their group. It isn't limited to meaning being responsible (it goes way beyond that) and it does not mean just keeping people from immoral acts. It *does* mean changing people's actions if they are different from what they think they should be doing. In abusive groups, accountability means monitoring each other's activities and pressuring fellow members into conformity.

EXCESSIVE CONFESSION
CONCERNING NON-MORAL ISSUES

In Applewhite's group, it was wrong not to expose an offense the same day it was committed.[18] It was wrong to "do an act on 'the sly.'"[19]

In abusive groups, there is also an obsession with confessions. Confession in Heaven's Gate did not mean just confessing immoral acts but also if members broke "any instruction or procedure"[20] or refused advice.

In abusive groups, it is also wrong, indeed sinful, to do anything secretively even though the actions may not be wrong. Your entire life must be open—especially through confessions—or you will be accused of being secretive.

ELITISM

Applewhite's followers felt that they were being led by God more closely than was anyone else.

Destructive cults and abusive Bible groups believe that their understanding of God is superior to all others.

WEEDING OUT THINKERS

At one point, Applewhite offered $1,000 to anyone who wanted (dared?) to leave.

To leave was a sign that one was not strong enough to stay. To accept the money would mean a loss of respect compounded by the belief that it signified turning one's back on God. Why would Heaven's Gate want people to leave? In destructive cults, leaders encourage members to leave if they don't believe they are totally committed. This way, they won't infect anyone else with doubt. If abusive groups are unsuccessful in ridding themselves of "undesirables," they often rebuke them and intimidate them until they leave "on their own." If this doesn't work, controlling churches may excommunicate members who challenge and question the leaders.

Controlling churches and cults don't want people around who think for themselves or are critical of the groups or their leaders. Whereas, a truly loving church openly accepts the weak and the strong, the questioning, and those who challenge.

NO CRITICISM OF THE LEADERS

One of the rules at Heaven's Gate was that there be no "Criticizing or finding fault with [the]... classmates or teachers."[21] In Applewhite's group, this was considered a serious offense.

If you criticize the leaders in abusive churches behind their backs, other members will tell you that you need to discuss it only with the leader. You will be told that you are sin if you are critical about the leader to anyone but that head person.

If you do go to the leader, however, it often results in your being called down for being in some kind of sin. It is a great control tactic for any leader to convince the entire group that it is always wrong to criticize the teacher or your group. What a con game! Beware of anyone that uses these tactics.

Keeping pressure continually on the victim causes the person to stay in an impressionable state of mind or altered state. The combination of pressure and environment usually keeps the victim from thinking objectively. In this type of controlled environment, most of the members will blindly obey whatever the leader suggests—even if it means committing suicide.

Endnotes for the Epilogue

[1] *U.S. News & World Report*, April 7, 1977, pp. 26-35.

[2] Ibid. p34.

[3] *Newsweek*, April 14, 1997, "The Last Insider's Untold Story," Mark Miller, p32.

[4] Ibid. (the same page as in the preceding note).

[5] Ibid. (the same page as in the preceding note).

[6] *Newsweek*, April 14, 1997, "www.massuicide.com," Mark Miller, p32.

[7] *Newsweek*, April 14, 1997, "The Last Insider's Untold Story," Mark Miller, p32.

[8] Blackaby, Henry T. and King, Claude V. *Experiencing God— Knowing and Doing the Will of God.* (Life Way Press, Nashville, TN. 1993), p. 27.

[9] *The Chattanooga Times*, Friday, March 28, 1997, "Cultists Expected to Board UFO," Scott Lindlaw, pA4.

[10] *U.S. News & World Report*, April 7, 1997, "The Eternal Quest for a New Age," Erica Goode, p34.

[11] *The Chattanooga Times*, March 28, 1997, "Contradictions Abound in Wake of Cult Deaths," Nichell Lock, pA4.

[12] *Newsweek*, April 14, 1997, "The Last Insider's Untold Story," Mark Miller, p32.

[13] *Chattanooga Free Press*, March 28, 1997, "Cultists' Suicides Took Over 3 Days," pA2.

[14] *Newsweek*, April 14, 1997, "The Last Insider's Untold Story," Mark Miller, p32.

[15] Ibid. (the same page as in the preceding note).

[16] Ibid. (the same page as in the preceding note).

[17] Ibid. p37.

[18] *Newsweek*, April 14, 1997, "The Last Insider's Untold Story," Mark Miller, p32.

[19] Ibid. (the same page as in the preceding note).

[20] Ibid. (the same page as in the preceding note).

[21] Ibid. (the same page as in the preceding note).

Appendix 1

REFERENCES AND RESOURCES

Each discipleship group is somewhat unique. If your group stayed within traditional Christianity but included elements of control, here are some books that can be helpful:

The Subtle Power of Spiritual Abuse
David Johnson & Jeff VanVondersen (Bethany House Publishers, 1991)
"Recognizing and escaping spiritual manipulation and false Spiritual Authority within the church." (Front cover statement)

When God's People Lets You Down
Jeff Van Vondersen (Bethany House Publishers, 1995)

Churches That Abuse
Ronald Enroth (Zondervan Publications, 1992)
Numerous true stories from ex-members of controlling churches.

Recovering From Churches That Abuse
Ronald Enroth (Zondervan Publications, 1994)
Helps victims of spiritual abuse and their families cope with reentry into the Christian mainstream.

Damaged Disciples
Ron & Vicki Burk (Zondervan Publications, 1992)
The story of this couple's involvement with shepherding (a form of discipling). Their painful experiences are typical of those suffered by most in these movements. Reading can be healing for many.

The Boston Movement
Carol Giambalvo & Herbert L. Rosedale, Eds. (American Family Foundation, 1996)
Critical perspectives on the International Churches of Christ.

Unholy Devotion
Harold L. Bussell (Zondervan Publications, 1983)
Excellent, easy to read. Explains overemphasis of subjective religious experiences, justification of actions, acceptance of religious leaders based on their ability to sway emotions, and insights into other deceptions to which Christians may fall prey.

Scripture Twisting: 20 Ways the Cults Misread the Bible
James Sire (InterVarsity Press, 1980)
Discusses common errors made in using the Bible.

Healing Spiritual Abuse: How to Break Free from Bad Church Experiences
Ken Blue (InterVarsity Press 1993)

Regaining Faith After Boston
Sharen Meyers (Star Bible Publications 1997) 1-800-433-7507

Wisdom Hunter
Randall Arthur (Questar Publishers, Inc. 1991) (novel)

The Shunning
Randall Arthur (Questar Publishers, Inc. 1991) (novel)

1984
George Orwell (Open University Press 1945) (novel)

FAITH MOVEMENT & PROSPERITY DOCTRINE

If your teachers claimed that any of the following were authorities or sources of information, they were probably promoting the "positive faith movement doctrine": Kenneth Copeland, Kenneth E. Hagin, Oral Roberts, Benny Hinn, John Avanzini, Essek William Kenyon, Frederick K. C. Price, Robert Tilton, Marilyn Hickey, Paul Yonggi Cho (David Cho), Charles Capps, Jerry Savelle, Morris Cerullo, Paul Crouch—unfortunately there are a host of others too numerous to mention.

If your group admired or promoted in a positive light the teachings of the Faith Movement or any kind of "prosperity doctrine," you will find the following books helpful:

Counterfeit Revival
Hank Haegraaff (Word Publishing, 1977)

Christianity in Crisis
Hank Haegraaff (Harvest House Publishers, 1993)

A Different Gospel
D. R. McConnell (Hendrickson Publishers, 1988)

The Many Faces of Deception
Florence Bulle (Bethany House Publishers, 1989)

PSYCHOLOGICAL MANIPULATION

These books may help you understand the psychological manipulation you have experienced:

Cultic Studies Journal - Women Under the Influence
Volume 14. No. 1, 1997 (American Family Foundation, P O Box 2265, Bonita Springs, FL 34133)

Cults In Our Midst
Dr. Margaret Thaler Singer with Janja Lalich (Jossey-Bass, 1995)

Recovery From Cults: Help for Victims of Psychological and Spiritual Abuse
Edited by Michael D. Langone (W. W. Norton and Company, 1993)

Combatting Cult Mind Control
Steven Hassan (Park Street Press, 1988)

Influence
Robert B. Cialdini, Ph.D. (Quill, 1984)
Explains the psychology of manipulation.

Toxic Faith
Stephen Arterburn & Jack Felton (Oliver Nelson Publication, 1991)

OTHER RESOURCES

Wellspring Retreat and Resource Center
P O Box 67
Albany, Ohio 45710
614/698-6277
Rehabilitation and counseling for persons emerging from total-ist/cult experiences. This is the only "live-in" facility for treatment; specializes particularly in destructive Bible groups.

ORGANIZATIONS THAT COLLECT INFORMATION AND DO RESEARCH ON DESTRUCTIVE GROUPS

Cult Resource Center
Ecumenical Ministries of Oregon
0245 S.W. Bancroft St. S.
Portland, OR 97201
Tel: (503) 221-1054, 221-9924

American Family Foundation
P O Box 2265
Bonita Springs FL 33959
(941) 514-3081

International Cult Education Program
P O Box 1232, Gracie Station
New York, NY 10028
(941) 514-3081

Cult Clinic Jewish Board of Family & Children Services
120 West 57th Street
New York, NY 10019
(212) 632-4640

Personal Freedom Outreach
P O Box 26062
St. Louis, MO 63136
(314) 388-2648

ESPECIALLY FOR FORMER CATHOLICS

Many Bible groups have a tendency to degrade other churches, especially the Roman Catholic Church. If this has happened to you, here are some books and audio tapes that might help:

Jesus, Peter & The Keys
Scott Butler, Norman Dahlgreen, David Hess (order from Queenship Publishing 1-800-647-9882)

What Catholics Really Believe: Setting the Record Straight
Karl Keating (Servant Publications, 1992)

Catholicism and Fundamentalism
Karl Keating (Ignatius Press, 1988)

Surprised by Truth
Patrick Madrid, Editor

These books can be ordered from:

Catholic Answers	Catholic Apologetics Intl.
P O Box 17490	P O Box 2247
San Diego, CA 92177-9821	Columbia, MD 21045
(619) 541-1131	(800) 531-6393

The Vatican's Pastoral Letter "Challenge of New Religious Movements, Sects, or Cults" (May 7, 1986), outlines and warns against the widespread problem of new religious groups both within and outside the Catholic Church. The groups described in this Pastoral Letter use manipulative techniques to persuade and control members. They sometimes use Catholic orthodoxy to recruit new members, exploiting the providential imprudence of youth and pastoral-parental naivete.

Scholars listed in this section of the appendix are recommended because of expertise in their particular field of doctrine, history, or Scripture and not necessarily because they have knowledge of manipulative groups within the Catholic Church. I have personally warned some scholars about groups using destructive methods of control within the Catholic Church. Because these manipulative groups taught correct church doctrine, some Catholic scholars have defended them. These scholars sometimes have recommended that Catholics join one of these manipulative groups. Even orthodox Catholic scholars can be naive concerning the methods of control used to undermine the free will. This only proves that you must study all sides of the situation before you become involved with any group that demands an intense commitment.

Recommended reading: *Parents' Guide to Opus Dei*
                                          Sicut Dixit Press
                                          305 Madison Avenue; Suite 1146
                                          New York, New York 10165

CANADIAN RESOURCES

Info Cult
5655 Park Ave., Suite 208
Montreal, Quebec
H2V 4H2
(514) 274-2333

Manitoba Cult Awareness Center
Box 31, Norwood Grove
Winnipeg, Manitoba
R2H 3B8
(204) 488-0741

Crossroads Family Centre
P O Box 5100
Burlington, Ontario
L7R 4M2
(905) 335-7100

FAMILY INTERVENTION
AND CONSULTATION SERVICES

For consultation concerning freeing victims of controlling churches, accountability groups, and similar cult-like organizations, contact:
Control Techniques, Inc.
Telephone: (423) 698-9343

Your comments and suggestions are welcome!

What information could we add or delete to make this book better for your situation? Although we cannot reply to all of your letters, all constructive suggestions and sincere requests will be considered in future revisions of *Twisted Scriptures*.

Please write! Tell us how you have used this book, and what success resulted from sharing *Twisted Scriptures*. We hope to start a newsletter based on your comments and stories so that other families can be helped. Address your comments to:

Twisted Scriptures Comments
P O Box 8021
Chattanooga, TN 37414-8021

Appendix 2

SHEPHERDING/DISCIPLESHIP/ACCOUNTABILITY GROUPS: A BRIEF HISTORY

There are differences of opinion regarding the origin of the shepherding/discipleship movement. Tom Yoder gives his first-hand knowledge of the movement.

It seems to have sprung up simultaneously in several groups in the United States and South America during the late 1960s and early 1970s. The best known of the early groups combined beliefs and practices from several sources. One source in the late 1960s was an inner city Episcopalian church in Houston, Texas, that used a form of shepherding in caring for people with special needs who were brought into church members' homes. Later, that shepherding system expanded to include most of the members of the church's charismatic community. During this same time, former leaders of the aberrant 1950s Pentecostal "Latter Rain Movement" taught that the proper church governmental model was the "Five-Fold Ministries." The phrase refers to the presumed hierarchical ordering of the apostles, prophets, evangelists, pastors, and teachers found in Ephesians 4:11-13. This group taught that the ultimate purpose of these ministries was to unite all believers, and to acquire a divine nature. The Five-Fold Ministries doctrine also held that there are living apostles who are to rule the church and eventually the world.

In 1966, former Communist Douglas Hyde wrote an influential book, Dedication and Leadership: Learning From the Communists, in which he urged Christians to adopt Communist cell group methods to recruit, inspire, and train new members. Some of the shepherding leaders adopted Hyde's book as a guide. Although not a misguided loyalty, it was a misguided methodology. Those adopting communistic methods did not understand their inherent evil.

The most prominent shepherding leaders were Bob Mumford, Derek Prince, Don Basham, Charles Simpson, and Ern Baxter who formed the Christian Growth Ministries in Fort Lauderdale, Florida, along with others not mentioned here. Steve Clark and Ralph Martin, leaders of an early charismatic covenant community in Ann Arbor, Michigan, called The Word of God, introduced two of these men to the specific goals and methods of shepherding around 1972. Together with Kevin Ranaghan and Paul DeCelles (leaders of the covenant community called People of Praise in South Bend, Indiana), and Larry Christenson and Don Pfotenauer, these men formed the somewhat secretive "General Council," which directed the main elements of the shepherding movement from 1974 through the early 1980s. The Council sponsored the National Men's Shepherding Conferences in the mid to late 1970s. The men of this General Council controlled the major charismatic media of the day: New Covenant, Pastoral Renewal, New Wine, and Servant Publications. They attempted to influence Cardinal Suenens and other bishops in the Pope's efforts to bring the Catholic Charismatic Renewal into the heart of the Catholic Church. That is, the Council attempted to keep control of the Charismatic Renewal out of the hands of the Catholic hierarchy. They attempted to form a single network of eighty or more Catholic charismatic covenant communities under their control consisting of those connected to the Word of God, the People of Praise, and the Gulf Coast Fellowship. It should be noted that many Shepherding groups never came under the umbrella of these men.

In 1974, several years after discipleship began, Juan Carlos Ortiz came to the United States from Argentina. With the help of the late Jamie Buckingham, Ortiz wrote Call to Discipleship in 1975. This was one of the first books that widely spread this particular type of discipleship in the charismatic movement.[1]

Discipleship programs became popular because the culture had become permissive and Christians wanted to remove themselves from such ungodliness. Many were looking to dedicate their lives to God in a closer way. Discipleship leaders in general promised they had "the way" to total commitment to Jesus. Their answer to helping Christians grow fully was found in their improper concept of being "more accountable." This was the shepherding error again, with just a few differences.

The result of their corrupted teaching soon showed a dark side. It was not because of imperfect men that this corruption grew, as is generally blamed, but mainly due to the non-Biblical teaching of what "being more accountable" supposedly meant. In practice, this teaching of "more accountability" frequently meant suppression of freedom of expression and action, and pressure to give up one's own convictions when these differed from those of the leaders. This in turn created mental anguish and moral dilemmas for many disciples. A Christian magazine reported in 1990 that:

> *..the movement quickly became elitist, exclusive. Operating on the basis that everyone needs to be accountable to a pastor, "sheep" were assigned to various "shepherds"—many of whom were young, immature, sometimes arrogant and often proud of their new authority. Havoc followed and horror stories abounded. Families were sometimes forced to relocate from one city to another at the whim of a shepherd. Churches split... Mumford and Simpson in particular took the heat from the critics, who charged they dominated those under them... Critics cited numerous examples of "shepherds" who required their "sheep" to ask their permission before they dated, changed jobs, or made major decisions.[2]*

The shepherding leaders responded that they were teaching a renewed Biblical understanding of God's government: delegated authority, and covenant loyalty. But soon other national leaders opposed them. During a *700 Club* broadcast, Pat Robertson called Mumford, Simpson, and Prince *"false teachers,"* and compared the discipleship movement to the cult led by Jim Jones, saying the only difference was *"the shepherds had not yet served Kool-Aid,"*[3] a reference to the mass suicide of more than 900 members of Jones's group who drank poisoned Kool-Aid on his command. Robertson banned the shepherding leaders from appearing on any of his radio or television outlets.

The conflict over the shepherding movement seemed to reach a turning point in 1990, when a Christian magazine quoted on their cover:

> *Discipleship was wrong. I repent. I ask forgiveness... discipleship resulted in unhealthy submission resulting in perverse and un-Biblical obedience to human leaders... for the injury and shame, I repent with sorrow and ask for your forgiveness.[4]*

This admission of unhealthy submission and non-Biblical obedience to human leaders shook the foundation of discipleship in America. Many leaders in this movement followed and repented of the abuses. *"All the men except Simpson and Baxter 'released' their disciples to find their own way."*[5] No longer were these disciples to be in complete obedience to men who were in spiritual oversight of their souls. Since that time, discipleship programs have been dropped by literally hundreds of thousands of people. The movement has continued to shrink as the abuses and the non-Scriptural base of some of the teachings are exposed. But it spawned eggs that even today continue to hatch.

In 1991, The *Word of God* Community in Ann Arbor, Michigan released their people from those in spiritual oversight. The leaders of this community recognized that many members were being emotionally harmed by their submission in this movement. These leaders asked Reverend James LeBar, a specialist on cults, to organize a seminar along with psychologist Margaret Singer and several other experts. During this seminar, the nature of the abuses was explained to the entire membership. The program was a great success in healing this abused flock.

The problems in the *Word of God* group, according to Tom Yoder, an eight-year former member, were:

...militancy, control, elitism, thought control, hierarchicalism, total-itarianism, black and white interpretations, unnecessary shame, pressure to perform, loss of identity, loss of personal dignity, loss of freedom-spirit and soul, suppression of the "created" self, dependency, loss of personal initiative, turning away and terminating membership of those thought undesirable, "arranged" marriages, extreme negative world view, extreme sex role differentiation, extreme loyalty, extreme secrecy, and hidden agendas.[6]

The far-reaching nature of the problems identified by Yoder makes it look like this group of Christians were pretty "far out." Yet in actuality, the former members repeated many times how subtle it was. That is one reason they stayed for so long in this discipleship program.

The discipleship movement in the mainline *Church of Christ* caused a church split. We will examine some of the problems that caused the discipleship program to be expunged. An in-depth study of this group was done by Flavil Yeakley, who summarized his findings in the book, *The Discipling Dilemma*.

Yeakley was asked to investigate charges that the discipleship program in this group was causing abnormal personality changes within committed members. Yeakley was at the time director of the *Church Growth Institute at Abilene Christian University*. He used the Myers-Briggs Type Indicator (MBTI), one of the leading tests for ascertaining personality traits. Yeakley measured the distribution of personality types in both new and longer-term members within the discipleship group, and then compared these results to a similar group from the *Church of Christ* mentioned above.

People are born with a specific type of temperament, which includes such factors as whether they are sensing or intuitive, extroverted or introverted, thinking or feeling, judging or perceiving. Although people grow mentally and mature emotionally, this personality remains the same. Even Christian conversion does not change the personality type.

Jesus' method of discipling did not change the personality of His disciples, either. His Apostles, after they were fully trained by Him and carried on their mission after Him, were indeed like Jesus in many ways. Yet they were clearly different in other ways. There were obvious differences between Peter and John and the other Apostles. Peter was apparently the most extroverted of the Apostles during his time with Jesus, and he continued to be that way afterward. The others were apparently more introverted, and continued to be so. The Apostle Paul was no less outgoing and analytical after he was a Christian; he just used his personality for different ends.

Yeakley therefore expected to find a distribution of personality types in each of the groups that was similar to that found in society in general. He was surprised to find that in the discipleship group, longer-term members showed a high level of personality change with a clear pattern of convergence toward a single type of personality. This pattern was not found among the newer group members or among the members of the mainline church.

Yeakley writes...

> Results of the psychological type study among members of the Boston Church of Christ clearly indicate that something is causing their members to deny their true type and try to become copies of someone else... There is something in the discipling methodology producing this unhealthy pattern. Whatever it is, it should be changed... They cannot deny that the psychological type scores are changing and converging in a single type. They cannot deny that the members are being made over after the image of the group norm. They cannot deny that the discipling methodology is producing this effect.[7]

... and he concluded...

You need to be able to reach and restore the many dropouts who will be harmed psychologically and spiritually by their participation in this movement. The time when these problems are most likely to develop is when the young people in this movement reach mid-life. Falsification of psychological type (trying to change your personality to imitate that of another) produces a serious mid-life crisis. There will be major burn-out problems, serious depression, and a variety of other psychological and spiritual problems to resolve.[8]

Yeakley extensively interviewed members of an abusive group led by Kip McKean (founder of the *International Church of Christ*). This statement proved to be almost prophetic as, in the years that followed, counselors in virtually every city where this radical movement exists were, and are now flooded with clients who are the psychological, emotional, and spiritual victims of this movement.

In his own assessment of spiritual leaders, Jesus Christ gave this standard...

By their fruits you will know them (Matt. 7:16).

And now, after many years, the fruits of broken hearts, damaged psyches, and disillusioned spirits are becoming more and more evident. Several former leaders echo these same complaints and observations...

Pastors like myself have spent large amounts of time over the last 15 years picking up the pieces of broken lives that resulted from distortion of truth by extreme teachings and destructive applications on discipleship, authority, and shepherding.[9]

Victims of this movement are usually born-again Christians and are fundamentalist and evangelical in their orientation. The errors are covered in many different terms, such as delegated authority, covering, unquestioned submission, covenant, commitment to a fellowship, etc. ... Terms change from time to time. Submission may be called "commitment," "covenant relationship," or "divine order" in church government. Often terms aren't used at all, but it is the actions that tell you what is going on.[10]

Endnotes for Appendix 2

[1] Excerpted from an unpublished paper: "The Shepherding / Discipleship Movement" by Tom Yoder (a former member of People of Praise).

[2] Buckingham, Jamie. "The End of the Discipleship Era." *Ministries Today*, January-February 1990, p. 46.

[3] Ibid.

[4] Ibid.

[5] Ibid.

[6] Yoder, Tom. "Leaving the Promised Land" - unpublished article by this eight-year former member of the Word of God Community, Ann Arbor, Michigan.

[7] Yeakley, Falvil R. Jr. *The Discipling Dilemma* (2nd Printing 1988) (Gospel Advocate Co., Nashville, TN.) p. 45.

[8] Ibid.

[9] Buckingham, Jamie. "The End of the Discipleship Era." *Ministries Today*, January-February 1990, p 48.

[10] Trusty, Gilbert. *Recovering from Abusive Authority*. (Conference Evangelical Ministries to New Religions in Philadelphia, PA. Sept. 14, 1994).

Appendix 3

A SUMMARY OF ABUSES

Remembering and recognizing the abuses is extremely important, because there may be days when you think you've made a mistake by leaving your (destructive) group. Sometimes this can cause *floating, spacing out,* or *dissociation* (describing an altered state of conciousness). This can happen especially when you are depressed or lonely. Bringing yourself out of this lapse and back into objective and critical thinking is partly the goal of this next exercise.

Muriel Mooney, Peter Clark, and Jo Noetzel left an abusive shepherding/discipleship community inside a mainline church. Together, they came up with a list of abuses perpetrated by the group. I've enlarged slightly on their list.[1] For each of these abuses, ask yourself questions such as: Was this applicable for my group? Did I always think or act this way before I became involved with the group? In respect to this point, what did our group teach that other churches don't normally stress?

Start a journal as you study the following list of abuses. Circle the ones that apply to your former group. A few weeks later, go over the list and see how many new examples you have recalled. Use a different color pen so you can take note of how many more abuses you can recall compared to the first time you reflected. Do this several times throughout the year and make additional entries for abuses not listed. Whenever you start to feel confused about having left the controlled environment, pick up your journal and start reading to focus yourself.

In your group, did you see that...

➤ Leadership was excessively esteemed?

➤ Leaders were not accountable to members?

➤ You were led to think that good solid teaching outside this group was rare?

➤ Doctrine often focused solely on behavior to the exclusion of theology?

➤ The group wanted you to give as much time as you possibly could to their activities?

➤ Everyone was expected to act together?

273

- ➤ There was a legalistic emphasis on external behaviors which resulted in loss of focus on Jesus?

- ➤ There was an excessive emphasis on commitment to the group? "Our commitment is a full commitment, a commitment that involves our whole lives."

- ➤ Guilt was an important emotional lever for producing compliance and conformity?

- ➤ Appropriate feelings were denigrated at times?

- ➤ Members were taught not to feel for themselves or their own needs but to think of the group and not complain?

- ➤ Denial and repression of feelings encouraged mood-altering addictive behaviors?

- ➤ There was a feeling that there wasn't any security outside the group?

- ➤ "Confidentiality" was used to isolate members from each other?

- ➤ There was control over channels of communication and information, and that some teachings and/or policies were kept secret?

- ➤ Withholding of information sometimes impaired sound judgments?

- ➤ Many were led to believe that the church represents all that was good and necessary to meet our needs?

- ➤ Your leaders had a corner on wisdom?

- ➤ Members needed extensive teaching to be led to Christian maturity?

- ➤ Members needed extensive accountability to other men to be led to Christian maturity?

- ➤ You were taught to be very concerned about your commitment to each other?

- ➤ Members were constantly asked to subordinate their own experiences to the group's teachings, mission, and expectations?

- ➤ Former life experiences and lessons were less valuable than what you learned in the group?

- ➤ At times, there was enormous pressure to conform in areas of non-moral issues?

- ➤ Some members' identities/personalities were reshaped in the process of discipling: dress changed, voice changed, vocabulary changed, appearance changed, and objectivity decreased?

- ➢ Women were taught to have a gentle and quiet spirit in order to keep them from asking questions or becoming leaders?
- ➢ Criticism, analytical thinking, free exchange of opinion, and an opportunity to verify facts were sometimes denied?
- ➢ Some members regressed to child-like dependency?
- ➢ Group-will often took precedence over an individual's will for the sake of unity?
- ➢ Individuality was perceived to be bad, conformity and uniformity as good?
- ➢ Unity depended on submission?
- ➢ Leaders were responsible for directing the body, leading it forward in unity; the rest were expected to submit to their direction?
- ➢ God's way was very narrow and specific (more so than in the Bible), so that it often seemed that there was only one way to do anything?
- ➢ A wrong choice could mean leaving God's protection?
- ➢ You were to ignore your inner self and instead trust authority?
- ➢ "Gatherings are a matter of commitment; we're not simply free to decide"?
- ➢ Attendance at all community gatherings usually took precedence over visiting families or friends?
- ➢ Members were expected to renounce good or neutral values simply because they held them prior to becoming group members?
- ➢ Your group provided a "new family" which became the focus of relationships previously sustained by your natural family?
- ➢ There were weddings in which the group was more involved than the couples' own families?
- ➢ Teachings may have encouraged a pessimistic world view at variance with Christian hope?
- ➢ Your own reality testing was diminished by relying largely on your leaders for their opinions?
- ➢ A discipler sometimes assumed the power to decide whether a member had a valid reason for not sticking to a commitment?
- ➢ Leaders had unilateral power to decide who could be asked to leave?
- ➢ Members were led to believe that without intense accountability from another person, they could not grow as fast?
- ➢ "Something bad" might happen if you left the group?

➤ Members who wanted to leave were told: "Each one of you, individually, is leaving the Community that you belong [to]... Each one of you, individually, is dropping the... relationship you have with the church you belong [to] and with the other brothers and sisters who are in that church... you will be leaving a... relationship"?

➤ Jargon or clichés were used to dismiss your legitimate concerns?

➤ Calling people into "accountability" was often a euphemism for controlling and meddling?

➤ Words were redefined, amplified, or given new meanings?

➤ Disciplers were not just persons "coming alongside" for guidance but became instruments for coercing conformity?

➤ Members were often told they were "working on something" or "struggling" because leaders didn't think they were measuring up?

➤ Disciplers often developed pride and arrogance?

➤ The group believed that the way to live a good Christian life was to get discipled; almost as if the leaders, teachings, structure, and committed relationships could save us?

➤ Often carrying out certain agreed-to actions became a sign of one's commitment?

➤ The group environment (shaped by legalism) bred a critical, judgmental spirit?

➤ Members used each other, expecting each other to drop all prior commitments and reschedule to help out a brother or sister in various ways?

➤ It was sometimes easier to say yes than deal with the guilt if one said no?

➤ Discipling was elevated to a place of primacy equal to our baptismal or marriage vows?

➤ There was a belief that one should be in a discipling relationship for his or her whole life?

➤ There was sometimes concealment of, or coloration of, the truth about why members left or were asked to leave?

➤ There was a selective recruitment process–leaders wanted only people who were willing to be totally dedicated to the program leaders?

➤ Leaders overwhelmed newcomers with love, acceptance, and lots of attention at the onset?

➤ Teachings used *layers of truth*, revealing existing policies a step at a time?

➤ There was a certain order of learning the group's teachings? (For example, one should experience the care of a discipler before learning about commitment to the discipler.)

➤ Many members felt pressure to reach unrealistic standards of behavior?

➤ Your group had odd traditions, such as refraining from giving presents at Christmas?

➤ There was little respect for diversity?

➤ Certain kinds of deception were legitimized? (For example, *Word of God* had front groups such as UCO, MCA, Men's Breakfast, Delta Chi Rho; when an event was advertised, they often didn't show *Word of God* as the sponsor.)

➤ Members were taught that people outside cannot understand what we believe, and it is right not to disclose this information?

➤ Those who wanted to leave had difficulty in moving out of the group?

➤ Members' self-worth and hope for salvation were tied to staying in the group?

➤ There were often subtle messages like: Are you going to leave after all we have done for you?

➤ *Dying to self* was exaggerated into becoming over-responsible for others and under-responsibile for oneself?

➤ Teachings about selflessness reinforced the idea of an exaggerated call to sacrificial service?

➤ Your group stressed looking for opportunities to lay down your life?

➤ Healthy relationships (with friends in the group) were not to be expected to continue once you left?

➤ Members were encouraged to make smug remarks about those who left?

➤ Members were taught to interpret the Golden Rule "Love thy neighbor, forget thyself" instead of *loving your neighbor AS yourself*?

➤ Legitimate goals and dreams of members were often reshaped?

➤ Assertive women often were turned into doormats?

➤ The importance of unity was emphasized, instead of discovering the value of one's uniqueness?

➤ The prevailing attitude was that objections and questions from members stemmed not from reasoned and fairly objective analysis but rather from the person's spiritual or emotional problems?

➤ There was extreme teaching on subordination, obedience, submission instead of Matt. 20:25-28, Acts 11:1-4, or Gal. 2:14-21?

➤ The tendency to listen, believe, and obey resulted in an atrophy of critical and analytical thinking skills?

➤ Leadership fostered a sense of urgency in order to gain cooperation?

➤ Dissenting was always bad?

➤ Group policy of extreme submission often produced oppression of women?

➤ The group's ideal of Christian womanhood promoted dependency?

➤ An overemphasis on subordination of women in order to produce a quiet, gentle spirit contributed to passivity, confusion, repressed anger, depression, and at times compulsive behavior on the part of female members?

➤ In your group, women were not seen as men's peers?

➤ Motherhood and homemaking were so highly praised as to give the impression that (for females) other interests were far inferior?

➤ Women who expressed or shared difficulties in their marriages were usually advised to submit, love, serve, and respect their husbands more?

➤ Members were rarely advised to seek professional counsel?

➤ It was usually decided that the one who needed to change was the woman instead of the man in order to put the marriage back on track?

➤ Men were encouraged to "have more distance" from their emotions or not to respond to them?

➤ The value of feelings and emotions was often disdained when these conflicted with the leaders' point of view?

➤ The underlying concept was that emotions are not a reliable guide to our actions, even when they are valid?

➤ Making a choice other than the one recommended by leaders was usually thought unwise or rebellious?

➤ Husbands were given an all-encompassing responsibility for their households–directing wives in all areas at all times—not just when problems arose?

➤ Sometimes mistrust was fostered in marriages as the husbands became more trusting of the disciplers?

➤ Some fathers were told to be "uncompromising" with children without regard to sensitivity for the children?

➤ This uncompromising attitude often led to emotional distance and unavailability of fathers?

➤ Single men were called on to give many hours of service?

➤ The group reduced marriage to merely a functional relationship?

➤ Friendships between men and women were often discouraged?

➤ Dating and courtship were highly controlled?

➤ Most members believed they were only to date/marry other members?

➤ Disciplers demanded so much time that little was left to pursue old friendships outside the group?

➤ Some members were disillusioned because they expected as a participant in discipleship that life should go better?

➤ Many experienced disappointment and anger because compliance and faithfulness to the system went unrewarded?

➤ Many who once defended and promoted controlling leaders now feel that their integrity was compromised?

➤ There was a general mistrust of others outside the group?

➤ There was a general loss of personal privacy?

If you don't understand how any one of these is detrimental, be sure to talk with an objective person to gain some perspective, otherwise you may miss some essential points.

Endnote for Appendix 3

[1]   Unpublished paper by Muriel Mooney, Peter Clark, and Jo Noetzel.

Endnotes

Chapter 2

[1] Buckingham, Jamie. "The End of the Discipleship Era." (*Ministries Today.* January-February 1990) p. 46.

[2] Ibid. pp. 46, 48.

[3] Ibid. p. 46.

[4] Ibid. pp. 46-48.

[5] Trusty, Gilbert. *Recovering from Abusive Authority.* (Conference Evangelical Ministries to New Religions in Philadelphia, PA. Sept. 14, 1994).

[6] Ibid.

[7] Hanegraaff, Hank. *Christianity in Crisis.* (Harvest House Publishers, Eugene, WA. 1993) Back cover.

Chapter 3

[8] Trusty, Gilbert. op. cit.

[9] Green, Scott. Audio tape from a 1988 Leadership Conference in *What Does the Boston Church of Christ Teach?* Vol. 1. edited by Jones, Jerry, Th.D. (Mid-America Book & Tape Sales, Bridgeton, MO. 1990) p.14.

[10] Ha, Rubin. Audio tape from a 1988 Leadership Conference in *What Does the Boston Church of Christ Teach?* Vol. 1. edited by Jones, Jerry, Th.D. (Mid-America Book & Tape Sales, Bridgeton, MO. 1990) p.14.

[11] Furguson, Theresa. "Forever Growing" in *What Does the Boston Church of Christ Teach?* Vol. 1. edited by Jones, Jerry, Th.D. (Mid-America Book & Tape Sales, Bridgeton, MO. 1990) p.11.

[12] McKean, Kip. "Discipleship Partners" in *What Does the Boston Church of Christ Teach?* Vol. 1. edited by Jones, Jerry, Th.D. (Mid-America Book & Tape Sales, Bridgeton, MO. 1990) p.10.

[13] Jones, Jerry, Th.D. "II. Discipling" in *What Does the Boston Church of Christ Teach?* Vol. 1. edited by Jones, Jerry, Th.D. (Mid-America Book & Tape Sales, Bridgeton, MO. 1990) p.12.

[14] Moore, Terry. "Trust Me! The Key to Being Discipled - Part I" in *What Does the Boston Church of Christ Teach?* Vol. 1. edited by Jones, Jerry, Th.D. (Mid-America Book & Tape Sales, Bridgeton, MO. 1990) p.12.

[15] Fike, Byron. "Authority and Discipleship" in *What Does the Boston Church of Christ Teach?* Vol. 1. edited by Jones, Jerry, Th.D. (Mid-America Book & Tape Sales, Bridgeton, MO. 1990) p.167.

[16] Ibid. p. 169.

[17] Paone, Anthony J., S.J. *My Daily Bread.* (Confraternity of the Precious Blood, Brooklyn, NY. 1954) p. 325.

[18] Ibid. p.169.

[19] Trusty, Gilbert. *Recovering from Abusive Authority.* (Conference Evangelical Ministries to New Religions in Philadelphia, PA. Sept. 14, 1994).

[20] Garmon, Joe. "The Attitude of Christ Jesus," Part I. in *What Does the Boston Church of Christ Teach?* Vol. 1. edited by Jones, Jerry, Th.D. (Mid-America Book & Tape Sales, Bridgeton, MO. 1990) p.7.

Chapter 4

[21] "Prayer Requests, Sunday, Sept. 11, 1988." (edited for space) in *What Does the Boston Church of Christ Teach?* Vol. 1. edited by Jones, Jerry, Th.D. (Mid-America Book & Tape Sales, Bridgeton, MO. 1990) p.15.

[22] McKean, Kip. "Why Do You Resist the Spirit?' in *What Does the Boston Church of Christ Teach?* Vol. 1. edited by Jones, Jerry, Th.D. (Mid-America Book & Tape Sales, Bridgeton, MO. 1990) p. 9.

[23] The Bible, Revised Standard Version (American Bible Society, New York 1971) Matthew 18:15.

[24] A personal letter from a discipleship leader.

[25] *The Word*—The Bible in 26 Translations (Mathis Publishers, Inc., Moss Point, NY. 1988) Weymouth, translated by Richard Francis. *The New Testament in Modern Speech.* 1 Timothy 5:19.

[26] *The Word*—The Bible in 26 Translations (Mathis Publishers, Inc., Moss Point, NY. 1988) Weymouth, translated by Kenneth N. Taylor; 1 Tim. 5:19.

[27] *The Word*—The Bible in 26 Translations (Mathis Publishers, Inc., Moss Point, NY, 1988) Weymouth, translated by New American Standard Bible; 1 Tim. 5:20.

[28] *Englishman's Greek and Hebrew Concordance.* Baker Book House.

Chapter 5

[29] Excerpted from a privately circulated paper. (Note: The writer has asked to remain anonymous.)

[30] Excerpted from a personal letter written by a former member of The People of Praise Community to the author.

[31] Lifton, Robert Jay. *Thought Reform and the Psychology of Totalism.* (University of North Carolina Press, Chapel Hill, NC. 1961) p. 429.

[32] Weeden, Larry. *Pleasing God—Leader's Guide.* (Here's Life Publishers. San Bernardino, CA. 1985) p. 13.

Chapter 6

[33] Blackaby, Henry T. and King, Claude V. *Experience God.* (Life Way Press, Nashville, TN. 1990).

[34] Ibid. p. 36.

[35] Ibid. p. 20.

[36] Ibid. p. 36.

[37] Personal letter on audio tape from Dr. Harry Krux. Approximate date—early 80's.

[38] Paone, Anthony J., S.J. *My Daily Bread.* (Confraternity of the Precious Blood, Brooklyn, NY. 1954) p. 188.

Chapter 7

[39] Rasnake, Eddie. *What Should I Do, Lord?* — *Following the Signs That Lead to God's Will.* (Here's Life Publishers, San Bernadino, CA. 1992) p. 30.

[40] Ibid. p. 32.

[41] Ibid. p. 78.

[42] Blackaby, Henry T. and King, Claude V. *Experiencing God.* (Life Way Press, Nashville, TN. 1993) p. 62.

[43] Ibid. p. 106.

[44] Ibid. p. 62.

[45] Ibid. p. 35.

[46] Ibid. p. 19.

[47] Ibid. p. 19.

[48] Ibid. p. 84.

[49] Ibid. p. 19.

Chapter 8

[50] *Ecclesiastical History*. Eusebius, Book 8, Chapter 14—p.341, Baker Book House Edition, 1955-1977.

Chapter 9

[51] Kelly Sr., Gratia, S.M.S.D. *Totus Tuus II: There Is Still a Window for God's Mercy*. Excerpted from audio tape.

[52] De Bertodano, Teresa. *Daily Readings with Mother Teresa*. (Harper Collins, 1993) pp. 82-83.

Chapter 10

[53] Laurie Jacobson—My Experience in YWAM, A Personal Account and Critique, in *Cultic Studies Journal*. Vol. 3, No. 2. (American Family Foundation, Bonita Springs, FL. 1986) pp. 205-12.

[54] Ibid. pp. 210-211.

[55] Ibid. p. 211.

[56] Ibid. p. 212.

[57] Ibid. p. 211.

[58] Adrian J. Reimers—More than the Devil's Due, in *Cultic Studies Journal*. Vol. 11, No. 1. (American Family Foundation, Bonita Springs, FL. 1994) p. 77.

[59] *Shaken*. A privately circulated article (the author wishes to remain anonymous and the names have been changed).

Chapter 11

[60] Rasnake, Eddie. "What Should I Do, Lord?" (Here's Life Publisher, San Bernadino, CA. 1992) p. 54.

[61] *The Word*—The Bible in 26 Translations (Mathis Publishers, Inc., Moss Point, NY. 1988) Williams 2 Cor. 6:14-18.

Chapter 12

[62] Rasnake, Eddie. Op. cit. p. 164.

[63] Ibid. p. 164.

Chapter 13

[64] Lifton, Robert Jay. *Thought Reform and the Psychology of Totalism*. (University of North Carolina Press, Chapel Hill, NC. 1961) pp. 419-437.

[65] Ibid. p. 422.

[66] Ibid. p. 423.

[67] Ibid.

[68] Ibid.

[69] Quebedeaux, Richard. *I Found It!* (Harper & Row, San Francisco, CA. 1979) p. 108.

[70] Lifton, Robert Jay. op. cit. pp. 427-428.

[71] Margaret Thaler Singer with Janja Lalich. *Cults in Our Midst.* (San Francisco: Jossey-Bass Publishers, 1995) p. 70.

Chapter 15

[72] Lifton, Robert Jay. *Thought Reform and the Psychology of Totalism.* (University of North Carolina Press. 1961) p. 422.

[73] *Shaken.* A privately circulated article (the author wishes to remain anonymous and the names have been changed).

[74] *Vine's Dictionary*; Greek Dictionary in NAS Exhaustive Concordance, #5463.

[75] *Clarke's Commentary on the Bible.* Clarke, Adam, L.L.D., F.S.A., M.R.I.A. Published in 1831. p. 857.

[76] Ibid.

[77] Hoo, Ray. *Called to Serve.* (The Navpress, Colorado Springs, CO. 1982) p. 15.

[78] Ibid. pp. 19-20.

[79] *Men Who Hate Women and The Women Who Love Them:* Dr. Susan Forward and Joan Torres (Bantam Books, New York. 1986) p.30.

[80] Ibid. p. 33.

[81] Ibid. p. 48.

[82] Paone, Anthony J., S.J. *My Daily Bread.* (Confraternity of the Precious Blood, Brooklyn, NY. 1954) p. 162.

Chapter 16

[83] Extracts from a 1994 audio tape made during a discipleship class. Held anonymous to avoid embarrassment to this particular Southern Baptist Church.

Chapter 17

[84] Excerpted from an unpublished paper: *The Shepherding/Discipleship Movement* by Tom Yoder (a former member of People of Praise).

[85] *Children of Faith.* A Newscenter 13 Probe Report with Tom Cochrun, WTHR, Channel 13 Video. Indiana, Inc., Indianapolis, 1983. Interview of Hobart Freeman, leader of Faith Assembly.

[86] Blackaby, Henry T. and King, Claude V. *Experiencing God.* (Life Way Press, Nashville, TN. 1993) p. 128.

[87] Yoder, Tom. *Leaving The Promised Land.* (Unpublished article by this eight-year former member of the "Word of God Community," Ann Arbor, Michigan).

[88] From a lecture by Dr. Paul Martin. Transcribed by Tom Yoder.

[89] Ibid.

[90] Ibid.

Index

ABOUT THE AUTHOR

Mary Alice Chrnalogar, a dedicated Christian, has spent more than 19 years working to rescue victims who are extremely controlled by leaders or destructive groups. Miss Chrnalogar is a respected international consultant in the field of cult education and has assisted with family interventions throughout the United States as well as in Australia, Canada, France, Israel, and Spain.

Her extensive work with those injured by mind control gives her a valuable insight into the thinking of these misguided persons and knowledge of how they keep themselves from thinking critically and objectively. This book is the foundation of the unique program Miss Chrnalogar uses to break the excessive and improper influences of leaders and abusive discipleship.

Miss Chrnalogar states: "It is one of my greatest joys to receive phone calls weekly from individuals who are so grateful to me for writing this book because the information freed them from an unhealthy church." "My favorite thank-you was a message sent to me by an ordained minister. He wrote, 'Chrnalogar's book was a godsend to me. I left an abusive system five years ago but her book has given me new meaning to life. The scriptures that used to haunt me no longer do because Miss Chrnalogar places them in the correct context.'"

The author comments, "My greatest happiness in life is knowing that many will be healed after they read this book that the Lord inspired in my heart."